"Stephen Betchen continues to be a leader in the integration of couple and sex therapy. A master clinician, he has now provided a long-awaited manual designed to guide the supervisors of couple and sex therapy trainees. Betchen has, once again, filled a significant gap in our professional literature by graciously sharing the practices and processes he has passed on to the many fortunate supervisees who have had the benefit of his guidance. This book is certain to boost the number of qualified supervisors of couple and sex therapy and fill a critical need in our profession."

Daniel N. Watter, *PhD, CST, CSTS, past president, The Society for Sex Therapy and Research (SSTAR)*

"Betchen's groundbreaking book addresses a long-standing gap in the clinical literature by offering a comprehensive guide dedicated to the supervision of therapists working with couples experiencing relationship and sexual difficulties. With his brilliant and analytic case examples and clinical interpretations, Betchen has outlined a structured supervisory model informed by psychodynamic conflict and systemic theories. An essential reading for supervisors, advanced clinicians, and trainees in couple and sex therapy, Couple and Sex Therapy Supervision offers a much-needed roadmap for training the next generation of therapists working at the intersection of intimacy, sexuality, and relationships."

Sabitha Pillai-Friedman, *PhD, CST, CSTS, adjunct associate professor, Center for Human Sexuality Studies, Widener University*

Couple and Sex Therapy Supervision

This book recognizes the inextricable link between conflict in intimate relationships and sexual problems, providing clinical couple and sex therapy supervisors with essential tools and considerations to help their supervisees better understand, address, and treat couples who experience a variety of sexual problems.

Dr. Stephen Betchen utilizes his psychoanalytic conflict-systems theory model as a base from which to demonstrate and teach supervisors of all developmental stages how to conduct supervision in treating couples with conflict – both sexual and nonsexual in nature. Chapters illustrate how supervisors can expand and adapt their therapeutic model of supervision, addressing the need for structure and boundary-setting in the supervision process. This book also emphasizes the importance of considering gender, race, and other sociocultural factors, as well as transference-countertransference and parallel process.

Filled with supervision cases for clinical and theoretical support, this is an invaluable guide for therapists and supervisors wishing to seamlessly integrate couple and sex therapy. This book is essential for clinicians who supervise trainees and supervisees of all levels, particularly those who work with couples that present with a wide range of sexual challenges and symptoms.

Stephen J. Betchen, DSW, is a licensed marriage and family therapist, and a certified sex therapist. He is also an AAMFT-approved and AASECT-certified supervisor. He maintains a private practice in New Jersey specializing in couple and sex therapy.

Couple and Sex Therapy Supervision

A Supervisor's Guide to Treating Couples with Sexual Problems

Stephen J. Betchen

Routledge
Taylor & Francis Group
NEW YORK AND LONDON

Designed cover image: Getty Images

First published 2027
by Routledge
605 Third Avenue, New York, NY 10158

and by Routledge
4 Park Square, Milton Park, Abingdon, Oxon, OX14 4RN

Routledge is an imprint of the Taylor & Francis Group, an informa business

ISBN: 9781041078913 (hbk)
ISBN: 9781041078890 (pbk)
ISBN: 9781003642732 (ebk)

DOI: 10.4324/9781003642732

Typeset in Sabon
by Newgen Publishing UK

Alanna, perhaps you and your generation will do it better than we did.

Contents

About the Author

Stephen J. Betchen is a licensed marriage and family therapist and a certified sex therapist. He completed a joint masters/doctorate program (MSW/DSW) at the University of Pennsylvania with a specialization in marriage and family therapy (MFT), and trained at the Marriage Council of Philadelphia, Department of Psychiatry, University of Pennsylvania School of Medicine. He followed with a post-doctoral fellowship in psychology of psychiatry with a specialization in sex therapy at the New York Hospital-Cornell University Medical Center, and subsequently completed the Clinical Psychoanalytic Fellowship Program at the Institute of the Philadelphia Association for Psychoanalysis, the Intensive Psychoanalytic Psychotherapy Program at the William Alanson White Institute of Psychiatry, Psychoanalysis and Psychology, and the Object Relations Theory and Practice Program at the International Psychotherapy Institute.

Dr. Betchen is the author of approximately 200 scholarly articles and chapters, magazine pieces and blogs (including blogs for *PsychologyToday.com*), over 500 newspaper columns, and 8 books on relationships including the critically acclaimed, *Intrusive Partners Elusive Mates: The Pursuer-Distancer Dynamic in Couples*. He is a former adjunct clinical professor in the Graduate Department of Couple and Family Therapy at Thomas Jefferson University, and Chief of Supervision in the Post-Graduate Sex Therapy Program at the Council for Relationships. He is certified as a supervisor by both AAMFT and AASECT and currently maintains a private practice specializing in the treatment and supervision of couples/sex therapy in New Jersey.

Preface

The areas of couple therapy and sex therapy have grown significantly as individual specialties, but the move to integrate the two has been slow and yet to garnish the attention it deserves. While there are many reasons for this which will be elaborated on in this book, two prominent reasons include added training and financial restraints. For many years individuals who wanted to treat couples with sexual problems would have to complete their core degree (e.g., psychiatry, psychology, social work), then seek post-graduate training in MFT followed by additional training in sex therapy. Very few institutes trained in both at the time, as did the Marriage Council of Philadelphia (renamed the Council for Relationships). In recent years, however, with the advent of a professional degree in MFT, individuals need only to follow with sex therapy training or find an MFT program with a built-in sex therapy track. But most promising are the dual certificates now offered in couple and sex therapy by organizations such as the Modern Sex Therapy Institutes and the Sexual Health Alliance – programs approved by the American Association of Sexuality Educators, Counselors and Therapists (AASECT). To take true advantage of these options, however, individuals should be certain they want to practice couple and sex therapy before embarking on such expensive and time-consuming endeavors.

Most individuals who have chosen to practice couple and sex therapy have found the process challenging, often taking years to feel comfortable and competent. One of the biggest hurdles is finding an adequately trained supervisor. Because there are relatively few therapists who specialize in this area, there is a shortage of supervisors to choose from; a limitation also reflected in the literature. For example, while there are many books on the supervision of MFT, I have found only one book on the supervision of sex therapy, and none dedicated exclusively to the supervision of couple and sex therapy. I believe that *Couple and Sex Therapy Supervision* is the only book dedicated to the supervisor of couple and sex therapy, with the purpose to provide a guide from which to educate and train the supervisee who wishes to work with couples who suffer from sexual problems. A short description of each chapter follows.

- "Chapter 1: The Evolution of Couple and Sex Therapy" explores the growth of both the couple therapy and sex therapy fields. Outcome studies are cited which show the importance and efficacy of both fields.
- "Chapter 2: Integrating Couple and Sex Therapy" provides a history of the integration of couple therapy and sex therapy, and confirms the need for this linkage. The barriers that challenge integration, both practical (i.e., time, money, and burnout) and personal (i.e., past traumas, intrusiveness, religious values, and cultural bias) are explored. Shifts in society and their impact on integration also are addressed.
- "Chapter 3: The Need for Integrative Supervision" addresses the need for supervision of this most theoretically and clinically challenging form of treatment. Case examples are provided to illustrate this need.
- "Chapter 4: Structuring Supervision" promotes the necessity for organizing the supervision process and presents a universal structure for supervision that can be easily applied to the supervision of couple and sex therapy. The structure includes forming alliances and joining, contracting and goal setting, limit setting and establishing appropriate boundaries, managing control struggles, and navigating clinical crises including suicidal behavior. Two detailed sections address the pros and cons of telesupervision, and different modalities of supervision (i.e., one-on-one; one-on-two; and one-on-four supervision) are discussed.
- "Chapter 5: Sociocultural Influences" addresses how ethnicity and culture, race, religion, gender-role conflict, gender identity and diversity, and sexual orientation play important roles in the supervision of couple and sex therapy.
- "Chapter 6: Therapeutic Approaches and Supervision" emphasizes that most supervisors base their supervisory models on their therapeutic approaches. Highlighted is the author's model of supervision which is grounded in psychodynamic and systemic conflict theory and designed specifically to treat couples with sexual issues. This chapter also addresses some of the pros and cons of having multiple supervisors.
- "Chapter 7: Conflict Theory Supervision in Practice" demonstrates how conflict theory is utilized in the supervision process. It details how to construct and use a genogram, recognize contradictions in a couple's family of origin and in their interactional style, determine, recognize, and expose a couple's shared internal conflict and connect it to their sexual symptoms, and suggesting clinical interventions. Cases are used to illustrate how the conflict model is applied in supervision.

- "Chapter 8: Transference-Countertransference (and Parallel Process)" illustrates the ways in which transference-countertransference and parallel process can impact the supervisory and treatment processes. The following concepts are discussed in detail and illustrated *via* case examples: the supervisee's transference reactions to each partner of the couple and to the supervisor; the supervisor's countertransference reactions to the supervisee; and to each partner of the supervisee's couple. Examples of positive, negative, and sexual transferences are discussed.
- "Chapter 9: Premature Termination and Termination of Supervision" offers detailed descriptions of both premature termination and some common causes of it, as well as the formal termination process. Questions are suggested that the supervisor can ask the supervisee to prevent termination or to determine why it might have occurred.
- "Chapter 10: Supervision Case Studies" provides six case examples detailing a six-step conflict theory supervisory model of couple and sex therapy. To demonstrate the breadth and depth of the model, the cases presented represent couples from a variety of sociocultural backgrounds who are experiencing male and female sexual issues, including: delayed ejaculation, erectile disorder (ED), male hypoactive sexual desire disorder (MHSDD), genito-pelvic pain/penetration disorder (GPPPD), and female sexual interest/arousal disorder (FSIAD). Open relationships are also addressed.

Acknowledgments

My heartfelt thanks to all the supervisees, who have bravely taken on the challenge of increasing their clinical acumen at the risk of exposing their own personal and professional vulnerabilities.

And to my Editor Julia Giordano, for giving me another opportunity to write and publish a book under her watch.

Chapter 1

The Evolution of Couple and Sex Therapy

Growth of Couple and Sex Therapy

Couple Therapy

Approximately 20 years ago, Orlinsky and Rønnestad (2005) – in the largest international study conducted about psychotherapists – found that 70% of the clinicians treated couples as part of their general practice. Yet Norcross et al. (2013) accurately predicted that couple therapy would continue to grow even greater. Once considered a minor mode of treatment, couple therapy is now a prominent intervention modality (Lebow & Snyder, 2022).

In a recent workforce study by the American Association for Marriage and Family Therapy (2022), 40% of respondents now held a specialized credential in marriage and family therapy, 30% wished to pursue one, and 43% of those individuals were primarily interested in pursuing clinical work with couples. Data USA (2022) suggested there were 26,365 marriage and family therapists (MFTs) employed in the United States of which 70.3% were White, 14.8% Black, and 14.2% Hispanic; 77.5% were women and 22.5% men. This year, the U.S. Bureau of Labor Statistics (2025) estimated that there are now approximately 76,000 MFTs practicing with a projected growth of 16% from 2023 to 2033 – the fastest rate for all occupations.

From a financial perspective, Marriage Counseling Services Global Market Report (2025) predicted that the industry of marriage counseling would grow from $12.9 billion in 2024 to $14.38 billion in 2025, at a compound annual growth rate (CAGR) of 11.5%. It also forecasted the industry would reach $21.99 billion in 2029. Research and Markets (2025) predicted marriage counseling services to expand to $19.79 billion by 2028. According to Ingalls (2023), 37% of those living with a partner attended couple therapy at least once throughout their relationship, 35%

DOI: 10.4324/9781003642732-1

started treatment before moving in together, and 34% started before marrying.

Couple therapy has also become an increasingly valuable vehicle for lesbian, gay, bisexual, transsexual, and queer (LGBTQ) couples. According to various scholars (Coolhart, 2023; Schwartz et al., 2020), these groups find it relatively safe to discuss their relationship issues within the confines of couple therapy. Medina and Mahowald (2023) reported that lesbian, gay, transgender, queer, intersex, asexual, and other sexual identities, gender identities, and any added, related identities (LGBTQI+) continue to report discrimination in the workplace "including being fired; being denied a promotion; having work hours cut; or experiencing verbal, physical, or sexual harassment" (p. 1). As society becomes less discriminatory against these minorities, *couple-level minority stressors* should decrease, leading more minority couples to seek couple therapy. Couple-level minority stress may be experienced by either one partner of a couple, or jointly by the couple because of the stigma attached to status of their relationship (Frost et al., 2017; Le Blanc et al., 2015).

Khoddam (2023) attributed the growth of couple therapy to divorce rates, widespread couple distress, the adverse effects of relationship strife on the emotional and physical well-being of both adults and children, and an increase in the expectation of relationship satisfaction. Doss et al. (2018) contended that couple therapy has benefitted from modern technology that has made it more accessible. And Research and Markets (2025) reported that technology has evolved to be more inclusive, collaborative, and sensitive to diverse communities such as LGBTQ individuals. Ingalls (2023) found that 56% of couples attend both in-person and online couple sessions.

Roddy et al. (2020) claimed that couple therapy can have a great effect on relationship satisfaction, especially in key domains such as communication, emotional intimacy, and partner behavior. Specifically, couple therapy has proven to be effective in treating infidelity (American Association for Marriage and Family Therapy, 2016), psychosexual problems, intimate partner violence (Carr, 2018), and a wide variety of issues related to both the mental and physical health of individuals such as anxiety and depression (Babinski & Sibley, 2022; Whisman & Collazos, 2023), as well as chronic pain, cardiovascular disease, substance abuse, and post-traumatic stress disorder (Marano, 2023). Not surprisingly, it was also found that by alleviating parental stress, couple therapy can serve to benefit the health of children (Bernet et al., 2016).

Lebow and Snyder (2022) reported that couples undergoing couple therapy are better-off than 70–80% of those not receiving treatment.

According to the American Association for Marriage and Family Therapy (2025):

> After receiving treatment, almost 90% of clients report an improvement in emotional health, and nearly two-thirds report an improvement in their overall physical health. A majority of clients report an improvement in their functioning at work, and three-fourths of those receiving marital/couples or family therapy report an improvement in the couple relationship.
>
> (p. 1)

These results are consistently positive when extended to treatment using telehealth services, especially videoconferencing, which is conducted in real-time between therapist and client. The use of videoconferencing has been a topic of research for many years consistently showing high satisfaction rates, strong efficacy, and positive outcomes (Backhaus et al., 2012; Andersson et al., 2019; Keller et al., 2021). A public opinion poll conducted by the American Psychiatric Association (APA) (2021) found that four in ten Americans have used telehealth and that the majority have used the services since the start of the pandemic (82%). And approximately 40–45% of the respondents found that telehealth provided the same quality of care as in-person treatment. White, Black, and Hispanic respondents said they would use telehealth for mental healthcare (between 58% and 61% each).

The use of videoconferencing in conducting couple therapy has been found to be just as, if not more, effective in treating couples than in-person treatment. Videoconferencing has proven to be efficacious in forming therapeutic alliances or connecting a couple and therapist together as well as producing relationship satisfaction, desired and perceived change, mental health (i.e., a reduction in anxiety and stress) and happiness (Kysely et al., 2022).

Hogan (2022) reported that couple videoconferencing may be more accessible, convenient, and cost effective than in-person couple therapy. The author specifically noted that it reduces barriers to scheduling and childcare needs. And de Boer et al. (2021) conducted a systematic review of over 7,112 abstracts and 37 papers in examining the efficacy, feasibility, and acceptability of couple and family therapy (CFT). In tune with other studies, telehealth was reported as a feasible and acceptable delivery method of CFT.

In the event of another pandemic, or whatever else may impede couples from accessing treatment, telehealth, especially videoconferencing, has proven a viable delivery of clinical service. For many it has grown to become the first option further demonstrating the value of couple therapy to those seeking to improve their relationships. Telesupervision will be addressed in more detail in Chapter 4.

Sex Therapy

Sex therapy has come a long way since Masters and Johnson (1966, 1970) published their seminal books *Human Sexual Response* and *Human Sexual Inadequacy*. Both illustrated how the researchers conceptualized, diagnosed, and treated sexual problems such as Erectile Disorder (ED), Premature Ejaculation (PE), and Female Orgasmic Disorder (FOD), to name a few. Their offering of the "Human Sexual Response Cycle" is one of their greatest contributions. The cycle is composed of four stages: excitement, plateau, orgasm, and resolution.

Kaplan (1977, 1979) later streamlined the response model by adding the concept of desire and excluding the plateau and resolution stages. Her preference was to focus on the psychological aspects of sexual response. Kaplan's three-stage stage model thus consisted of: desire, excitement, and orgasm. Nevertheless, the discoveries of Masters and Johnson were especially pivotal in influencing the founding, in 1967, of the first certifying organization for sex therapists: The American Association of Sex Educators, Counselors and Therapists (AASECT). AASECT is reportedly stable with a little over 1,000 certified sex therapists.

The field of sex therapy is experiencing significant growth. For example, data shows a 3.6% rise in sex therapy practices in 2024 compared to the previous year. The demand for sex therapists is projected to grow to 17% by 2028 (Zippia, 2021). From a financial perspective, IBISWorld has shown a huge increase in sex therapy revenues from a CAGR of 4.4% over the past five years equaling approximately 177.6 million in 2024, with couples representing the largest market for sex therapists (Curran, 2024).

Sexual disorders affect 43% of men and 31% of women. Low desire is experienced by 30% of women and 15% of men. ED and sexual arousal in women are 10% and 20% respectively. Orgasmic disorders in women are 10–15%. PE is the most common complaint in men at 30%. Sexual pain is reported at 10–15% of women and less than 5% of men (Rosen et al, 2000). These sexual disorders are usually associated with psychological distress (Frühauf et al., 2013), and may impact well-being, a sense of self-worth, and quality of life (Arcos-Romero et al., 2023; Vasconcelos et al., 2024).

The efficacy rates reported in various studies have helped to validate the value of sex therapy interventions. For example, in a long-term study of 140 couples who entered sex therapy, Hawton et al. (1986) found that successful follow up primarily by interview was possible with at least one partner in 75% of the cases. While recurrence of sexual difficulties was common, coping strategies were identified which often helped overcome relapses. Improvements in couple's general relationships resulting from treatment were usually sustained. Long term outcome was excellent for vaginismus, good for erectile dysfunction, but poor for PE and female impaired sexual interest. Zilbergeld and Kilmann (1984) reviewed short- and long-term clinical studies and found the best results were associated with treatment for PE and women who have never had orgasms. Least successful was treatment for ED and women with situational orgasm complaints. The authors concluded that with these results, sex therapy was still the treatment of choice.

Mestre-Bach et al. (2022) found that cognitive-behavioral and mindfulness therapies were successful in treating female dysfunctions. In a study measuring the effectiveness of sex therapy using cognitive-behavioral, mindfulness-based, and integrative approaches, Abolghasemi et al. (2023) found significant difference in sexual satisfaction and sexual desire among married women with sexual dissatisfaction in the three methods compared to the control group, with integrative showing the most improvement. The researchers concluded that sex therapy treatment is effective in reducing sexual dissatisfaction and increasing sexual desire and intimacy.

Günzler and Berner (2012) conducted a systematic review of the research concerning the efficacy of psychological treatment in male sexual dysfunction and found that overall, psychosocial interventions improved sexual functioning. One study concluded that psychotherapy is superior to medication while another found the opposite. In men with PE, behavioral techniques proved to be effective. Frühauf et al. (2013) agreed that psychological interventions in the context of sex therapy proved promising in the treatment of sex issues.

Hummel (2017) reported on the efficacy of internet-based cognitive behavioral therapy (CBT) in improving sexual functioning of breast cancer survivors (BCS). The author concluded that internet-based CBT has salutary effects on sexual functioning, body image, and menopausal symptoms in BCSs with a sexual dysfunction. Velten et al. (2024) found that online cognitive-behavioral sex therapy and online mindfulness-based sex therapy for low sex drive in women showed that compared to the control condition both demonstrated significant improvements in sexual desire and sexual distress at 3-month and 6-month follow-up. Results were sustained at 12-month follow-up, with 35% and 41% demonstrating reliable improvements and an additional 20% and 24% achieving clinically significant improvements in sexual desire after both methods. With regards to sexual distress or anxiety, frustration, and worry about sexual issues, 49% and 42% exhibited reliable change with an additional 37–42% achieving clinically significant improvement. The results supported the overall long-term efficacy of psychological therapies in treating low sex drive in women. And Kleinplatz et al. (2022) reported that in-person and teletherapy group couple therapy proved equally effective, and that interventions were found to be enduring for treating low sexual desire or frequency in women.

Siegel (2019) advocated for the integration of sex therapy and sexual medicine, finding it most effective in treating sexual problems. Atallah et al. (2021) combined medical and psychological interventions in treating ED. The author's results indicated that a combination of psychological intervention (PI) and phosphodiesterase-5 inhibitor (PDE-5i) was most effective in treating psychogenic ED.

Althof (2006) found that combining medical and psychological interventions for individuals or couples with sexual dysfunction offers an alternative approach to therapy that enhances: efficacy, treatment and relational satisfaction, and decreases patient discontinuation. Perelman (2005) supported these findings.

In a later study Althof (2016) found combining pharmaco- and psychotherapy is the most promising intervention for lifelong and acquired PE and offers superior efficacy to drug alone. And in a more recent study Althof (2023) contended it is best to use psychosexual counseling as an adjunct to pharmacotherapy in the treatment of erectile dysfunction.

While successful outcome research has attributed to the growth of sex therapy, there are several other reasons for its expansion. According to de Lucena and Abdo (2017), sex therapy has become more popular in the last several decades primarily because it now focuses on relieving sexual distress and promoting sexual satisfaction rather than exclusively attributing sexual symptoms to unconscious conflicts. In the article, "Therapy has never been sexier: Why sex therapy is growing," Torres (2024) agreed that sex therapy is now believed to be less taboo because it is aimed at increasing intimacy; it is not trauma focused and that psychology, beyond physiology, is playing a more crucial role in treating sexual health. Virtual sessions have also allowed sex therapy to be more accessible.

Greater diversity among sex therapists has also helped to increase the popularity of the field. A 2021 survey conducted between 2010 and 2021 found that 64.1% of sex therapists are women with racial and age diversity – a sharp increase over the past decade. Most sex therapists were recently found to be 62.4% White, 17.3% Hispanic, and 9.2% Black (Zippia, 2025).

The field of sex therapy has proven to be adaptable as made evident by the trends cited by Meana and Jones (2011): (1) Combining psychological and medical interventions; (2) Considering contextual influences and new theoretical perspectives; (3) Focusing primarily on sexual satisfaction over sexual functioning; (4) Championing realistic expectations especially in the context of sex and aging; (5) Applying new technologies in the field; and (6) Recognizing diversity in the context of sexual experience.

According to Weir (2019), emerging directions of sex therapy include:

- Mindfulness-based interventions – Mindfulness-based cognitive therapy that is geared towards sexual issues (Bossio et al., 2018). Many clients present with a poor sense of self and a disconnection from their bodies. Mindfulness techniques may help these individuals to integrate both mind and body to enhance sexual experience.
- Psychotherapy interventions over medications – Psychosocial factors are considered risk factors for sexual dysfunction (McCabe et al., 2016); medications alone do not cure most sexual disorders (Althof, 2002).
- Inclusivity – Considers gender identity, including transgender and gender nonbinary people, same-sex couples and non-monogamous relationships, in the human sexual experience.
- Couple perspective – Sexual dysfunction is usually the responsibility of the couple system (Brotto et al., 2016).
- Changing attitudes toward sex – Sex is seen as less taboo.
- Cybertherapy – Use of proven technology to treat a variety of sexual problems in men and women (Connaughton & McCabe, 2017).

References

Abolghasemi, S. J., Panahali, A., & Shalchi, B. (2023). A comparative study of the effectiveness of sex therapy using cognitive-behavioral, mindfulness-based, and integrative approaches on sexual satisfaction and sexual desire in married women with sexual dissatisfaction. *Journal of Propulsion Technology*, *44*, 6667–6683.

Althof, S. (2002). When an erection alone is not enough: Biopsychosocial obstacles to lovemaking. *International Journal of Impotence Research*, *14*, S99–S104. doi:10.1038/sj.ijir.3900799

Althof, S. (2006). Psychological approaches to the treatment of rapid ejaculation. *Practicing Medicine*, *3*, 180–186.

Althof, S. (2016). Psychosexual therapy for premature ejaculation. *Translational Andrology and Urology*, *5*, 475–481. doi: 10.21037/tau.2016.05.15

Althof, S. (2023). Role of psychosexual counseling as an adjuvant to pharmacotherapy in the treatment of erectile dysfunction. *Journal of Sexual Medicine*, *20*, 236–239. doi: 10.1093/jsxmed/qdac042

American Association for Marriage and Family Therapists (2016). *Infidelity*. www.aamft.org/AAMFT/consumer_updates/infidelity.aspx

American Association for Marriage and Family Therapists (2022). *2022 MFT Industry Workforce Study*. www.aamft.org/aamft/workforce_study/home.aspx
American Association for Marriage and Family Therapists (2025). *About marriage and family therapists. What is marriage and family therapy?* www.aamft.org/AAMFT/AAMFT/About.aspx
American Psychiatric Association. (2021). *New nationwide poll shows an increased popularity for telehealth services*. www.psychiatry.org/News-room/News-Releases/New-Nationwide-Poll-Shows-an-Increased-Popularity
Andersson, G., Titcov, N., Dear, B. F., Rozental, A., Carlberg, P. (2019). Internet-delivered psychological treatments: From innovation to implementation. *World Psychiatry*, *18*, 20–28. doi: 10.1002/wps.20610
Arcos-Romero, A. I., & Calvillo, C. (2023). Sexual health and psychological well-being of women: A systematic review. *Healthcare*, *11*, 3025. doi: 10.3390/healthcare11233025
Atallah, S., Haydar, A., Jabbour, T., Kfoury, P., & Sader, G. (2021). The effectiveness of psychological interventions alone, or in combination with phosphodiesterase-5 inhibitors, for the treatment of erectile dysfunctions: A systematic review. *Arab Journal of Urology*, *19*, 310–322.
Babinski, D. E., & Sibley, M. H. (2022). Family-based treatments for attention-deficit/hyperactivity disorder: A review of family functioning outcomes in randomized controlled trials from 1020 to 2019. *Journal of Marital and Family Therapy*, *48*, 83–106. https://doi.org/10.1111/jmft.12572
Backhaus, A., Agha, Z., Maglione, M. L., Repp, A., Ross, B., Zuest, D., Rice-Thorp, N. M., Lohr, J., & Thorp, S. R. (2012). Videoconferencing psychotherapy a systematic review. *Psychological Services*, *9*, 111–131. doi: 10.1037/a0027924
Bernet, W., Wamboldt, M. Z., & Narrow, W. E. (2016). Child affected by parental relationship distress. *Journal of the American Academy of Child & Adolescent Psychiatry*, *55*, 571–579. doi: 10.1016/j.jaac.2016.04.018.
Bossio, J. A., Basson, R., Driscoll, M., Correia, S., & Brotto, L. A. (2018). Mindfulness-based group therapy for men with situational erectile dysfunction: A mixed-methods feasibility analysis and pilot study. *The Journal of Sexual Medicine*, *15*, 1478–1490. https://doi.org/10.1016/j.jsxm.2018.08.013
Brotto, L., Attallah, S., Johnson-Agbakwu, C., Rosenbaum, T., Abdo, C., Byers, E. S., Graham, C., Nobre, P., & Wylie, K. (2016). Psychological and interpersonal dimensions of sexual functions and dysfunctions. *The Journal of Sexual Medicine*, *13*, 538–571. https://doi.org/10.1016/j.jsxm.2016.01.019
Carr, A. (2018). Couple therapy, family therapy and systemic interventions for adult-focused problems: The current evidence base. *Journal of Family Therapy*, *41*, 492–536. https://doi.org/10.1111/1467-6427.12225
Connaughton, C., & McCabe, M. (2017). Internet-based sex therapy. In Z. D. Peterson (Ed.), *The Wiley handbook of sex therapy* (pp. 483–502). John Wiley & Sons Ltd.
Coolhart, D. (2023). Therapy with queer couples. In J. Lebow & D. K. Snyder (Eds.), *Clinical handbook of couple therapy* (6th ed., pp. 512–530). Guilford Press.

Curran, J. (2024). Sex therapists in the US – Market research report (2014–2029). IBISWorld. www.ibisworld.com/united-states/industry/sex-therapists/6436//
Data USA (2022). *Marriage and Family Therapists*. https://datausa.io/profile/soc/marriage-and-family-therapistsde
Boer, K., Muir, S. D., Nedelijkovic, M., Seabrook, E., & Meyer, T. N. (2021). Videoconferencing psychotherapy for couples and families: A systematic review. *Journal of Marital and Family Therapy*, *47*, 259–288. doi: 10.1111/jmft.12518
de Lucena, B. B., & Abdo, C. H. N. (2017). Sex therapy: Brief historic and current perspectives. *Women's Health*, *5*, 287–289. doi: doi.10.15406/mojwh.2017.05.00134
Doss, B. D., Feinberg, L. K., Rothman, K., Roddy, M. K., & Comer, J. S. (2018). Using technology to enhance and expand interventions for couples and families: Conceptual and methodological considerations. *Journal of Family Psychology*, *31*, 983–993. doi: 10.1037/fam0000349
Frost, D. M., LeBlanc, A. J., de Vries, B., Alston-Stepnitz, E., Stephenson, R., & Woodyatt, C. (2017). Couple-level minority stress: An examination of same-sex couples' unique experiences. *Journal of Health and Social Behavior*, *58*, 455–472. https://doi.org/10.1177/0022146517736754
Frühoff, S., Gerger, H., Schmidt, H. M., Munder, T., & Barth, J. (2013). Efficacy of psychological interventions for sexual dysfunction: a systematic review and meta-analysis. *Archives of Sexual behavior*, *42*, 915933. doi: 10.1007/s10508-012-0062-0
Günzler, C. & Berner, B. M. (2012). Efficacy of psychosocial interventions in men and women with sexual dysfunctions—a systematic review of controlled clinical trials: pat 1-the efficacy of psychosocial interventions for male sexual dysfunction. *Journal of Sexual Medicine*, *9*, 3108–3125. doi: 10.1111/j.1743-610.2012.02965.x
Hawton, K., Catalan, J., Martin, P., & Fagg, J. (1986). Long-term outcome of sex therapy. *Behaviour Research and Therapy*, *24*, 665–675. https://doi.org/10.1016/0005-7967(86)90062-8
Hogan, J. (2022). Conducting couple therapy via telehealth: Special consideration for virtual success. *Journal of Health Service Psychology*, *48*, 89–96. https://doi.org/10.1007/s42843-022-00060-x
Hummel, S. B., van Lankveld, J. J. D. M., Oldenburg, H. S. A., Hahn, D. E. E., Kieffer, J. M., Gerritsma, M. A., Kuenen, M. A., & Aaronson, N. K. (2017). Efficacy of internet-based cognitive behavioral therapy in improving sexual functioning of breast cancer survivors: Results of a randomized controlled trial. *Journal of Clinical Oncology*, *35*. https://pubmed.ncbi.nlm.nih.gov/28240966/
Ingalls, N. (2023). The positive impact of couples therapy is nearly universal, Verywell Mind survey finds. *Verywell Mind*. www.verywellmind.com/relationships-survey-7104667
Kaplan, H. S. (1977). Hypoactive sexual desire. *Journal of Sex & Marital Therapy*, *3*, 3–9. doi:10.1080/00926237708405343.
Kaplan, H. S. (1979). *Disorders of sexual desire*. Brunner/Mazel.
Keller, A., Babl, A., Berger, T., & Schindler, L. (2021). Efficacy of the web-based PaarBalance program on relationship satisfaction, depression and anxiety – A

randomized controlled trial. *Internet Interventions, 23*, 1–9. https://doi.org/10.1016/j.invent.2020.100360

Khoddam, R. (2023). Why couples therapy is on the rise: Finding the right therapist. *Retrieved from* https://www.psychologytoday.com/ca/blog/the-addiction-connection/202308/why-couples-therapy-is-on-the-rise?msockid=1b95d396938b612a0b2fc4da926960f9

Kleinplatz, P., Charest, M., Paradis, N., Rosen, L. & Ramsay, T. O. (2022). 083 The effectiveness of in-person versus remote group couples therapy for the treatment of low sexual desire or frequency. *The Journal of Sexual Medicine, 19*, S156–S157. https://doi.org/10.1016/j.jsxm.2022.03.359

Kysely, A., Bishop, B., Kane, R. T., McDevitt, M., De Palma, M., & Rooney, R. (2022). Couples therapy delivered through videoconferencing: Effects on relationship outcomes, mental health and the therapeutic alliance. *Frontiers in Psychology, 12*, 1–13. doi:// 10.3389/fpsyg.2021.773030

LeBlanc, A. J., Frost, D. M., & Wight, R. (2015). Minority stress and stress proliferation among same-sex and other marginalized couples. *Journal of Marriage and Family Therapy, 77*, 40–59. https://doi.org/.10.1111/jomf.12160

Lebow, J. L., & Snyder, D. K. (Ed.). (2022). *Clinical handbook of couple therapy* (6th ed.). The Guilford Press.

Marano, H. A. (2023, June). How does couples therapy work? *Psychology Today.* www.psychologytoday.com/us/basics/therapy/how-does-couples-therapy-work?msokid=1827006fadbc6dd73d3a15e7acae6c99

Marriage Counseling Services Global Market Report (2025). Market size, trends, and global forecast 2025–2034. https://www.marketresearch.com/Business-Research-Company-v4006/Marriage-Counseling-Services-Global-40632999/t

Masters, W., & Johnson, V. (1966). *Human sexual response.* Little, Brown & Company.

Masters, W., & Johnson, V. (1970). *Human sexual inadequacy.* Little, Brown & Company.

McCabe, M. P., Sharlip, I. D., Lewis, R., Atalia, E., Balon, R., Fisher, A. D., Laumann, E., Lee, S.W., & Segraves, R. T. (2016). Risk factors for sexual dysfunction among women and men: A consensus statement from the fourth. *International Consultation on Sexual Medicine, 13*, 153–167. doi:10.1016/j.jsxm.2015

Meana, M., & Jones, S. (2011). Developments and trends in sex therapy. *Advances in Psychosomatic Medicine, 31*, 57–71. doi:10.1159/000328808

Medina, C., & Mahowald, L. (2023). Discrimination and barriers to well-being: The state of the LGBTQI+ community in 2022. *Center for American Progress.* www.americanprogress.org/article/discrimination-and-barriers-to-well-being-the-state-of-the-lgbtqi-community-in-2020/

Mestre-Bach, G., Blycker, G. R., & Potenza, M. N. (2022). Behavioral therapies for treating female sexual dysfunctions: A state-of-the-art review. *Journal of Clinical Medicine*, 11, 2794. https://doi.org/10.3390/jcm11102794

Norcross, J. C., Pfund, R. A., & Prochaska, J. O. (2013). Psychotherapy in 2022: A Delphi pole on its future. *Professional Psychology: Research & Practice, 44*, 363–370.

Orlinsky, D. E., & Rønnestad, M. H. (2005). *How psychotherapists develop: A study of therapeutic work and professional growth*. Washington, DC: American Psychological Association. https://doi.org/10.1037/11157-000

Perelman, M. (2005). Psychosocial evaluation and combination treatment of men with erectile dysfunction. *Urologic Clinics of North America*, *32*, 431–445. doi: 10.1016/j.ucl.2005.08.010

Research and Markets (2025). Marriage counseling services market report 2024. htpps://www.researchandmarkets.com/reports/6035580/marriage-counseling-services-market-report#product-toc

Roddy, M. K., Walsh, L. M., Rothman, K., Hatch, S. G., & Doss, B. D. (2020). Meta-analysis of couple therapy: Effects across outcomes, designs, timeframes, and other modalities. *Journal of Consulting and Clinical Psychology*, *88*, 583–596. doi: 10.1037/ccp0000514

Rosen, R., Brown, C., Heiman, J., Leiblum, S., Meston, C., Shabsigh, R., Ferguson, D., & D'Agostino, R. (2000). Female sexual function index (FSFI): A multidimensional self-report instrument for the assessment of female sexual function. *Journal of Sex & Marital Therapy*, *26*, 191–208. doi: 10.1080/009262300278597

Schwartz, A., Yarbrough, E., & McIntosh, C. A. (2020). Sex and relationships issues in work with the LGBT community. *Focus: The Journal of Lifelong Learning in Psychiatry*, *18*, 277–284. doi: 10.1176/appl.focus.20200014

Siegel, R. (2019). The integration of sex therapy and sexual medicine. In J. C. Wadley & R. Siegel (Eds.), *The art of sex therapy supervision* (pp. 4–9). Routledge.

Torres, G. (2024). Therapy has never been sexier: Thanks to pop culture, more couples than ever are seeking professional help in service of better sex. *Yes! Magazine*. www.yesmagazine.org/issue/connections/2024/03/04/therapy-has-never-been-sexier

U. S. Bureau of Labor Statistics (2025). Marriage and family therapists. *Occupational outlook handbook*. www.bls.gov/ooh/community-and-social-service/marriage-and-family-therapists.htm

Vasconcelos, P., Carrito, M. L., Quinta-Gomes, A. L., Patrão, A. L., Nóbrega, A. A. P., Costa, P. A., & Nobre, P. J. (2024). Associations between sexual health and well-being: A systematic review. *Bulletin of the World Health Organization*, *102*, 873–887. doi: 10.2471/BLT.24.291565

Velten, J., Hirschfeld, G., Meyers, M., & Margraf, J. (2024). Results of a randomized waitlist-controlled trial of online cognitive behavioral sex therapy and online mindfulness-based sex therapy for hypoactive sexual desire dysfunction in women. *Journal of Consulting Clinical Psychologist*, *92*, 742–755.

Weir, K. (2019). CE corner: Sex therapy for the 21st century: Five emerging directions. *Monitor on Psychology*, *50*, 30. American Psychological Association.

Whisman, M. A., & Collazos, T. (2023). A longitudinal investigation of marital dissolution, marital quality, and generalized anxiety disorder in a national probability sample. *Journal of Anxiety Disorders*, *96*, 102713–102720. https://www.sciencedirect.com/science/article/abs/pii/S0887618523000518

Zilbergeld, B., & Kilmann, P. R. (1984). The scope and effectiveness of sex therapy. *Psychotherapy*, *21*, 319–326. https://doi.org/10.1037/h0086092
Zippia. (2021). Job outlook for sex therapists in the United States. *Zippia* www.zippia.com/sex-therapist-jobs/trends/
Zippia. (2025). *Sex therapist demographics and statistics in the US. Zippia*. www.zippia.com/sex-therapist-jobs/demographics/

Chapter 2

Integrating Couple and Sex Therapy

Couple therapy and sex therapy are often treated as separate fields "to the detriment of couples who need to address intimacy and sexuality problems" (McCarthy & Thestrup, 2008, p. 139), but in fact, they are intricately linked. Johnson et al. (2018) stated: "Sexual issues always present in the relational context typically have a significant impact on intimate relationships" (p. 65). And Hertlein et al. (2020) wrote: "Couples therapists and sex therapists alike have found that sexual problems reflect and exacerbate relationship problems" (p. 363).

Manjula et al. (2021) also deemed that sexual disorders and marital intimacy are reciprocal. In a sample of 155 couples, the author reported that 82% of those with sexual disorders suffered from moderate-to-severe marital distress. Emond et al. (2021) found that in 48.5% of 169 couples sampled, at least one partner reported a sexual problem significant enough to bring them to therapy. LGBTQ couples are no exception. While this population experiences unique stressors (Medina & Mahowald, 2023), Schwartz et al. (2020) wrote that many of the sexual and relationship issues these couples face, are indistinguishable from these experienced by heterosexual couples.

Many clinicians and theorists have valiantly tried to promote the integration of couple therapy and sex therapy (McCarthy, 2001, McCarthy & Thestrup, 2008; Scharff & Scharff, 1991; Schnarch, 1991, 1997; Weeks & Hof, 1987), and some continue to do so (Betchen, 2022, 2024, Betchen & Davidson, 2018; Borden & Allan, 2024; Gambescia et al., 2021; Guttman, 2020; Hertlein et al., 2019, 2020; Johnson et al., 2018; Nelson, 2020; Weeks et al., 2020). Some institutes also provide integrative training like the Council for Relationships (formerly the Marriage Council of Philadelphia), the Modern Sex Therapy Institutes, and the Sexual Health Alliance. But integrating the two fields is still not as common as it should be in clinical practice.

DOI: 10.4324/9781003642732-2

Some colleagues have told me they do not see the need for specialized training in both areas. They believe that sexual issues are merely symptoms that can be alleviated with effective couple's therapy – a position I will argue against in this book. Others claim that most of the couples they treat do not suffer from sexual issues, and if they did, they would refer them to a sex therapist. I suspect in many of these cases the therapist might be colluding with the couple by neglecting to take an adequate sexual history or ask significant sex-related questions. Others might ask a fleeting general question like: "How is your sex life?" But fail to follow up with more detailed questions to determine how the couple's responses may link to their relational dynamics.

When one partner suffers from a specific sexual disorder, it is important that the therapist gather as much detail as possible. Sex-related detail is "vital" in accurately diagnosing a sexual problem and for constructing a proper treatment plan (H. S. Kaplan, personal communication, October 7, 1987). But this task might prove especially challenging for the therapist who is uncomfortable with the subject area. For example, if a client suffers from ED, the therapist would do well to ask what the client's definition of ED is: when he first experienced it; the frequency of the problem; and if he masturbates with success and how often, to name a few key questions. In my experience many therapists do not ask enough questions to determine whether the problem is acquired or lifelong; or is specific to the client's partner.

A colleague requested a consultation about a couple in which the husband was having an affair. The colleague could not understand why this man would risk losing such a smart, beautiful wife, and alienating his three young children. When I inquired about the couple's sex life, the colleague answered, "according to the husband it could have been better," but she did not follow-up by asking in what ways. Only with my urging did she find the husband was extremely unhappy with his wife's "rigid and conservative approach" to lovemaking. In contrast, his lover was adventurous and spontaneous. My colleague admitted that discussing sex-related material in too much detail made her anxious. She said that she "feared being intrusive," and "worried" the husband would embarrass both she and his wife with sex-related information. While these concerns are not uncommon, in this case the couple turned out to be more comfortable exploring their sex life than the therapist.

To successfully combine couple and sex therapy, the clinician must recognize the intricate link between them and that a couple's nonsexual dynamic may reveal something about them sexually, and *vice versa*. For example, Tom, a divorcee, was baffled by the chronic delayed ejaculation he was experiencing with his fiancée, Janine. Tom claimed that he was very attracted to Janine and that he had never experienced this problem with anyone else from his past. Once he realized that his sexual withholding represented a withholding of a part of himself out of fear he might be abandoned by a second wife, he was finally able to ejaculate into Janine.

Tom had been through a traumatic divorce, and his delayed ejaculation unconsciously defended against experiencing another trauma. In this sense, Tom felt safer by not being "all-in." During a presentation of this case a senior colleague and supervisor interrupted and asked whether Tom withheld affection or financial support in his relationship with Janine. I was initially confused by the question, but the supervisor was in fact, emphasizing the point that Tom's sexual disorder may also reveal something about his nonsexual traits or tendencies.

In another example, Ginny could not achieve orgasm when having intercourse with her fiancée, Jed. Her sexual history revealed a pattern: she could orgasm if her relationships were temporary. Since she and Jed were planning a future, their relationship qualified as long-term. Ginny was close to her father growing up. He was very protective and would do his best to keep the boys away from her. When Ginny did manage to bring a young man home, her father used intimidating tactics to chase him away. Her father also ridiculed Ginny if she dressed sexually provocatively. Because Ginny loved her father, she rarely challenged his authority. When she and Jed presented for treatment, she had no idea that her orgasm difficulty was representative of being disloyal to her father or choosing another man over him.

Despite evidence of the connection between couple therapy and sex therapy, there are few MFT programs that include sex therapy (Zamboni & Zaid, 2017), and even fewer dedicated to the integration of couples and sex therapy. Some MFT programs do offer "sex therapy tracks" in their curriculum but many of these are not adequate to produce knowledgeable and skillful human sexuality professionals. Therapists who wish to achieve competence in both disciplines must usually complete two training programs: one in marriage and family therapy, and one in sex therapy (Zamboni & Zaid, 2017). But this does not necessarily mean they will be taught how to integrate the two when treating couples.

A supervisee told me the following story of his experience at a sex therapy institute: A young, newly married couple presented for treatment because the wife could not achieve an orgasm. Despite the supervisee's protest, the supervisor insisted that the husband be released from treatment so that the supervisee could focus exclusively on his wife's anorgasmia. According to the supervisee, within the next three sessions the wife admitted that she saw her husband as domineering and controlling. And while she did feel guilty because she could not orgasm, she terminated the treatment because she believed she was being "solely" blamed by her husband, and by both supervisee and supervisor.

True integration is more likely to happen when one program offers both disciplines and specifically trains students to embrace an integrative approach. But the question remains why there is a shortage of these programs? There are two specific barriers to integration that I believe must be examined to attempt to answer this question: 1. Practical Barriers and 2. Personal Barriers.

Barriers to Integration

Practical Barriers

Time and Money

Training programs are time-consuming – most tend to run from 1 to 4 years, full-time. Integrative programs may take longer to complete and cost more because therapists must train in two disciplines. Many young graduates are deep in debt by the time they are ready to pursue post-graduate training. One young woman told me that she was against borrowing any more money; she did not think the cost-benefit ratio of attending a training program was good enough. She strongly felt the fiscally responsible thing for her to do was to get a job as soon as possible. Her philosophy was that the sooner she started working, the more money she could save for her future.

As a potential solution to this dilemma, many of my students and supervisees open private practices as soon as they have completed graduate school – without attending a post-graduate program – and before they might be clinically ready. This can sometimes lead to serious clinical errors and heighten the importance of and need for well-trained supervisors.

In the not too recent past, it was relatively unheard of to open a private practice before honing one's craft in a mental health agency or two. I was told by my first supervisor that I should spend a few years working in agencies/clinics before I ventured out on my own. She warned me that treating couples was fraught with potential clinical dilemmas and the more experience I have the better I will be able to navigate these issues. I took this advice and worked at several clinics for many years before opening my practice.

In all fairness to today's young therapist, however, interest rates were lower in my time, and scholarship and grant money plentiful. Many therapists must also become dues-paying members of at least one professional organization such as the American Psychological Association (APA), the National Association of Social Workers (NASW), or the American Counseling Association (ACA).

Adding organizations that represent a specialty such as the American Association for Marriage and Family Therapy (AAMFT), the American Association of Sexuality Educators, Counselors and Therapists (AASECT), or the Society for Sex Therapy and Research (SSTAR), for example, create even more expense. This is in addition to the cost of licensing fees and continuing education credits required to maintain licenses and certificates.

Burnout

Another practical reason why students do not pursue post-graduate work is because of what is commonly known as the "burnout factor." Once finished with graduate school, many individuals are too mentally exhausted to train for a specialty. I hear this more often from those clinicians who obtained doctorate degrees. A supervisee told me that he went straight into a post-doctorate training program and could barely stay awake. "I was exhausted. I would doze off in class. I just couldn't read one more book." Another student claimed that following the completion of his internship and dissertation continued training was the farthest thought from his mind.

While some therapists might consider the preceding examples dramatic, many of the young therapists I have spoken to carefully measure the amount of time they will invest in any activity beyond maintaining a basic, steady income. Some committed to agency work while maintaining small practices to ensure available health benefits.

Personal Barriers

While therapists who have sex therapy training might avoid training in couple therapy for practical reasons, those with couple training tend to shy away from sex therapy training because of a discomfort with sex. For example, empirical studies suggest that many therapists have difficulty talking about sex with clients (Dermer & Brachenberg, 2015; Harris & Hays, 2008; Moore, 2018; Timm, 2009). Both Moore and Timm found this especially true for beginning therapists with little supervision and clinical experience. The authors contended that therapists' attitudes, comfort, or willingness to discuss sex were not significant in these findings. In contrast, Harris and Hays conducted a survey of 175 clinical members of AAMFT and found that their "perceived sexual knowledge, and their comfort with sexual material influenced their willingness to engage in sexually-related discussions with their clients" (p. 239).

I have experienced similar reactions from relatively inexperienced couple therapists. For example, a young, male MFT seeking supervision forewarned me he would not be comfortable treating couples with sexual symptoms because of a prior personal trauma. He asked if we could somehow "work around" sex. A female MFT supervisee who had just completed a post-graduate program told me that she could not treat couples who presented with sexual problems, but she would not say why.

I have also experienced similar reactions to sexual material with veteran therapists. For example, although I was specifically asked to speak on male and female sexual disorders to a group of counselors, a male in the audience was uncomfortable enough to continuously interrupt my talk. The only way I could stop him was to point out his discomfort and recommend that he get help. He remained quiet the rest of the evening. A group of clinical social workers were openly hostile when I showed a sex therapy treatment video. Some claimed they were embarrassed by the video and would have preferred that I simply read from my notes.

The following are more reasons therapists might have difficulty with sex and sex therapy and therefore resist integrating it in their treatment with couples. Some of these reasons overlap, but are important enough to merit individual attention:

Sexual Abuse

Supervisees are not exempt from having experienced sexual abuse. In a national survey of 500 psychologists (with a 58% return rate), two thirds of the women and one third of the men experienced some form of physical or sexual abuse, with sexual abuse being predominant (Pope & Feldman-Summers, 1992).

As victims of sexual abuse, therapists may be likely to distance from or refer sex-related cases, or to refrain from discussing sex in treatment (Walsh et al. 2010). One female supervisee admitted she was sexually abused as a child and would only address the topic in supervision if I left my office door open – which I obliged to do when no one was in the waiting room.

It is common for people who were sexually abused to experience a sense of powerlessness, and in turn, exert more control over their environment even if they have repressed the memories of their abuse, supervisees included. Others find discussing the topic dredges up internalized shame and embarrassment. It is not, however, unethical or illegal for a therapist to "limit the scope of practice" under appropriate conditions. Marschall (2024) wrote:

> Sometimes, a therapist will limit their scope of practice based on personal needs. A therapist who is being treated for their own trauma

might be aware that they cannot competently treat clients who have experienced similar trauma without their own triggers coming up.

(p. 1)

Intrusiveness

Sex is considered very personal. As mentioned, some supervisees do not like to pry into this part of a couple's life fearing they will make themselves and their clients uncomfortable (Kauppi, 2024). Some therapists have told me they like to wait until joining sufficiently with clients before asking them about their sex lives (Gambescia, November 9, 2016). At times I find this to be a prudent therapeutic approach. But more often, the therapist is projecting personal anxiety onto the couple to defend against upsetting them or losing them to premature termination.

A seasoned female supervisee told me that she did not take the sexual history of a couple because she felt that it would be "going too deep, too fast." But when she finally questioned them about their sex-life she found that the couple was disappointed it took her so long to do so. They told her they were considering replacing her with another therapist.

My personal philosophy is to always take a sexual history at the beginning of treatment – I usually start in the first session – whether the couple present with a sexual problem or not. I believe this should especially hold true for couples who present sexual problems. Why would they have a problem with this if they specifically sought out a sex therapist to help them? It would only be logical that they would appreciate the therapist engaging them in as natural a way, and as soon as possible.

Religious Values

A supervisee's religious values may serve to restrict the confrontation of sexual issues in treatment and in turn, the integration of sex into their work with couples. Kaur (2025) reported that religion may shape someone's view of human sexuality. The author lists four major ways in which religion influences sexuality: (1) Beliefs about sexual behavior – Religions establish guidelines about what is sexually moral; (2) Expectations around gender roles – Religion may specify the roles man and women and the nonbinary play in relationships; (3) Shame and Stigma – Religion may stigmatize certain sexual practices or identities such as LGBTQ+; and (4) Importance and Modesty – Some religions promote modesty which can impact body image and in turn, sexual feelings and behaviors.

Shafrir et al. (2022) examined the differences between secular and religious psychotherapists participating in an intervention supervision program. The researchers found that the therapists' attitudes about sex – whether religious or secular – could lead to feelings of shame and embarrassment, or to avoiding the topic altogether. Both groups perceived discussing sex as socially taboo. In some cases, only normative sexual practices were discussed. That is, there was more difficulty addressing atypical or abusive sexuality such as fetishes, or bondage and discipline, dominance and submission, sadism and masochism (BDSM).

Reactions from the religious therapists depended on their level of religiosity and were correlated with their religious morals and values, especially those values that promoted modesty and were against promoting knowledge about sexual issues. While the secular therapists sought to change their attitudes regarding sexuality, the religious therapists preferred adapting their attitudes about sex to their religious morals and values.

Cultural Bias

The supervisee's cultural background helps to determine how he or she will process sex-related material. For example, according to the Global Promiscuity Index, some countries with relatively liberal cultural mores like Australia, Brazil, Germany, Italy, Switzerland, and Thailand are relatively unbiased and open to sexual difference. Other countries such as China, India, and Iran are least sexually open. Variables measured by the Index were: age at loss of virginity, number of sexual partners, rates of sexually transmitted diseases (STDS), premarital sex and whether it is viewed as moral, and if a country has legalized prostitution (Hales, 2025).

A supervisee originally from Iran referred a couple to me because he found himself unbalancing the treatment in favor of a jealous husband. He said that his personal values were getting in the way, and he either needed to address them in supervision, or continue to refer certain couples to unbiased therapists. He claimed that he tried to control himself but because of his strict background he was unable to.

The husband in this case, Ahmed, was from Egypt, and the wife, Carrie was American. Apparently, every time Carrie spoke to another man in Ahmed's presence, Ahmed would intervene and accuse the man of trying to flirt with Carrie. He would then call Carrie names like "slut" or "whore."

No explanation could satisfy Ahmed, who would threaten to beat both the man and Carrie. Ahmed was also obsessed with his Carrie's sexual history, considering it shameful because she had slept with 10 men before she met him. In a rage, Ahmed would say to her: "Once a slut, always a slut." Carrie was fed up with Ahmed's behavior and was threatening to divorce him.

The culturally sensitive supervisee will be better able to adapt to and join with a diverse range of couples suffering from a variety of sexual disorders. They may also be more empathic and willing to treat the sexually marginalized, such as LGBTQ+ couples. Integrating sex therapy into couple therapy would be a natural process for a culturally liberal therapist.

Societal Shifts

There is reason to believe that the integration of couple and sex therapy will one day take a prominent place in the field of psychotherapy, and I believe the reason for this optimism lies with the younger generations. Just as we have experienced a series of social shifts in the 1960s which led to a more sexually liberated United States (i.e., the counterculture and civil rights movements, effective contraception, and effective treatments for STDS), a shift has occurred in the way sex and sexual differences are viewed and reacted to. For example, both Millennials (born between 1981 and 1996) and Gen Z (born between 1997 and 2012) have demonstrated a greater openness to discussing sex than previous generations. They both are supportive of diversity (Parker et al., 2019) and less likely to discriminate against same-sex relationships (Parker & Igielnik, 2020). Millennials are more open to premarital sex and support consensual nonmonogamy (CNM) (Hawkins & Smith, 2019; Twenge et al., 2015).

While Gen Z average less sex and favor monogamy, they have also championed gender fluidity and in this sense have managed to fit traditional values into a contemporary sexual context. This does not mean they are sexually inexperienced. According to a joint study, "*The State of Dating: How Gen Z is Redefining Sexuality and Relationships*" (Feeld & Lehmiller, 2024), Gen Z are perhaps the kinkiest generation, taking a special interest in BDSM with 56% reported having BDSM fantasies compared to 52% of the generally more sexually permissive Millennials. The proliferation of and easy access to porn, the mainstreaming of kink, and a reduction in sexual stigma were found to be causal factors.

These new and open attitudes towards sex make integration more likely. Most Millennial and Gen Z supervisees, for example, have little difficulty addressing sexual issues with their clients. Many consider this an important part of every treatment. These groups are also considered "sex positive." That is, they have a positive view of sexuality without attaching shame.

According to Pitts and Greene (2019), a sex positive professional is accepting of a diversity of sexual activities, and that sanctions people to enjoy the kind of sex they want without being discriminated against. In this type of therapeutic atmosphere, clients are more likely to feel accepted and safe, which in turn makes it easier for them to freely express themselves without fear of consequences. In short, the more comfortable supervisees are when addressing sexual issues, the better the chance they are likely to consider sex as a potentially significant factor in their therapeutic work, especially with couples.

References

Betchen, S. (2022). *Couples in conflict: Clinical techniques for navigating sexual and relationship control struggles*. Routledge.

Betchen, S. (2024). *Unmet expectations in couple and sex therapy: Helping couples negotiate realistic relationships*. Routledge.

Betchen, S., & Davidson, H. (2018). *Master conflict therapy: A new model for practicing couples and sex therapy*. Routledge.

Borden, L., & Allan, R. (2024). Integrating sex therapy with emotionally focused therapy to treat sexual desire discrepancy. *The Family Journal*, *32*, 522–530.

Dermer, S., & Bachenberg, M. (2015). The importance of training marital, couple, and family therapists in sexual health. *Australian and New Zealand Journal of Family Therapy*, *36*, 492–503. https://doi.org/10.1002/anzf.1122

Emond, M., Byers, E. S., Brassard, A., & Tremblay, N., & Péloquin, K. (2021). Addressing sexual issues in couples seeking relationship therapy. *Sexual and Relationship Therapy*, *39*, 115–130. https://doi.org/10.1080/14681994.2021.1969546

Feeld & Lehmiller, J. J. (2024). The state of dating: How Gen Z is redefining sexuality and relationships. www.sexandpsychology.com/blog/2024/9/4/how-gen-z-is-redefining-sexuality-and-relationships/

Gambescia, N., Weeks, G., & Hertlein, K. (Eds.). (2021). *A clinician's guide to systemic sex therapy* (3rd ed.). Routledge.

Guttman, G. (2020). Sex and couples therapy: Biopsychosocial and relationship therapy. In Nelson, T. (Ed.), *Integrative sex & couples therapy: A therapist's guide to new and innovative approaches* (pp. 9–19). PESI Publishing & Media.

Hales, D. (2025, June 4). *Which countries are the most promiscuous?* NapLab. https://naplab.com/guides/which-countries-are-the-most-promiscuous/

Harris, S. M., & Hays, K. W. (2008). Family therapist comfort with and willingness to discuss client sexuality. *Journal of Marital and Family Therapy*, *34*, 239–250. https://doi.org/10.1111.j.1752-0606.2008.00066.x

Hawkins, A. J., & Smith, H. (2019, September 11). National survey reveals generational differences in consensual non-monogamy. *Institute for Family Studies*. https://ifstudies.org/blog/national-study-reveals-generationa-differences-in-consensual-nonmogamy

Hertlein, K., Gambescia, N., & Weeks, G. (Eds.). (2019). *Systemic sex therapy* (3rd ed.). Routledge.

Hertlein, K., Tim, T. M., & D'Aniello, C. (2020). Integrating couple therapy into work with sexual dysfunctions. In K. S. Wampler & A. J. Blow (Eds.), *The handbook of systemic family therapy: Systemic family therapy with couples* (pp. 363–383). Wiley Blackwell. https://doi.org/10.1002/9781119438519.ch75

Johnson, S. M., Simakhodskaya, Z., & Moran, M. (2018). Addressing issues of sexuality in couples therapy: Emotionally focused therapy meets sex therapy. *Current Sexual Health Reports, 10*, 65–71. https://doi.org/10.1007/s11930-018-0146-5

Kauppi, M. (2024, December). Every therapist should talk with their clients about sex. *Psychology Today*. www.psychologytoday.com/us/blog/relational-intimacy/202412/every-therapist-should-talk-with-their-clients-about-sex?msockid=035bd4366df7696609ddc37b69f79f76bf3c

Kaur, N. (2025, February 3). The role of religion and culture in sex therapy. *Safe Space Counseling*. www.safespacecounseling.com/post/the-role-of-religion-and-culture-in-sex-therapy

Manjula, V., Munivenkatappa, M., Navaneetham, J., & Mariamma, P. (2021). Quality of marital relationship and sexual interaction in couples with sexual dysfunction: An exploration study from India. *Journal of Psychosexual Health, 3*, 332–32. doi: 10.1177/26318318211047547

Marschall, A. (2024). What your therapist's scope of practice means for you. *Verywell Mind*. www.verywellmind.com/what-is-scope-of-pracice-for-therapists-5323826

McCarthy, B. (2001). Integrating sex therapy strategies and techniques into marital therapy. *Journal of Family Psychotherapy, 12*, 5–53. https://doi.org/10.1300/j085v12n03_03

McCarthy, B., & Thestrup, M. (2008). Integrating sex therapy interventions with couple therapy. *Journal of Contemporary Psychotherapy, 38*, 139–149. https://doi.org/10.1007/s10879-008-9083-3

Medina, C., & Mahowald, L. (2023). Discrimination and barriers to well-being: The state of the LGBTQI+ community in 2022. *Center for American Progress*. www.americanprogress.org/article/discrimination-and-barriers-to-well-being-the-state-of-the-lgbtqi-community-in-2020/

Moore, B. (2018). Therapists' attitudes, knowledge, comfort, and willingness to discuss sexual topics with clients [Unpublished doctoral dissertation]. Walden University College of Social and Behavioral Sciences.

Nelson, T. (2020). (Ed.). *Integrative sex & couples therapy: A therapist's guide to new and innovative approaches*. PESI Publishing & Media.

Parker, K., Graf, N., & Idielnik, R. (2019). Generation Z looks a lot like Millennials on key social and political issues. *Pew Research Center*. www.pewresearch.org/social-ternds/wp-content/uploads/sites/3/2019/01/generations-full-report_final_1.18.pdf

Parker, K., & Idielnik, R. (2020). On the cusp of adulthood and facing an uncertain future: What we know about Gen Z so far. *Pew Research Center*. www.pewresearch.org/social-trends/2020/05/14/on-the-cusp-of-adulthood-and-facing-an-uncertain-future-what-we-know-about-gen-z-so-far/

Pitts, R. A., & Greene, R. E. (2019). Promoting positive sexual health. *American Journal of Public Health*, *110*, 149–150. doi: 10.2105/AJPH.2019.305336

Pope, K. S., & Felman-Summers, S. (1992). National survey of psychologists' sexual and physical abuse history and their evaluation of training and competence in these areas. *Professional Psychology: Research and Practice*, *23*, 353–361.

Scharff, D., & Scharff, J. S. (1991). *Object relations couple therapy*. Aronson.

Schnarch, D. (1991). *Constructing the sexual crucible: An integration of sexual and marital therapy*. Norton.

Schnarch, D. (1997). *Passionate marriage: Sex, love, and intimacy in emotionally committed relationships*. Norton.

Schwartz, A., Yarbrough, E., & McIntosh, C. A. (2020). Sex and relationships issues in work with the LGBT community. *Focus: The Journal of Lifelong Learning in Psychiatry*, *18*, 277–284. doi: 10.1176/appl.focus.20200014

Shafrir, N., & Balahur, C. (2022). The differences in attitudes towards sexuality between religious and secular therapists as a result of participation in an intervention supervision program. *Psychology*, *13*, 1009–1024. doi: 10.4236/psych.2022.137069

Timm, T. M. (2009). Do I really have to talk about sex? Encouraging beginning therapists to integrate sexuality into couples therapy. *Journal of Couple & Relationship Therapy*, 8, 15–33. https://doi.org/10.1080/15332690802626692

Twenge, J. M., Sherman, R. A., & Wells, B. E. (2015). Changes in American adults' sexual behavior and attitudes, *1972–2012*. *Archives of Sexual Behavior*, *44*, 2273–2285. doi: 10.1007/s10508-015-0540-2

Walsh, K., Fortier, M. A., & DiLillo, D. (2010). Adult coping with childhood sexual abuse: A theoretical and empirical review. *Aggression and Violent Behavior*, *15*, 1–113. doi:10.1016/j.avb.2009.06.009

Weeks, G., & Hof, L (Eds.). (1987). *Integrating sex and marital therapy: A clinical guide*. Brunner/Mazel.

Weeks, G., Gambescia, N., & Hertlein, K. (2020). The intersystem approach to sex therapy. In K. Hertlein, N. Gambescia, & G. Weeks (Eds.), *Systemic sex therapy* (pp. 1–12). Routledge.

Zamboni, B. D., & Zaid, S. J. (2017). Human sexuality education in marriage and family therapy graduate programs. *Journal of Marriage and Family Therapy*, *3*, 605–616. https://doi.org/10.1111/jmft.12214

Chapter 3

The Need for Integrative Supervision

Supervision is critical for therapists who treat couples, especially those with sexual disorders. Couple therapy is a complex process in which the therapist must join and build a relationship with more than one individual, track transference-countertransference reactions related to both partners, maintain a dyadic balance, set limits and appropriate boundaries, assess any problematic disparity in sociocultural values, regulate highly charged emotions, process different communication styles and power dynamics, all of which will be addressed later in this book.

Doherty (2002) stated that couple therapy was the hardest of all psychotherapies. D. Scharff (personal communication, November 19, 2025) said: "Couple work is the hardest work I do; much harder than individual work." I compare couple therapy to walking in a minefield. The therapist must struggle, sometimes mightily, to maintain objectivity as partners vie for attention and favor. A supervisor skilled in working with couples can help the therapist to set and maintain therapeutic structure, deftly avoid pitfalls, and navigate the treatment towards a successful outcome.

When a couple presents with a sexual dysfunction, be it Erectile Disorder (ED), Female Sexual Interest/Arousal Disorder (FSIAD), Female Orgasmic Disorder (FOD), Male Hypoactive Sexual Desire Disorder (MHSDD), or something else, supervision may be especially important to help the therapist determine whether the disorder is the cause or the result of a couple's dynamics. Too many couples focus on their sexual symptoms and ignore their relationship dynamics. I have long warned therapists to pay equal homage to process (e.g., couple dynamics) and content (e.g., sexual symptoms) when treating couples (Betchen, 2022, 2025, Betchen & Davidson, 2018). But this is easier said than done.

A couple came to see me soon after the wife, Mary, fired their sex therapist for apparently ignoring the couple's presenting problem: the husband, Hank's, low sexual desire. Mary was already angry about Hank's

DOI: 10.4324/9781003642732-3

low desire, and the therapist further angered her by insisting the couple put their sexual concerns on hold and focus solely on their relationship dynamics. The therapist saw their relational dynamics (process) as the underlying problem and Hank's low desire as a symptom (content) of this dynamic. The therapist firmly believed if the couple dynamics were treated their sex symptom would most likely dissipate.

After taking an extensive general and sexual history, and observing the couple's interactional process, I too agreed with the former therapist's assessment. But rather than ignore the couple's sexual issues, I integrated the two by treating the dynamic and symptom simultaneously. I did this by weaving back and forth between the two throughout the treatment process until the couple saw their symptoms from a broader perspective. For example, when Hank failed to meet a nonsexual need and Mary attacked him for it, I pointed out that this dynamic looked very much like what happens to them with sex: Hank withholds sex, and Mary attacks him for it. This technique kept the couple in treatment long enough to improve their dynamic and alleviate their symptoms.

In no other mode of psychotherapy is therapeutic resistance a larger factor than in sex therapy. Sexual exercises, for example, may be offered, sabotaged, and medical treatment easily ignored or the subject of procrastination (Betchen, 2024). Adequate supervision by someone knowledgeable and skilled in both couples and sex therapy can be a significant asset to both supervisee and couple. The value is such that I have supervisees with private practices in couples and sex therapy continuing their supervision with me long after formal graduation from their respective postgraduate programs; the same is true with therapists who work in clinics that do not offer such supervision.

A seasoned supervisee – but not in couple and sex therapy – told me of a case in which the wife, Beatrice, had been complaining for many years that her husband, Ronald, refused to have sex with her. The supervisee was at his wit's end and against my recommendation decided to press Ronald to choose a time to approach Beatrice for sex. I offered: "What makes you think the wife wants to have sex?" The supervisee found the question absurd: "That's all she has been complaining about for years. Of course she wants to have sex." Considering this a learning opportunity I responded: "Okay, give it a try and get back to me."

While the supervisee did get Ronald to approach Beatrice, Ronald was rejected. Beatrice claimed that she was not feeling well but could not be specific about what was wrong with her. The very next day, however, Beatrice picked up where she left off – complaining about Ronald's refusal to have sex. In her defense, Beatrice said that her mysterious illness was an anomaly that should not count against her desire for Ronald to pursue her for sex. The supervisee was shocked by the dynamics of this case, but he did learn something about couple dynamics and the integration of couple and sex therapy.

Another good reason for the need of supervision for those who are attempting to integrate couple therapy and sex therapy is because a couple's sexual issues can be associated with medical problems, which are sometimes at their root. For example, it is common knowledge that ED may be associated with cardiovascular disorders (Köhler et al., 2024), diabetes and hypertension (Kitaw et al., 2024), and spinal disease (Zizzo et al., 2022). Premature Ejaculation (PE) may also be associated with penile sensitivity (Chen et al., 2018), diabetes, hypertension, and hyperthyroidism (Raveendran & Agarwal, 2021), endocrine disorders (Coskuner & Ozkan, 2022), and urological problems (Przydacz et al., 2024; Schecter & Gruenwald, 2024).

FOD may be associated with diabetes, multiple sclerosis, or conditions that cause physical pain as well as changes related to childbirth (Mozhdehipanah et al., 2025). Genito-Pelvic Pain/Penetration Disorder (GPPPD) may be associated with vulvodynia, endometriosis, and interstitial cystitis (Adedipe & Chukwujama, 2021). And FSIAD may be associated with menopause as well as cardiovascular and neurological disorders (Adebisi & Carlson, 2024).

A supervisor with a medical background, or extensive training in sex therapy will be a better guide to help a supervisee recognize these issues or to make an appropriate referral to someone with the appropriate medical knowledge. I believe the following abbreviated case examples emphasize my point:

Peter, an LMFT supervisee with very limited experience in treating sexual problems, presented a 62-year-old married couple suffering from PE. The husband, Jim, would ejaculate within seconds of entering his wife, Tammy. This would in turn anger, disappoint, and frustrate Tammy primarily because intercourse was her primary avenue to orgasm.

A urological exam found Jim was free of any medical issues, but he was prescribed a selective serotonin reuptake inhibitor (SSRI), for anxiety and depression. Jim feared that Tammy would leave him if he continued to have difficulty, although there was no evidence to support this concern. To me, this was a projection on Jim's part. That is, Jim felt he deserved to be abandoned.

Peter claimed to be "lost" and "over his head." He said that he feared the couple would soon fire him. I calmed him as best I could and told him to be patient. I then recommended that Peter tell Jim to try using a condom. And while this did extend Jim a few more thrusts, it was not enough to please Tammy.

The more Jim and Tammy failed, the more anxious Peter got. But I calmed him and told him we could solve Jim's mystery together. I then recommended that Peter try something I had success with in in similar cases. I told Peter to check with Jim's urologist (with Jim's permission) to see if it would be safe to add an ED drug (off-label) – which it was. I then recommended Peter tell Jim and Tammy to shorten their foreplay time, use a condom, only attempt intercourse in the female superior position (Tammy on top), and to employ the quiet vagina technique (Jim enters Tammy but does not thrust until acclimated). I reminded Peter that no steps were to be skipped or changed.

After a sabotage or two by both partners, Jim was soon able to perform long enough to enjoy sex with Tammy, and for Tammy to orgasm. As Jim gained confidence, he was able to stop using a condom. He was not, however, confident enough to cease taking medication.

Peter learned several things by treating Jim and Tammy: (1) the many ways in which a couple can sabotage straightforward sex therapy exercises; (2) the creative ways in which couple and sex therapy can be applied; and (3) the importance of having some specialized sex therapy experience when working with couples with sexual problems. Without specialized supervision in sex therapy, I highly doubt Peter would have lasted very long as Jim and Tammy's therapist.

William was in his MFT program's sex therapy track. Although he had been trained to treat some sexual disorders, he admitted that he needed an experienced supervisor to help him negotiate difficult cases. For example, William presented a married couple, Harold and Lena, who were unable to have children primarily because Lena had vaginismus – as diagnosed by an obstetrician-gynecologist (OB-GYN) William referred her to. While William had heard of this issue, and knew many therapists treated it with dilators, this was the extent of his knowledge about pain disorders. Lena's physician prescribed dilators, but William was at a loss when Lena reached the third of four dilators and Harold suddenly left the relationship. William was shocked by this development. He was sure that Harold would be ecstatic because Lena was close to having intercourse with him, but this only showed William's lack of experience.

As William's supervisor, I warned him that Harold was not used to getting what he wants in life as evident by his genogram. Therefore, if Lena was finally able to have sex with him, he might be uncomfortable. I told William that it was relatively normal for a man such as Harold to create a disturbance like revealing an affair, or leaving the relationship, to avoid getting what he said he wanted: sex from his wife. I further warned him that this usually occurs when the third dilator is introduced.

I recommended that William speak to Harold about my theory. It might challenge him to own what he deserves rather than reject it. When the case came to a successful conclusion with Harold and Lena regularly engaging in intercourse, William admitted that he would never have figured out what was going on without supervision.

References

Adebisi, O. Y., & Carlson, K. (2024). Female sexual interest and arousal disorder. *National Library of Medicine* and *National Center for Biotechnology Information*. www.statpearls.com/point-of-care/157560

Adedipe, T. O., & Chukwujama, U. (2021). Vulvar endometriosis mimicking as primary vulvodynia in a young nulliparous woman: Algorithm of care following a rapid literature review. *Journal of Clinical Gynecology & Obstetrics*, *10*, 35–39. https://jcgo.org

Betchen, S. (2022). *Couples in conflict: Clinical techniques for navigating sexual and relationship control struggles*. Routledge.

Betchen, S. (2024). *Unmet expectations in couple and sex therapy: Helping couples negotiate realistic relationships*. Routledge.

Betchen, S. (2025). *Commitment in couples therapy: A therapist's guide to assessing relationship durability*. Routledge.

Betchen, S., & Davidson, H. (2018). *Master conflict therapy: A new model for practicing couples and sex therapy*. Routledge.

Chen, X., Wang, F. X., Chao, H., Nian-Qin, Y., & Ji-Can, D. (2018). Penile sensory thresholds in subtypes of premature ejaculation implications of comorbid erectile dysfunction. *Asian Journal of Andrology*, *20*, 330–335. doi: 10.4103/aja.aja_62_17

Coskuner, E. R., & Ozkan, B. (2022). Premature ejaculation and endocrine disorders: A literature review. *World Journal of Men's Health*, *40*, 38–51. doi: 10.5534/wjmh.200184.

Doherty, W. (2002). Bad couples therapy: How to avoid doing it. *Psychotherapy Networker*, *26*, 26–33.

Kitaw, T. A., Abate, B. B., Tilsahun, B. D., Yilak, G., Rede, M. B., Getie, A., & Haile, R. N. (2024). The global burden of erectile dysfunction and its associated risk factors in diabetic patients: An umbrella reviews. *BMC Public Health*, *24*, 1–12. doi: 10.1186/s12889-024-20300-7

Köehler, T. S., Kloner, R. A., Rosen, R. C., Burnett, A. L., Blaha, M. J., Ganz, P., Goldstein, I., Kim, N. N., Lue, T., McVary, K. T., Muhall, J. P., Parish, S. J., Sadeghi-Nejad, H., Sadovsky, R., Sharlip, I. D., & Miner, M. (2024). The Princeton IV Consensus: Recommendations for the management of erectile dysfunction and cardiovascular disease. *Mayo Clinic Proceedings*, *99*, 1500–1517. doi: 10.10.16/j.mayocp.2024.06.002

Mozhedehipanah, H., Sharifi, N., & Mirzadeh, M., (2025). The prevalence of sexual dysfunction and its contributors among the women with multiple sclerosis. *BMC Women's Health*, 25, 1–12. https://doi.org/10.1186/s12905-025-03653-y

Przydacz, M., Rajwa, P., De Cillis, S., Guillot-Tantay, C., Herve, F., Fernandez, A. T., Tutolo, M., Culha, M. G., Geretto, P., Shenhar, C., Miszczyk, M., Chlosta, P., Phe, V., & Osman, N. (2024). Lower urinary tract symptoms correlate with erectile dysfunction and premature ejaculation but not with men's sexual activity: Results from a large population-representative study. *Healthcare*, *12*, 1–12. https://doi:10.3390/healthcare12141408

Raveendran, A. V., & Agarwal, A. (2021). Premature ejaculation – current concepts in the management: A narrative review. *International Reproductive BioMedecine*, *19*, 5–22. https://doi.org/10.18502/ijrm.v19i1.8176

Schecter, A., & Gruenwald, I. (2024). New technologies developed for the treatment of premature ejaculation. *International Journal of Impotence Research*, *36*, 700–705. https://doi.org/10.1038/s41443-024-00875-w

Zizzo, J., Gater, D. R., Hough, S., & Ibrahim, E. (2022). Sexuality, intimacy, and reproductive health after spinal cord injury. *Journal of Personalized Medicine*, *12*, 1–12. 10.3390/jpm12121985

Chapter 4

Structuring Supervision

Studies show there is a need for a framework or structure to treat couples efficiently and effectively (Gurman, 2010; Weeks & Fife, 2014); others show it is an important organizing factor when supervising the therapists who treat them (Celano et al., 2010). The following is the general organizational structure I use when supervising couple and sex therapy. Although much of what I present can be applied to the supervision process in any context, note that the supervisor and supervisee working together in a private practice setting have more flexibility and control over their process compared to those working or training at an institution. The latter individuals must follow policy and accept who they are assigned to work with (see **Figure 4.1**).

Forming an Alliance/Assessing Compatibility and Experience

Just as a therapist-couple fit is important for therapeutic success, it is equally important for supervisor and supervisee to form a positive and functional alliance. Holloway (2016) wrote: "The relationship of supervision is central to the learning alliance between supervisor and supervisee" (p. 15). According to Watkins (2014): "The supervisory alliance has come to be increasingly regarded as the crucial and pivotal component in the successful prosecution of the supervision relationship, considered to substantively affect and contribute to its ongoing process and eventual outcome" (p. 42). Cheon et al. (2009) believed a good working alliance was a strong predictor of supervisee satisfaction. And Martin et al. (2014) found that a strong supervisor–supervisee fit leads to higher quality supervision, even when using telesupervision.

In my opinion, from the point of initial contact – be it by email, telephone, or in person, the potential supervisor and supervisee should feel comfortable personally and professionally. This is not to suggest that

DOI: 10.4324/9781003642732-4

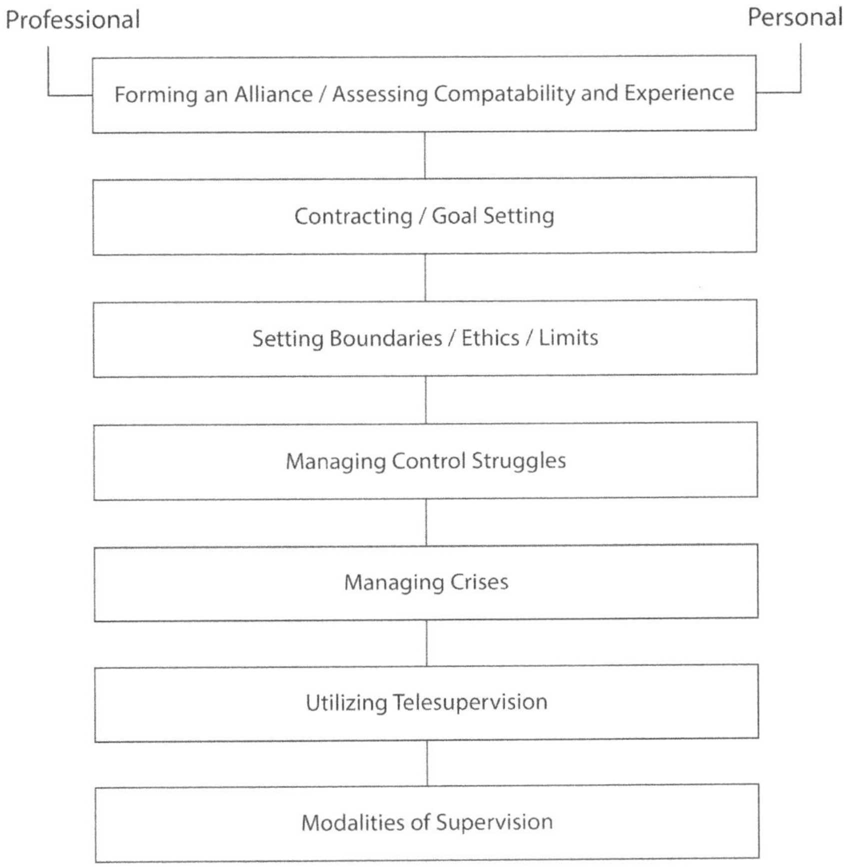

Figure 4.1 Structuring Supervision

initial discomfort and perceived differences cannot eventually be worked through by clarifying them with an open and frank discussion along with patience on the part of all participants – many can (Tracey, 2006). But first impressions count when contemplating entering any new relationship. I have heard far too many therapists, supervisors, and supervisees express regret over ignoring their first impressions in the match process, especially when their intuition told them the match would be problematic.

As mentioned, not all supervisors can choose their supervisees, especially those who work in clinics or teaching institutes. In these instances, the supervisor will have to make a concerted effort to align with the supervisee. One way I do this is to look for some strength in the supervisee;

something admirable or a trait that shows potential. A supervisee may have a somewhat challenging personality, but he or she may also be brilliant and have a great future. A young graduate student I supervised joined exceptionally well with couples and had obvious clinical talent. But she neglected to follow clinic policy and fell far behind on her paperwork. I had no idea that she was neglectful in this way until I received a call from the director of supervision threatening to terminate her. Knowing this would be a great loss, I joined with the supervisee in her hatred of paperwork but helped her to understand that she was sabotaging her career. I told her that losing her would be a great loss for the clinic, his university, and the public. Thankfully, she made a surge, caught up on her paperwork, and graduated on time.

Some supervisees are late bloomers that only prosper with the patience of a calm and confident supervisor. A young post-graduate supervisee overreacted to constructive clinical criticism and lost emotional control. My initial thought was to report her to the director of the program. But instead, I kept it to myself and processed her sensitivity with her. By the middle of her second year, she developed into one of my strongest supervisees. I apparently had to weather her storms and give her the time and space to grow. Rothwell et al. (2021) found that some of the barriers to effective clinical supervision were a lack of time, space, and trust.

Professional Compatibility and Experience

Interests

One of the first questions I ask a potential supervisee is: What kind of supervision are you looking for? Because I only do couple and or sex therapy and prefer to train how to integrate the two, I limit my supervision to a supervisee who has the same interest. While I am less rigid about this, I also look for someone willing to consider my conflict model of supervision. They may have been previously trained in other models, but they must be open to learning something new or applying aspects of my approach to their pre-existing model. I am hesitant to accept a supervisee who is looking for a fundamentally different model of supervision or one outside my realm of expertise. For example, if someone insists on cognitive-behavioral therapy (CBT) supervision it would serve them better to find a CBT supervisor. As mentioned, in an institutional setting both supervisor and supervisee might have to work with someone they ordinarily would not, but I am more discriminatory in the private practice setting.

Psychotherapy has become so specialized that when legally deposed or issued a subpoena, the first thing the therapist is challenged on is credentials.

The process will most likely be easier if a therapist has specialized training; a few publications in the area may help to establish authority and expertise. I will, however, give myself some clinical leeway. For example, I may not be a specialist in a certain area, such as sexual abuse, but I feel I know enough about it to be able to adequately supervise someone looking for help in this area.

Being a sex therapist does afford me a certain amount of general expertise that I can rely on to best serve the client and supervisee. Nevertheless, once you choose to treat or supervise someone it's hard to end the relationship. And a rejected individual may not take it too lightly. Treat the supervisory process as if you are entering into a potentially long-term relationship with someone – someone you look forward to being with. If you can wait for the right fit, it is well worth it to get someone you enjoy working with.

Openness

Supervising someone in couple and sex therapy requires the supervisee to be open to a myriad of sexual problems that couples might present, some of which the supervisee might find triggering. I will work with supervisees who are at least open to becoming more comfortable discussing sexual issues, but I am reluctant to accept someone in supervision if they are unable to confront these issues. Bjorn (2023) wrote: "Without established and robust sex-positive frameworks in supervision, the clinical supervisor is exposed to incompetent practices that miss an adequate assessment, detection, and treatment, all critical elements of the conceptualization process" (p. 88). Again, practicing and supervising in an institutional setting may not afford such an option.

A young woman requested couple therapy supervision but distinctly told me that she would have to refer all couples who present with sexual symptoms and that she had personal reasons for taking this stance. I told her that I respected her position, but because I view the two areas as often linked, I did not think I would be a good fit for her. She was so adamant in her position that I did not feel it would have turned out well to give her a lecture on what critical issues she might miss in the couple's overall picture that could render the treatment ineffective.

Asking pertinent questions about a potential supervisee's background, interests, and career goals is one way to ensure a good professional supervisor–supervisee fit. This is especially true if the supervision is to take place in the supervisor's private practice. Another way is to request a supervisee's resume. This document can either support or refute the supervisee's initial assertions about his or her experience and interests.

If someone prefers to supervise in an institute or clinic, I recommend they try and do so in one that specializes in his or her area of expertise. For example, working for several years at the Marriage Council of Philadelphia (now Council for Relationships) which specialized in marital/couple and sex therapy, was the right place for someone with my professional credentials and goals. I was guaranteed to supervise trainees who held interests that were aligned with my own. Those who specialized in family therapy were more attracted to the now defunct, but once renowned Philadelphia Child Guidance Clinic.

Developmental Stages

I also question supervisees about their experience in treating couples with sexual problems. In private practice, I prefer to supervise experienced, licensed supervisees. In clinics and institutes, I do not have this luxury, and so my best advice is to supervise individuals in these settings more closely. To assess the experiential level of a supervisee, I look to the developmental models of supervision. These models are designed to track growth and delineate supervisees into dynamic stages of clinical competence and maturity. For example, McNeil and Stoltenberg (2016) categorize supervisees into three stages of development: beginner, intermediate, and advanced.

Beginner

Beginner supervisees usually need close monitoring and more clinical direction. It is vital that the supervisor pay attention to the types of couples the supervisee can handle. High conflict couples are usually not a good match for beginners – this kind of case will only decrease their confidence and increase their anxiety – which they have enough of in this stage. Expectations of both the supervisor and supervisee should be realistic. Couple therapy alone is hard enough to become competent in, let alone the integration of couple and sex therapy. That is why I tend to look at this stage as "educational," where I may explain theory to supervisees at this level and how it might fit with the cases they are presenting. Supervision is also more prescriptive in this stage. I go over with supervisees the basic sex disorders, their causes, and how they are generally treated. I may give beginner supervisees examples of integrating couple and sex therapy and refer them to various readings.

In the beginner stage, I strongly urge supervisees to first take non-sexual and sexual histories of each partner, including dating histories. I do not expect them to draw any ingenious hypotheses about the couple, but

I want them to get used to the idea of gathering important data, and to develop a framework for the treatment. Too many supervisees have presented cases to me without being able to answer some of my most basic questions about the couple. I find having a history of the couple makes it easier to spot a couple's interactional patterns, and to distinguish a couple's relational process from their sexual content. All this data should be recorded by the supervisee on the couple's genogram.

Intermediate

In this stage I can trust the supervisee to handle more difficult couples. I am, therefore, less prescriptive, focusing more on reinforcing the supervisee's clinical decision making. I do, however, challenge supervisees. That is, I expect supervisees at this stage to begin to demonstrate a theoretical understanding of clinical theory and to apply it to couple and sex therapy. I also challenge any countertransference reactions and expect supervisees to openly process these in supervision.

Advanced

In the advanced stage of supervision, supervisees are better able to handle cases – which they have little to no experience – by utilizing their advanced training and natural ability. I also expect them to be more creative in their interventions and to be able to assess a couple much more quickly than they could in earlier stages. The integration of couple and sex therapy should, in theory and practice, be almost seamless. The breadth and depth of their clinical experience and training, by now, should have familiarized them to a wider range of couple dynamics and a variety of sexual disorders they would ordinarily not have been exposed to.

Personal Compatibility

Not all people get along, and even the most seasoned of supervisors, who value objectivity, will not work well with everyone. The same can be said for choosing a supervisor. While professional differences should be taken seriously, personality-fit can be equally important. I recommend that supervisors try not to "fit a square peg into a round hole." That is, if you do not like something about somebody there is no use trying to force a relationship. It is preferable to understand what that potential supervisee is setting off inside you, or the transference-countertransference dynamic that is operating and to process with supervisees as soon as possible.

According to Heers (2022), ruptures are quite common in the supervision process, especially if a supervisee feels the supervisor is falling short of expectations, or if the supervisor is expecting too much. The author refers to this as the "storming stage" (p. 1). But some people cannot make a relationship work no matter how much it is analyzed. For example, as a young supervisor at a clinic, I was assigned a supervisee, Wyatt, who seemed to hate me from the moment he walked into my office. I tried to process this with him, but it would only anger him further. When I brought this up to my supervisor, she told me to "hang in there" and that the challenge would be "good for my professional growth." I disagreed but followed her orders.

As time went on, however, Wyatt became more belligerent and hostile until one day he told me that his psychiatrist thought he should request a new supervisor. As he was leaving, I asked why he disliked me so much given that I had never met him before. He told me that we both grew up in the same neighborhood and that he was bullied as a child. Although this jogged my memory, I knew nothing of his history of being bullied. I told him that I was sorry that he was in pain but that I had nothing to do with it. He said that he knows that I did not bully him, but because I was from the same neighborhood he automatically associated me with his torturers. Having heard this I told Wyatt that perhaps now might be a good time for us to process this transference, he disagreed and abruptly terminated treatment. I suspect he might have taken some sadistic pleasure in our dynamic.

As I will discuss later in the book, internalized conflicts drive partner choices in intimate relationships; the same is true in supervisor–supervisee relationships. In clinics where supervisors and supervisees are thrown together, like Wyatt and I were, there is not much choice. But in private practice, underlying conflicts are unconsciously drawn together. For example, the supervisees that I have had the most productive and lasting relationships with shared my internal conflict.

Jeannie, a brilliant and ambitious doctoral student, wanted to learn everything she could and would only train under the biggest names in the field. But another part of her disdained the spotlight and preferred to hide her talent. I have a similar conflict about being "big," but I had the opportunity to work on this conflict for years. Nevertheless, Jeannie and I worked together exceedingly well because I recognized the conflict and we were able to work it out. That is, I encouraged Jeannie to continue to seek the best training, but I refrained from pushing her into the limelight. She, on the other hand, was proud of my accomplishments but could be critical if she felt I was becoming too commercial.

While working at a clinic I was assigned a supervisee, Linda, who only wished to do the basics: get her degree, obtain her license, and open a practice. It was difficult to get her to commit to the field or to give back to it in any way. I even offered to write a journal article with her, but she resisted any extra work. She made it clear that although she found conflict theory useful with her couples, she did not want to change anything in her professional life. She said she had loans to pay back, and this was her major real goal. I got the message and decided not to push Linda beyond her comfort level if she was doing solid clinical work. I knew this would only escalate into something even more uncomfortable. Linda had her reasons for the way she felt, and although they were foreign to me, I respected them in the supervisory process. We both made it through the required semester of supervision, but whatever Linda's conflict was, it did not match with mine. I doubt either of us would have chosen the other if we had the option.

Contracting (and Goal Setting)

Osborn and Davis (2008) have cited five reasons that merit the need for a contract in clinical supervision: (1) clarify goals and expectations; (2) foster collaboration; (3) ensure ethical practice; (4) record services; and (5) align both the supervisory and therapeutic process. The authors also listed six terms to be included in a supervisory contract: (1) goals of supervision; (2) the context of the service provided; (3) how progress will be measured; (4) duties of both parties; (5) the maintenance of procedures agreed to; and (6) supervisor's scope of practice and supervision.

Contracting is certainly used to clarify the supervision process for both supervisor and supervisee, but it is especially needed in our litigious world. While I do not follow the recommendations of Osborn and Davis (2008) completely, I do draw up a contract that may help to protect me should any misunderstandings arise in the supervision process. Although the business-like terms may seem awkward given the nature of the relationship, these terms are important in both the client-therapist and supervisor–supervisee context.

As mentioned in the previous chapter, I limit my supervision to my scope of practice (i.e., couple therapy and sex therapy) and avoid dual relationships with supervisees as recommended by the American Association of Sex Educators, Counselors and Therapists (2024). I also make sure to include: the agreed upon length of the supervision process (e.g., one year); the fee and how missed supervisory sessions will be handled; how crises will be managed (e.g., when I will be available to the supervisee and their obligation to inform me of a crisis or potential crisis); the obligation of the supervisee to be HIPPA compliant; the need to take readable progress notes, especially during a crisis; and the types of cases I will be responsible for (e.g., cases not supervised by another supervisor). I want to make sure that the supervisee initially gives me a full list of the cases (and continuously update this list) rather than pick one or two problematic cases and fail to mention the rest. Previously, I allowed a supervisee to present the cases he or she was having difficulty with, but I soon learned the hard way that some supervisees fail to realize that they have less control over their cases than they think.

Mia presented what she thought were her problematic cases in weekly supervision. However, she failed to inform me that she had split a couple up for a session and inadvertently revealed to the wife that her husband told her in his confidential session that he hated his mother-in-law. The wife's sister, a therapist, convinced her to threaten my supervisee with an ethical violation. Forced to intervene, I had to find a way out of the situation, but it was a stressful time.

It is also safer practice to request that supervisees obtain a release form signed by their couples giving permission to present their cases for supervision. While couples being treated in an institution or teaching clinic are likely to know if their therapist is in supervision, couples being seen in private practice are not. While I have never experienced a problem in this context, it is better to be careful rather than risk a breach of confidentiality.

In institutional settings formal assessment is usually ongoing, including mid-term and final evaluations, along with the continuous signing of supervisee progress notes on each of their cases. While I do not assess the progress of a supervisee in private practice in a formal way, I do discuss this issue with all supervisees. To manage expectations, I have supervisees state their goals for the supervisory process in a space provided on the formal contract. I feel if I cannot help the supervisee achieve these clinical goals, I will not sign the contract. If I feel I can help them achieve their goals, but I believe that it will take longer than the time they agreed to stay in supervision, I will tell them so and note this in the contract. I may, for example, use the words "limited gains promised" next to a listed goal.

If a potential supervisee has unrealistic expectations about the supervision process it may be a sign of a conflict that will hinder the success of the supervisory process. Becoming proficient in both couple and sex therapy will usually take longer than supervision of couple therapy or sex therapy alone. My experience has been that a supervisee planning to train in this dual specialty should plan on a minimum of two years of supervision, but this will vary according to the supervisee's capabilities.

Setting Boundaries/Ethics/Limits

Just as winning the battle for structure (Whitacker & Keith, 1981) is vital in the therapeutic process, it is equally valuable in the supervisory process. Establishing boundaries and setting appropriate limits helps to further clarify the supervisor–supervisee relationship. And while almost all professional organizations have their ethical guidelines for the practice of supervision, I will only mention a few that I feel are especially applicable to couple and sex therapy.

While some supervisors prefer to see their supervisees as colleagues or peers, and believe that the supervision process should foster egalitarianism, I tend to modify this approach. If the supervisee believe they are colleagues, they may see themselves in partnership with the supervisor and believe they have equal say on what happens in supervision and with their couples. I let the supervisee know that there is a hierarchal structure. I also believe this helps to discourage any thought of intimacy or supervisory resistance. This boundary comes in handy especially in times of clinical crisis where some supervisees, feeling equal, might contest my decision on a matter of life or death. Less dramatically, it could lead to a couple's unnecessary divorce, or a legal issue that could have been avoided.

Supervisors are not God-like, but most do have a lot more clinical experience than their supervisees and may be able to see a serious problem developing it long before most supervisees do. Having said this, I do treat the supervisee with respect, and I foster mutual trust (Rothwell et al., 2021). I also refrain from treating rather than teaching the supervisee with an emphasis on learning and emotional growth (Frederickson, 2015).

Brittany was a young MFT candidate working with her first couple. She got into a control struggle with the wife, Janice, who wanted her husband, Todd, to find another job. Todd worked as a bouncer at an erotic strip club and hoped to open his own strip bar one day. He saw it as "a recession proof business." Janice, on the other hand, thought that the job was not only dangerous – Todd ended up in the hospital on more than one occasion because of physical altercations, including stabbings – but she also was concerned about sexual temptation. She claimed that Todd already had flings with two of the dancers. Todd, who dropped out of high school after his sophomore year, could not see himself doing anything else. Brittany decided to form a coalition with Todd and in the process drew Janice's ire.

While I suggested that Brittany was unbalancing the couple and provoking a control struggle with Janice, she did not seem to care. She in fact admitted that she has a problem when one partner tries to control the other and that her mother did the same to her father. She saw her countertransference as justified. Brittany was sure she was in the right, even if it destroyed the couple's marriage. I eventually had to contact the director of the program because Britanny was consistently putting the couple's marriage at risk by forming a coalition with the husband. Even more dangerous, Janice began to think that Brittany was showing interest in Todd.

Cruikshanks and Burns (2021) wrote: "Boundary violations happen when interactions deviate markedly from the social conventions of professional relationships. Sexual boundary violations happen when sexual behavior is introduced into the training relationship" (p. 1952). I also make it a priority to set clear sexual boundaries between myself and the supervisee and demand that the supervisee do the same with client-couples. It is especially important because, as I have said before, there is a natural attraction to someone with the same internal conflict.

While I do not raise this issue unless it becomes a factor, I always keep it in mind. Staying in control of oneself is especially important in the supervision of couple and sex therapy because much of the material discussed will be of a sexual nature and may stir up feelings that could complicate or deteriorate the supervisory process (Koenig & Spano, 2004). I have, however, confronted more than one supervisee on their provocative dress in supervision, and when treating couples. In my experience, this can indicate a need the supervisee has to seduce the supervisor and possibly a client. For example, Gina, my supervisee, seemed to wear low necklines in supervision until I finally had to gently request that she dress in a less-distracting manner. I explained that this would be best for both of us. Fortunately, she complied.

John, another of my supervisees, treated a woman, Jill, who was very flirtatious and provocative in treatment. Her flirtations with other men were in fact the reason her husband, Kevin, brought the couple in for treatment. The more flirtatious Jill was in treatment, however, the more excited and enabling John became, and the more depressed and helpless Kevin felt. I processed this triangle with John in supervision and requested that he curb his enabling. I also recommended that he begin confronting Jill on her behavior and work with Kevin on his powerlessness.

Perhaps the most egregious breach of boundaries that I have heard about in the context of supervision was relayed to me by a colleague. The colleague, another supervisor of couples and sex therapy, was contacted by an attorney representing the husband of a couple he was supervising. Apparently, the treating supervisee was having an affair with the wife of a couple he had been treating for months for sexual difficulty. The supervisee had told the wife that he could help her to achieve the orgasm her husband could not evoke in her.

When the affair was finally exposed, the husband, both angry and distraught, decided to take legal action. The supervisee, who was licensed at the time, was eventually suspended. I am not sure what the consequences were for my colleague, who claimed to feel shocked, guilty, and embarrassed about his supervisee's unethical behavior and his failure to prevent it.

It is important for the supervisor dealing with sexual issues to conform to the agreed-upon allotted supervisory time and refrain from spending time with the supervisee outside of the appointed supervisory session. These limits indicate to the supervisee that the supervisory relationship is purely professional. I also limit touching to handshakes, and I refrain from disclosing any information that may indicate I may be unhappy with certain aspects of my personal life, especially that of a sexual nature.

Affairs often begin with a mutual commiseration of partners, so I find it best not to communicate such information. I also maintain a certain seating distance from the couples I treat and the therapists I supervise. I once saw a female supervisee who claimed our chairs were "too far apart." While I allowed her to move somewhat closer, I noticed that she in fact moved her chair closer with every session until I became uncomfortable and insisted that she move back to her original spot.

It is optimal for supervisors, especially those working with sexual content, to do what they can to have as healthy a personal relationship as possible and to take care of themselves emotionally, spiritually, and physically to help to prevent burnout (Posluns & Gall, 2019). I also believe this helps them to function at a higher level clinically and to maintain better therapeutic boundaries. If, however, a supervisor is in poor physical health, feels emotionally drained, lonely, or even sexually deprived, it will be easier for a potentially dangerous countertransference to interfere with their work.

I have direct discussions with the supervisees about the consequences of forming any type of dual relationship with one or both partners of a couple. I discuss the potential consequences they might face if caught, and that I will feel obligated to report them as their supervisor. If this seems like an attempt to scare them straight, it is. The punishment for losing one's boundaries, especially sexually, can be quite severe from listening to colleagues who once lost their way. It is never worth it. Being accused and found guilty of unethical behavior of any kind can ruin a professional's life.

One of the most common limit-setting problems I see in supervision is when the supervisee fails to collect fees for service or fails to collect them in a timely fashion, thus allowing clients to build up debt. Therapists are natural caretakers, given that a good portion of them were parentified in their families of origin (Boszormenyi-Nagy & Spark, 1973; Lackie 1983; Sessions, 1986). Jung (1946/1966) is credited as referring to those in the mental health field as "wounded healers."

In my experience, getting some supervisees to charge an appropriate amount for their clinical services and to collect the fee can evoke guilt in individuals who were trained to give of themselves with little to no reciprocity. But failing to be financially reciprocated may lead to unrealistic expectations, enabling client dependency, and may give clients the wrong impression of the relationship between client and therapist. If the supervision takes place in an institute or clinic where it is against policy to ignore the collection of fees, the supervisee may face sanctioning or termination.

Jeremy was an intermediate level supervisee interning in a teaching clinic. He was an excellent clinician skilled in couple, family, and sex therapy but he had one big problem: he always seemed to feel sorry for his clients. Any hardship story he was told compelled him to request my authorization for a fee reduction. While some circumstances merited this and were granted, others did not. In fact, some of Jeremy's fees were set so low, they were almost negligible.

While I processed this issue with Jeremy several times in supervision, it did no good as he soon fell very behind in his fee collection duties. When I told him that the director of the clinic was getting angry, he became overtly obstinate and accused both me and the clinic of lacking empathy. The situation deteriorated to the point that I was ordered to terminate Jeremy's supervision if he did not comply with the clinic's standards within two weeks. Luckily, Jeremy finally gave in and was able to attribute his stance on this issue to his childhood parentification. To my pleasant surprise, supervision continued.

Managing Control Struggles

Control struggles in couples are defined as a disagreement in a context in which partners take the opposite side of the argument, and they cannot seem to break the gridlock (Betchen, 2022). In supervision this can happen between supervisor and supervisee. For the supervisor to maintain order and a hierarchical structure in the supervisory process he or she must avoid these struggles or break out of them – which is not easy.

I was supervising Alice, a first-year student in a marriage and family therapy program. Alice appeared to me to be very controlling, and she viewed me the same way. But when I noticed that she established a pattern of siding with the husbands of the couples she was treating in our clinic, I challenged her problem with "balance." Instead of appreciating my comment she took offense and told me that I could not know what was going on in her cases because I was not treating the couple. At first, I used an intellectual approach, trying to explain how the pattern could be destructive and unbalance the couples, but this only solidified her stance.

Alice was experiencing countertransference with her couples and a related transference with me in supervision.

I talked to Alice about our control struggle and emphasized that we needed to end it for everyone's sake. She then revealed the origin of her transference-countertransference: "My mother always held me back and if it were not for my father I would not even be in this program. It seems to me that it is always the wives who quash their husband's dreams." It was then obvious to both Alice and I that she saw her female clients, and me as her supervisor, as blocking her dreams and the dreams of the men she treated.

James was a first-year MFT graduate student who presented the case of a couple in which the husband had a drinking problem that was interfering with his marriage and his work. But when I called this man an alcoholic and questioned whether James had addressed this in treatment, James became enraged with me. He told me that alcoholism ran in his family and that he would know an alcoholic if he saw one. He said that he grew up with an alcoholic mother.

The problem in this case was that James was not only in denial about his client, but he was putting all of us, including the clinic, at risk because his client had suffered many blackouts. Warning James of the legal implications of his denial and the fact that his client could severely hurt himself, even die, did not seem to shake James out of his position on the case.

Unfortunately, not all control struggles can be processed in supervision, and this was one of those times. I therefore reported James to the director of supervision who sided with my view and threatened his prospects of graduating if he could not be more compliant in supervision. James finally acquiesced and referred his client for detox; our supervision then continued. James never apologized and I never held it against him either. Luckily, his tendency to enter a control struggle was limited to this one specific area, and we never again had a case like this. It could also be that James was concerned about extending his control struggle to the director.

It is prudent for the supervisor to determine early on whether a potential supervisee has a tendency for need to control. These individuals may want to learn but find it hard to be vulnerable enough to submit to the learning process. Often this oppositional behavior will show itself in the contracting phase of supervision. One unique example comes to mind.

While I request that couples sign a short HIPPA form to protect their confidentiality, a woman presenting for couple therapy with her husband insisted that my supervisee give her a complete copy of the Health Insurance Portability and Accountability Act regulations. When the supervisee complied, however, the woman sat in the waiting room and proceeded to read the entire binder of regulations. Her husband volunteered that it was his wife's way of letting both he and my supervisee know that she was in control. Appropriately, the supervisee let the woman read the entire book and charged the couple full fee for the 10 minutes they had left time for. The wife's husband was furious with her, but this incident set the treatment on its path.

I assess the potential for a control struggle in the very first contact with the supervisee. If I sense the supervisee can work through a control struggle, I will consider them. If I determine they cannot, I will refer them to another supervisor, even if I am in a clinic where my choices are less flexible; it will depend on how difficult I believe a supervisee will be. While winning the battle for structure in the supervisory process helps, it does not always serve as a deterrent for control struggles along the way.

Managing Crises

In the context of couple and sex therapy, crises tend to center around infidelity, or the threat of divorce over a chronic problem that has never been adequately addressed in the relationship. In extreme cases, these problems can lead to suicidal intent or behavior in at least one partner, but I have seen only a handful of such cases in over 40 years of practicing couple and sex therapy. Erring on the side of caution, however, I like to form working relationships with other professionals (e.g., psychiatrists) who I can call upon in an emergency such as a potential suicide, and I insist that the supervisee does the same.

The referral will come after the supervisee and I have assessed the client using an established safety plan. The approach I prefer is based on the five-step evaluation and triage plan developed by the Substance Abuse and Mental Health Services Administration (SAMHSA) (2024). This plan includes identifying risk factors, protective factors, conducting a suicide inquiry, determining risk level and intervention, and documenting all interactions. In case a referral needs to be made, other than to an emergency room, I urge all my supervisees to establish a relationship with two to three psychiatrists.

I make it clear that the supervisee is to contact me immediately if a crisis ensues. I give my cell phone number to all my supervisees, with the expectation that they can call me at any time for an emergency; they have never abused that privilege. In fact, I find if they make any mistake, it is because they try to handle crises by themselves. Experienced supervisees are more likely to pull this off, but younger ones tend to get into trouble. One of the most common miscalculations is when a young supervisee does not take the work of psychotherapy seriously enough. Since we do not work in the field of medicine, where there may be the constant threat of death, some supervisees woefully underestimate the risk. They do not yet understand how a few choice words can damage someone or that sexual issues can trigger past traumas and lead to depression and debilitation (Watter, 2023).

An inexperienced supervisee unilaterally (and without informing me) decided to hold an individual session with the wife of a couple she was treating. Because the wife seemed to be holding back vital information, the supervisee's goal was to determine the true cause of why the woman was contemplating leaving her husband. During the session, the wife finally confessed that she was quite dissatisfied with her husband's sexual performance and that it was inferior to her experience with a previous boyfriend. Although this was apparently serious enough to drive her out of her relationship, she did not want to confess the true cause of her unhappiness to her husband and therefore blamed her dissatisfaction with him on various other things such as his spending habits or his reluctance to do more of the chores around the house.

Making a bad situation worse, the supervisee let some of what she learned from the wife in confidence slip in a couple session and the husband left the session terribly depressed. The wife was very angry with the supervisee, even threatening to stop treatment. But in the following session the husband shared his feelings for the first time. Seemingly in great pain he told his wife and supervisee that the first girl he was "madly in love with," cheated and left him for someone she said was a "much better lover."

While the wife was grateful for her husband's revelation, she did not appreciate the supervisee's breach of confidence, and neither did I. The supervisee defended herself by claiming that she thought her breach would expose the couple's real issues. But for her efforts she was put on probation by her program and told never to split a couple unless it was first brought up in supervision.

An understandably scared supervisee received an emergency call that she immediately informed me about. The husband of a couple she was treating had just found out that his wife had an affair with someone at work. The husband called the supervisee in the middle of a panic attack and told her that he would consider suicide if his wife left him. My first reaction was to ask the supervisee what she wanted to do. This showed confidence in her and gave me an indication of her crisis management skills. The supervisee, a very competent clinician, wanted to hold an emergency conjoint session and refer the husband to a psychiatrist if she could not calm him. I agreed in part, because the husband only threatened suicide if abandoned, and the supervisee needed to discern whether this was a realistic concern.

The conjoint session was held within a couple of hours and in it the wife confessed to what she called "a brief fling." She said that she was not thinking about leaving her marriage and that her lover felt the same way about his – he had a wife and three children that he was not necessarily willing to sacrifice. The wife claimed that the transgression lasted approximately one month and that she stopped it two weeks ago out of tremendous guilt. According to the supervisee she then profusely apologized to her husband and said, "It was the dumbest thing I ever did, and I put all of us at risk." She claimed that she wanted to stay in treatment to better understand her issues with the marriage and that she hoped he would too because in her opinion he was complicit in the fling. I praised the supervisee for her diligence and told her that I had the utmost confidence in her moving forward. I pointed out that her initial anxiety was not a sign of weakness but a sign of caring and concern.

An inexperienced supervisee failed to take a young husband's threats to leave his brief marriage seriously. The couple suffered from Female Orgasmic Disorder (FOD). The supervisee stated that the wife was finally able to achieve orgasm manually, and making progress to having one with her husband when the husband decided to leave her. I first asked the supervisee why she thought the husband wanted his wife to achieve an orgasm to begin with. She then laughed and told me that it was an absurd question given all the fuss the man had been making about his limited and passionless sex life. I retorted that being in his position for so long might indicate that the man has a conflict about sex as well and that it may not reveal itself until he is offered what he wants, and he turns it down. I told her that it is not uncommon for a man to leave his relationship just as he is about to get what he wants. I illustrated this point earlier in a couple suffering from vaginismus. I told the supervisee that her unyielding belief in this man might be an indication of a countertransference.

While the supervisee smirked at me, within a few days she called in shock to tell me the man had just left his wife and rented a hotel room. This was a great teaching lesson in integrating couple and sex therapy: both partners were in conflict about enjoying sex. In processing the case in supervision, it unsurprisingly turned out that the supervisee had a conflict of her own: she wanted to believe that psychotherapy was a straight-forward business; not nearly as complicated as people would lead you to believe so she did not have to face that being insecure is part of inexperience.

I advise supervisees to follow my lead and avoid as many crisis-oriented cases as possible, especially if they cannot stomach them. This of course is easier said than done because a crisis may not show for some time. For example, intimate partner violence may only show itself in the middle of treatment. The supervisee will then merit special attention and enlightenment from the supervisor regarding the "cycle of violence," in which an individual who was subjected to violence when young may perpetuate it or be a victim of it as an adult (Wright & Fagan, 2014). Discussing the value of a safety plan with one's supervisee like the plan recommend by the National Center on Domestic and Sexual Violence (2025) might prove invaluable in a domestic crisis.

Because I have specific training in treating paraphilias, fetishes, and adult survivors of sexual abuse, I will supervise students who wish to specialize in these areas. But I recommend that supervisors and supervisees choose these cases carefully. Many can bring with them legal difficulties that neither supervisor nor supervisee may want to inherit. I do not have training in supervising cases concerning pedophiles, and I refer to those who do. My general mantra for supervision is to stick to what you know (or are willing to learn) and what you feel comfortable with. Given the nature of the practice of couple and sex therapy, I also recommend having at least one gynecologist, one urologist, and a specialist who may be more familiar with specific sexual issues the supervisor or supervisee are unfamiliar with.

Utilizing Telesupervision

According to the Health Resources & Services Administration (HRSA) (2022): "Telehealth is defined as the use of electronic information and telecommunication technologies to support long distance clinical health care, patient and professional health-related education, health administration, and public health" (p. 1). Some of these technologies include internet use, videoconferencing, and telephonic communications.

Hertlein and Blumer (2014) reported that the use of telehealth by couple and family therapists was slow moving prior to the coronavirus COVID-19 pandemic. The authors found that therapists were concerned about confidentiality, liability, licensing conflicts, and the training that would be required of them. However, when forced to embrace this new technology, especially videoconferencing where they could see the couple, they did so, and many now prefer to treat people from the comfort of their homes. In support of these findings, Hardy et al. (2021) reported that couple therapists were positive about the transition from in-person to telehealth therapy, with the majority noting they would continue providing teletherapy even after the pandemic had ended.

The outcome research on telehealth while somewhat limited, leaves room for optimism. Kysely et al. (2022) studied the efficacy of a behavioral couple's therapy program. In comparing videoconferencing to in-person treatment, the authors found that videoconferencing was comparable in relation to establishing a couple-therapist connection, positive therapeutic outcome, and overall treatment satisfaction. Hardy et al. (2021) found that regardless of the method they used while applying teletherapy to treat couples (i.e., emotional, cognitive, behavioral, systemic, family-of-origin, psychodynamic, or neuroscience), the teletherapy worked moderately well (33%), very well (38%), or extremely well (21%).

Steel et al. (2011) conducted a review of the literature on therapeutic interventions for chronic conditions. The authors found that interventions for both psychological and physical conditions delivered by videoconferencing produced similar treatment outcomes to in-person treatment. And Langarizadeh et al. (2017), in a systematic review of the literature, concluded that telemental health care was cost effective, yields promising outcomes, and is an invaluable way to get mental health services to those in under-developed communities.

Telesupervision is an outgrowth of the pandemic. In the words of Martin et al. (2017), it "offers an opportunity to overcome the tyrannies of distance, access and time" (p. 38). Perle and Zheng (2023) broadly defined telesupervision as "the supervision of a trainee from a distance through the use of technology (e.g., video, telephone, email)" (p. 2). In the context of couple and family therapy, Aviram and Nadan (2022) described telesupervision "as offering feedback on one's clinical work by electronic means, most often videoconferencing" (p. 1419).

Compared to teletherapy, there is little outcome-research on telesupervision. However, some studies have shown it to be an effective tool in training supervisees in their clinical work (Inman et al., 2018; Jordan & Fisher, 2016; Jordan & Shearer, 2019; Martin et al., 2017; Martin et al., 2023). Tarlow et al. (2020) compared the relative effectiveness between telesupervision and in-person supervision. The authors found "there was no significant decrease in participant-rated *supervision satisfaction* or *supervisory working alliance* after participants switched from the initial in-person supervision format to telesupervision" (p. 383).

Perle and Zheng (2023) have discussed what I refer to as some of the potential pros and cons of telesupervision:

Pros:

- Greater accessibility for training
- Promotes equity and inclusion by exposing supervisees to a greater number of supervisors
- Exposes supervisees to peers from different locations
- Allows for scheduling flexibility
- Reduces hierarchical issues between supervisor and supervisee
- Electronic communication lowers social inhibitions in the supervisee

- Allows the supervisees to become acquainted with the technology before treating clients

Cons:

- Potential confidentiality issues with the use of technology
- Interruptions by outsiders
- Requires a greater level of planning and a modicum of computer skill.
- Plan needed for clinical emergencies
- Greater potential for distractions

In agreement with Perle and Zheng (2023), and others (Appleton et al., 2021; Augusterfer et al., 2020), I, too, have also found telesupervision, especially videoconferencing, more flexible than in-person supervision (i.e., where the supervisor and supervisee are in the same room). It saves both supervisor and supervisee time and travel, and it does not limit the supervisor from supervising individuals who live beyond a feasible commute.

Prior to the advent of telesupervision, even though my clinical license allowed for it, I could not supervise those trainees who lived in the extreme northern part of the state – which would require at least a 2-hour drive to my office each way. Those who tried this commute would usually terminate their supervision within a month and I would end up losing most of these people to supervisors who held dual licenses in close neighboring states. Also, it is hard enough for a potential supervisee to find a supervisor trained in both couple therapy and sex therapy. The larger the geographical location they can pool from, the better. I prefer to meet with a telesupervision candidate in-person for the first session, and most comply. I rarely agree to hold telephone supervision unless I have already worked with an individual in-person or *via* telesupervision. I find supervision *via* the telephone a far too distant process.

From a clinical perspective, I have found telesupervision to be both less intimidating and embarrassing for supervisees, thus making it easier for them to address sexual issues. It allows me to supervise a wider diversity of supervisees, and several at the same time utilizing platforms such as "Zoom" where the content is shared within the group (Rousmaniere, 2014). But the distractions and interruptions that can come with telesupervision can be counterproductive and therefore limit-setting is somewhat different than when conducting in-person supervision. For example, there is a much greater chance that children, pets, maids, or handymen will interrupt supervision or may even be triangulated into the supervisory process. Consider the following example:

Kurt, a 32-year-old telesupervisee was referred for couple and sex therapy supervision by a former supervisee with whom I had a very positive experience. I initially found Kurt to be a very bright and talented clinician, but he also appeared somewhat controlling and fearful of criticism. Kurt presented a case to me in which he could only see the top of his client's heads on his computer. Although he complained about this, when I asked him to get the couple fix the screen, he resisted with little explanation. Because this continued, I suggested that this could be a sign of resistance from the couple – since they were in control of their screen – and that he will need to confront them. Once again, however, he resisted. It seemed to me that a parallel process, which will be discussed in detail in Chapter 8, was in play: the couple resisted Kurt's control and Kurt then resisted what he perceived as my need for control.

Faith, a 41-year-old supervisee conducted telesupervision from the confines of a quiet study. For the first two weeks of supervision all went well, but soon enough Faith demonstrated that she was fearful of constructive criticism and withheld some important information from me. This in turn made it harder for me to understand her cases and to help her. After confronting Faith, she began to employ a host of techniques to interrupt our supervision and cut the tension she was experiencing. For example, at the beginning of supervision Faith's dog was dying and Faith allowed her to stay in her study during supervision.

Although Faith would check on the dog from time to time, I did not find this disturbing enough to challenge. However, within a week of her dog dying Faith brought a puppy home that was quite disruptive. When I protested, Faith then followed with yet another puppy and soon the telesupervision was a circus with the puppies knocking over lamps and biting computer cords. Several times we lost our connection because of the antics of one or both puppies. When I pointed out that she was triangulating her dogs into supervision to cut her tension, she reluctantly moved them to another room during supervision. It was only another month before she totally terminated our supervision. I was not shocked in the least by the termination.

Discussing sexual issues is difficult enough but most couples are more protective of a discussion about sex in front of others, especially their children. Grames et al. (2022) mentioned that there is a tendency for both supervisors and supervisees to be distracted by their cell phones or to surf the internet during supervision. A colleague admitted to me that she likes telesupervision because it allows her to multi-task.

Danny, a young supervisee, was treating a wealthy, middle-aged couple in which the wife presented with Female Sexual Interest/Arousal Disorder (FSIAD); a problem which kept them from having sex for the past two years. The husband was angry and distraught about the situation but rather than continuing to fight directly with his wife, he reverted to expressing his feelings *via* constant sarcasm. Danny treated the couple online, and while they were compliant, they had a habit of allowing others to walk in and out of the room during their sessions.

Danny complained to me that no matter how uncomfortable he told the couple he was with this situation, they continued to allow their maid, or a child, to enter during their sessions. They then would stop talking until the person left. Danny said that this cut greatly into the couple's therapy time and made discussing sex almost impossible for him out of fear he would reveal something to the maid or even worse, to one of the couple's children.

I instructed Danny to take charge of the therapeutic structure by telling the couple that he could not conduct therapy under these conditions and if they insisted, he would have to refer them. I pointed out that the couple were trapped in their dilemma and that they were in turn trapping him by controlling the structure of the treatment – another example of parallel process. Danny took a couple more sessions to get up the nerve to confront the couple in part, because he said that he was afraid to lose them. Eventually he did, however, win back the structure and the couple acquiesced to Danny's wishes.

Despite the positive aspects of telesupervision, I admit that I find in-person supervision to be a more intimate process. I believe it can make both supervisor and supervisee feel more secure in the relationship, and it also demonstrates greater commitment to the supervisory process. Likewise, in-person supervision allows for more control over the supervisory process. That is, the supervisor can better control any distractions such as cell phone use or anybody else wandering into the office. Supervisors do not have to worry about technological difficulties, and it is especially more convenient in clinical emergencies. I also feel as if I can also get to know a supervisee on a deeper level. For all those reasons, in-person supervision is still primarily used in teaching clinics.

From an evaluative perspective, the supervisors who use telesupervision can witness their supervisee's actual treatment (in-person or one-way-mirror) *via* Remote Live Supervision (RLS) (Rousmaniere, 2014, Rousmaniere et al., 2014). According to Rousmaniere et al. (2014), this is where a webcam transmits live video of the interaction of the supervisee and couple to a supervisor in another location.

According to Wittenborn (2022), video feedback (VF) has been effective in the supervision of Emotionally Focused Therapy (EFT). This technology is used "to digitally make notations and flag important moments directly on a recording during live or video supervision" (p. 1060). All these methods usually require more preparation than most supervisors and supervisees are able or willing to put into the supervision process, especially those who provide private supervision out of their practices. Private practitioners prefer to rely on the supervisee's progress notes or case presentations.

The one-way-mirror method of supervision made popular by family therapists is still used in most teaching institutes and has proved to be an effective tool in supervising CBT trainees and psychoanalytic psychotherapists alike (Athar, 2021). Athar claimed that this method "brings out certain types of material, defenses and dynamics both in the patients and the therapists, which should be addressed in the supervisory relationship" (p. 97). He also stated: "The most apparent advantage of live supervision over post-hoc supervision is that the supervisor directly observes the sessions and gets an unedited picture of the running therapy sessions" (p. 99).

Audio and video recording are still used in some teaching institutes. And they have also proved to be effective in clinical supervision. According to McMahon and Ledden (2019), these methods enable learning, depict reality, and promote accountability. The negatives are increased anxiety and inhibition. The authors also warn of a greater potential for a breach of confidentiality which, according to Aveline (1992) merits attention to consent, and the security of tapes.

Topor et al. (2017) found video recording can increase a supervisor's objectivity and allow the supervisor to observe a supervisee's nonverbal behaviors. Benefits for supervisees include greater self-observation, self-reflection, and self-awareness. The biggest negative was heightened anxiety and the associated resistance to video-record.

I believe that supervisors should always keep in mind that no matter how well they structure the supervision process, and no matter how detailed the supervision contract is made to be, supervisees come with their own prejudices, perspectives, and conflicts, and these will inevitably show in the supervision process and test the supervisor no matter the medium.

Modalities of Supervision

There are many different supervisor–supervisee configurations. In this section I will address what I have found to be the most common, and only those that I have experienced. I therefore include one-on-one, one-on-two, and one-on-four supervision modalities.

One-on-One Supervision

This might be the easiest configuration for both the supervisor and supervisee. The supervisor only needs to join with one individual, and if the two are personally and professionally compatible, the supervision process will most likely be successful. In this context I often use the word "couple" metaphorically because while supervisor and supervisee are not in a romantic relationship, their relationship consists of up of two individuals working together towards a common goal.

I have had positive experiences with supervisees of both sexes. If supervisor and supervisee connect and like each other, the dynamic can be very productive. I have found that similar personalities and objectives tend to bring them together. I have always advocated for the success of my supervisees even if their goals were to eclipse my achievements – I take joy in that accomplishment. And while there is the potential, especially for a one-on-one configuration to evolve into an intimate relationship, I maintain focus on helping these individuals to grow, not to regress.

Perhaps the funniest but most meaningful thing a female supervisee has ever said to after completing supervision was: "I just want to thank you for not being weird." When I asked her to elaborate, she claimed that her experience with some male supervisors is that they somehow found a way to breach boundaries and make her feel uncomfortable. I thanked her for the compliment, but I could not help but feel sad for her that she had to endure those prior experiences. The following are some of the pros and cons that I have experienced, in one-on-one supervision:

<u>Pros:</u>

- More time to focus on and to have control over the supervisee's caseload.
- More time to process complex material.
- Offers more opportunity to bond.
- Easier for positive transference-countertransference to develop and be worked through.
- Can focus on one supervisee rather than worry about splitting time between others.
- The supervisor–supervisee couple can serve as a role model for a high functioning couple demonstrating good, clear communication and problem-solving capability.
- Less likely that triangulation will occur as it might with one-on-two supervisees.
- Less likely that destructive coalitions will form.

<u>Cons:</u>

- Tension cannot be diluted by the presence of other supervisees.
- Easier to stimulate negative transference and countertransference.
- Emotionally more difficult termination process.
- Easier for control struggles to develop.

- Greater potential for breaking personal and professional boundaries.
- Might be more difficult to discuss sex-related cases.
- The supervisee cannot share the cost of supervision.
- Misses the benefit of input, positive or negative, from peers.

I will admit that one-on-one supervision is only my second favorite mode of supervision. My favorite, although it can be more complex, is the one-on-two supervision modality.

One-on-Two Supervision

This mode of supervision in my opinion is a dynamic that best replicates working with a couple. The supervisor is in the therapist's position, and the two supervisees make up the couple. It might not be as intimate a process as the one-on-one mode, but I find it both interesting and stimulating. I especially like this mode of supervision when the supervisees are close colleagues and have a mutually vested interest in learning couple and sex therapy. This lends itself to an energy or excitement of learning in the air. Theories are passed back and forth, and therapeutic suggestions are usually in abundance. This is especially so if the supervisees were friends or colleagues prior to the supervision and that they mutually sought supervision out because of a shared need to become better or more informed clinicians.

I believe that when supervisees pursue supervision out of a need to learn as opposed to a need to satisfy certain requirements for certification or licensing, the clinical interest and energy is at its highest. In the former position supervisees act out of their own free will while in the latter situation there is a certain bureaucratic requirement to seek supervision, even though licenses and certifications are in place to protect clinicians and the public.

While supervisees and the supervisor will have certain differences, if they match up well enough in levels of energy, interest, and are close enough theoretically, supervision will be a fruitful experience. The following is a list of some of the pros and cons I have experienced in two-on-one supervision modality:

<u>Pros:</u>

- Best replicates a couple therapy session.
- Has the potential for greater energy and excitement.
- Supervisees can support each other.
- Wider variety of cases presented.

- Greater opportunity for different clinical and theoretical perspectives.
- May help to desensitize sexual content that might trouble one of the supervisees.
- Termination of supervision may be less intense.

Cons:

- Greater potential for a fixed triangle to form.
- Greater potential for coalitions to form.
- Supervisees may compete with one another in a destructive way.
- Greater potential for one supervisee to dominate.
- Greater potential for one supervisee to carry the load of supervision.
- More work for the supervisor to emotionally balance the supervisee-couple.
- More work for the supervisee to maintain objectivity.
- More work for the supervisor to make sure time is distributed equally.
- More difficulty to set limits and maintain appropriate boundaries.

My experience is that supervisees who know each other and choose to come together for supervision out of their own free will are usually of the same gender. And while this configuration has been generally productive, it can make it easier for a supervisee-couple to form a coalition against a supervisor – an experience I have had only once in my entire career.

Charlotte and Kate were mid-level supervisees who worked together in a private practice group and who were interested in achieving AASECT certification as sex therapists. The two were in sync theoretically with what they hoped to accomplish in the supervision process. Although Kate warned me that she had difficulty with men, especially authority figures, I made two erroneous assumptions: (1) I could find a way to join with Kate and help her to see that I was not interested in dominating her; and (2) Charlotte, who seemed the more pleasant of the two might help me balance this dynamic if it gets out of hand and possibly even take my side if appropriate. What I learned however, was that Kate's anger towards men ran deep, and that Charlotte was too afraid to cross her. While the process got better over time, the first several weeks were rough for all three of us. I simply refused to let Kate provoke me and eventually she tired of our dynamic and became more compliant.

In contrast, I had an unproductive experience with a mixed-gender couple who disliked each other prior to supervision. They were ordered to work together against their will by the institute they were training at when assigned to me and forced me into a mediating role to keep the peace until the end of the designated academic year. All this to say I have not found "gender" to be as significant a problem in the one-on-two supervision as I have "freedom of choice" and "theoretical and clinical harmony."

One-on-Four Supervision

Because I have never experienced the one-on-three mode of supervision, I will focus primarily here on the dynamic I am most familiar with: one-on-four supervision; sometimes referred to as "group supervision." According to Valentino et al. (2016): "Group supervision can provide unique opportunities to establish critical professional repertoires such as peer feedback skills and public speaking skills" (p. 320). I believe that this modality, however, is perhaps the most complex of all supervision configurations and the norm in institutes, especially those in which the number of supervisees outnumber qualified supervisors.

Most certifying organizations require a ratio of one supervisor to a maximum of four supervisees, and most institutions abide by this. The transference and countertransference reactions are plentiful and consistent not only between supervisees and supervisors, but between the supervisees. There is also greater opportunity for coalitions to be formed, and these could range from two against two to a more sadistic four against one.

The supervisor must be especially prepared to maintain objectivity and to make sure the supervision process is an equitable one. There is an excellent chance that the supervisor will favor one or more supervisees over the others, but this must be controlled. In fact, it is in this formation that I have had the most difficulty over the years. Out of four supervisees, it is likely that at least one will be especially challenging and disruptive. Sometimes it has been a disturbed supervisee who cannot curb their behavior; other times it is a more experienced supervisee who cannot tolerate the re-learning process, even if they are not yet proficient. Sometimes an older clinician who could not tolerate a young supervisor no matter how much they could offer the supervisee is a problem, and on occasion there will be a supervisee who disagrees with my model of treatment and supervision.

The structure of this modality can also be problematic because each supervisee must get time to present a case. I prefer to have each supervisee present their entire caseload before we dive into the supervision process. This way I can keep an eye on all cases and check back in with the supervisee to for progress or regression. I may request that a supervisee follow-up with me on a case I think might be problematic even if it cuts somewhat into another supervisee's time. I assume that supervisees also learn by listening to each other's presentations. The following lists sum up the pros and the cons I have experienced in one-on-four supervision:

Pros:

- Higher energy.
- Supervisees can support one another and provide greater feedback.
- More room for different clinical and theoretical perspectives.
- Greater opportunity to work with therapists from different sociocultural backgrounds.
- Supervisees help to enforce personal and professional boundaries within the group.
- May be more cost-effective.
- Can help create a greater referral network for supervisees.
- Greater variety of case-topics covered in less time.
- May help desensitize the anxiety associated with presenting in public.
- May desensitize sexual content that may be difficult for some supervisees to process.
- Termination of supervision might be less complicated.

Cons:

- Good chance of coalitions forming.
- One or two supervisees could ruin the supervision process for the rest.
- More work for the supervisor to maintain equity.
- More work for the supervisor to maintain order.
- Time restraints.
- Fewer cases covered overall.
- Less opportunity to address transference and countertransference.
- More likely to result in sociocultural clashes.
- Supervisor and supervisees might not have the freedom to choose one another.
- Crises-oriented cases might receive less time to process.

This following one-on-four supervision took place in a post-graduate sex therapy program affiliated with a university teaching clinic. The supervisees were all in the intermediate developmental stage with some couple therapy experience. Laila and Ayannia were two Black women, and Kelly and Laura were two white women. All supervisees were single and in their mid-20's. I served as their only supervisor.

This was by far my best supervisory experience in the one-on-four configuration, for many reasons. All four women were ambitious, motivated, and relatable. When cases were presented, they were supportive rather than competitive with one another, and they openly shared personal experiences which helped them to bond. They were very open to my clinical suggestions but were not afraid to challenge me when appropriate. Given our generational difference, they were especially liberal when it came to certain issues such as polyamory, which most were accepting of.

On the other hand, I have also had some rather unpleasant experiences in the one-on-four configuration. One such experience was with a supervisee I'll refer to as Donna. Donna was a mid-aged woman in the same post-graduate sex therapy program who had been in practice for many years and who disagreed with most of my clinical suggestions. She was argumentative and often disrupted the supervision process. Being nice and supportive did not alter Donna's behavior and confronting her only escalated matters. Although I suspected that she was competing with me for control of the group she was not open to exploring her countertransference. In fact, when I brought this up, it was met with sarcasm. Just before I contacted the director of the program to complain, however, the group turned on Donna. They told her that they felt it was unfair that she was disrupting their learning process, especially since they were paying for the program. One of the supervisees was firm but very nice in telling Donna that she may not need supervision, but that she did. Shocked by the group's aggressive stance, Donna backed down and kept a lower profile in the group until she graduated.

References

American Association of Sex Educators, Counselors and Therapists (AASECT). (2024). *Supervision Guidelines*. www.aasect.org/guidelines-supervision.

Appleton, R., Williams, J., Vera San Juan, N., Needle, J. J., Schlief, M., Jordan, H., Rains, L. S., Goulding, L., Badhan, M., Roxburgh, E., Barnett, P., Spyrideonidis, S., Tomaskova, M., Mo, J., Harju-Seppänen, J., Haime, Z., Casetta, C., Papamichail, A., Lloyd-Evans, B., Simpson, A., Sevdalis, N., Gaughran, F., & Johnson, S. (2021). Implementation, adoption, and perceptions of telemental health during the COVID-19 pandemic: Systematic review. *Journal of Medical Internet Research*, *23*(12), e31746. doi: 10.2196/31746

Athar, M. E. (2021). Remarks on using one-way mirror supervision method to train psychoanalytic psychotherapists. *The International Journal of Supervision in Psychotherapy*, *3*, 97–106. doi: 10.47409/ijsp.2021.3.7

Augusterfer, E. F., O'Neal, C. R., Martin, S. W., Sheikh, T. L., & Mollica, R. F. (2020). The role of telemental health, tele-consultation, and tele-supervision in post-disaster and low-resource settings. *Current Psychiatry Reports*, *22*, 85. doi: 10.1007/s11920-020-020-01209-5

Aveline, M. (1992). The use of audio and videotape recordings of therapy sessions in the supervision and practice of dynamic psychotherapy. *British Journal of Psychotherapy*, *8*(4), 347–358.

Aviram, A., & Nadan, Y. (2022). Online clinical supervision in couple and family therapy: A scoping review. *Family Process*, *61*, 1417–1436. doi: 10.1111/famp.12809

Betchen, S. (2022). *Couples in conflict: Clinical techniques for navigating sexual and relationship control struggles*. Routledge.

Bjorn, B. A. (2023). Sex-positive clinical supervision: A special commentary. *Journal of Counseling Sexology & Wellness: Research, Practice, and Education*, *4*, 88–90. hhtps://doi.org/10.34296/04S11076

Boszormenyi-Nagy, I., & Spark, G. (1973). *Invisible loyalties*. Harper & Row.

Celano, M., Smith, C. O., & Kaslow, N. (2010). A competency-based approach to couple and family therapy supervision. *Psychotherapy Research Practice*, *47*, 35–44. doi: 10.1037/a0018845

Cheon, H. S., Blumer, M. L. C., Shih, A. T., Murphy, M. J., & Sato, M. (2009). The influence of supervisor and supervisee matching, role conflict, and supervisor relationship supervisee satisfaction. *Contemporary Family Therapy*, *31*, 52–67. doi://10.1007/s1059-008-9078-y

Cruishanks, D. R., & Burns, S. T. (2021). Sexual boundary violations in counselor training and supervision. In I. Management Association (Ed.), Research anthology on rehabilitation practices and therapy (pp. 1952–1973). IGI Global Scientific Publishing. https://doi.org/10.4018/978-1-7998-3432-8.ch099

Frederickson, J. (2015). Countertransference in supervision. *Psychiatry*, *78*, 217–224. doi: 10.1080/00332747.2015.1069641

Grames, H., Sims, P., Holden, C., Rollins, P., Jeanfreau, M., & Fitzgerald, M. (2022). The changing face of telesupervision and digital training in response to COVID-19. *Journal of Family Therapy*, *45*, 211–222 doi://10.1111/1467-6427.12415

Gurman, A. (2010). (Ed.). *Clinical handbook of couple therapy* (pp. 1–20). Guilford.

Hardy, N. R., Maier, C. A., & Gregson, T. J. (2021). Couple teletherapy in the era of COVID-19: Experiences and recommendations. *Journal of Marital and Family Therapy*, *47*, 225–243. doi: 10.1111/jmft.12501

Health Resources & Services Administration (2022). Office for the Advancement of Telehealth. *What is Telehealth?* https://www.hrsa.gov/telehealth/what-is-telehealth

Heers, S. (2022, December 15). Navigating a rupture with your clinical supervisor. *FireLight Supervision*. https://firelightsupervision.com/navigating-a-rupture-with-your-clinical-supervisor/

Hertlein, K. M., & Blumer, M. L. C. (2014). *The couple and family technology framework: Intimate relationships in a digital age*. Routledge.

Holloway, E. L. (2016). *Supervision essentials for a systems approach to supervision*. American Psychological Association.

Inman, A. G., Soheilian, S. S., & Linh, L. P. (2018). Telesupervision: Building bridges in a Digital age. *Journal of Clinical Psychology*, *75*, 292–301. doi// 10.1002/jcip.22722

Jordan, K., & Fisher, U. (2016). *History and future trends*. In K. Jordan (Ed.), *Couple, marriage, and family therapy supervision*. Springer.

Jordan, S. E., & Shearer, E. M. (2019). An exploration of supervision delivered via clinical video telehealth (CVT). *Training and Education in Professional Psychology*, *13*, 323–330. https://doi.org/10.1037/tep0000245

Jung, C. G. (1946/1966). The practice of psychotherapy: Essays on the psychology of the transference and other subjects. Fundamental questions of psychotherapy. In H. Read, M. Fordham, G. Adler, & W. W. McGuire (Eds.), R. F. C. Hull (Trans.), *The collected works of C. G. Jung* (2nd ed.) (Vol. 16, pp. 163–240). Princeton University, Press.

Koenig, T. L., & Spano, R. N. (2004). Sex, supervision, and boundary violations: Pressing challenges and possible solutions. *The Clinical Supervisor*, *22*, 3–19. https://doi.org/10.1300/J001v22n01_02

Kysely, A., Bishop, B., Kane, R. T., McDevitt, M., De Palma, M., & Rooney, R. (2022). Couples therapy delivered through videoconferencing: Effect on relationship outcomes, mental health and the therapeutic alliance. *Frontiers in Psychology*, *12*, 1–35. https://doi.org/10.3389/fpsyg.2021.773030

Lackie, B. (1983). The families of origin of social workers. *Clinical Social Work Journal*, *11*, 309–322. https://doi.org/10.1007/BF00755898

Langarizadeh, M., Tabatabaei, M. S., Tavakol, K., Naghipour, M., Rostami, A., & Moghbeli, F. (2017). Telemental health care, and effective alternative to conventional mental care: A systematic review. *Acta Informatica Medica*, *25*, 240–246. doi: 10.5455/aim.2017.25.240-246

Martin, P., Copley, J., & Tyack, Z. (2014). Twelve tips for effective clinical supervision based on narrative literature and expert opinion. *Medical Teacher*, *36*, 201–207. doi://10.3109/014259X.2013.852166

Martin, P., Kumar, S., & Lizarondo, L. (2017). Effective use of technology in clinical interventions. *ScienceDirect*, *8*, 35–39. https://doi.org/10.1016/j.invent.2017.03.001

Martin, P., Lizarondo, L., Kumar, S., Jie Tian, E., Kondalsamy-Chennakesavan, S., & Argus, G. (2023). Characteristics of perceived effective telesupervision practices: A case study of supervisees and supervisors. *PLOS ONE*, *18*(7), e0288314. https://doi.org/10.1371/journal.pone.0288314

McMahon, A., & Ledden, K. (2019). Recording client sessions during psychotherapy training: From 'absurd idea' to 'potent learning'. *Counselling and Psychotherapy Research*, *19*, 241–251. https://doi.org/10.1002/capr.12209

McNeil, B. W., & Stoltenberg, C. D. (2016). *Supervision essentials for the integrative developmental model*. American Psychological Association.

National Center on Domestic and Sexual Violence (2025). *Domestic Violence Personalized Safety Plan*. https://www.ncdsv.org/uploads/1/4/2/2/142238266/2018-ncdsv-safetyplan.pdf

Osborn, C. J., Davis, T. E. (2008). The supervision contract: Making it perfectly clear. *The Clinical Supervisor*, *14*, 121–134. https://doi.org/10.1300/j001v14n02_10

Perle, J. G., & Zheng, W. (2023). A primer for understanding and utilizing telesupervision with healthcare trainees. *Journal of Technology in Behavioral Science*, *19*, 1–7. doi://10.1007/s41347-023-00322-5

Posluns, K., & Gall, T. L. (2019). Dear mental health practitioners, take care of yourselves: A literature review on self-care. *International Journal for the Advancement of Counselling*, *42*, 1–20. doi://10.1007/s10447-019-09382-w

Rothwell, C., Kehoe, A., Farrok, S. F., & Illing, J. (2021). Enablers and barriers to effective Clinical supervision in the workplace: A rapid evidence review. *BMJ Open*, *11*, e052929. doi://1135/bmjopen-2021-052929.

Rousmaniere, T. (2014). Using technology to enhance clinical supervision. In C. Edward Watkins, Jr., & D. L. Milne (Eds.), *The Wiley International Handbook of Clinical Supervision* (pp. 204–237). John Wiley & Sons, Ltd.

Rousmaniere, T., Abbass, A., & Frederickson, J. (2014). New developments in technology assisted supervision and training: A practical overview. *Journal of Clinical Psychology*, *70*, 1082–1093. www.researchgate.net/publication/265786216_New_Developments_in_Technology-Assisted_Supervision_and_Training_A_Practical_Overview

Sessions, M. W. (1986). *Influence of parentification on professional role choice and interpersonal style* [Doctoral dissertation, Georgia State University]. Dissertation Abstracts International, 47, 5066 (University Microfilms No. 87-06815).

Steel, K., Cox, D., & Garry, H. (2011). Therapeutic videoconferencing interventions for the treatment of long-term conditions. *Journal of Telemedicine and Telecare*, *17*, 109–117. https://doi.org/10.1258/jtt.2010.100318

Substance Abuse and Mental Health Services Administration (SAMHSA) (2024). SAFE-T Suicide Assessment: Five-step evaluation and triage https://library.samhsa.gov/sites/default/files/safet-flyer-pep24-01-036.pdf

Tarlow, K. R., McCord, C. E., Nelson, J. L., & Bernhard, P. A. (2020). Comparing in-person supervision and telesupervision: A multiple baseline single-case study. *Journal of Psychotherapy Integration*, *30*, 383–393. https://doi.org/10.1037/int0000210

Topor, D. R., AhnAllen, C. G., Mulligan, E. A., & Dickey, C. C. (2017). Using video recordings of psychotherapy sessions in supervision: Strategies to reduce learner anxiety. *Academic Psychiatry*, *41*, 40–43. doi: 10.1007/s40596-016-0605-0

Tracey, M. D. (2006). More effective supervision: Clinical supervision informed by research and theory can help trainees excel. *Monitor on Psychology*, *37*, 48. American Psychological Association.

Valentino, A. L., LeBlanc, L. A., & Sellers, T. P. (2016). The benefits of group supervision and a recommended structure for implementation. *Behavior Analysis in Practice*, *9*, 320–328. doi: 10.1007/s40617-016-0138-8

Watkins, C. E. (2014). The supervisory alliance: A half century of theory, practice, and research in critical perspective. *American Journal of Psychotherapy*, *68*, 19–55. doi://10.1176/appi.psychotherapy.2014.68.1.19

Watter, D. (2023). *The existential history of the penis*. Routledge.

Weeks, G., & Fife, S. (2014). *Couples in treatment: Effective approaches for effective practice* (3rd ed.), Routledge.

Whitacker, C. A., & Keith, D. V. (1981). Symbolic-experiential family therapy. In A.S. Gurman & D. P. Kniskern (Eds.), *Handbook of Family Therapy* (pp. 187–225). Brunner/Mazel.

Wittenborn, A. K., Subramaniam, S., Morgan, P. C., & Tseng, C. F. (2022). Effects of adding video feedback to emotionally focused therapy supervision: A concurrent multiple-baseline across subjects design. *Journal of Marital and Family Therapy*, *48*, 1059–1074. doi://10.1111.jmft.12586

Wright, E. M., & Fagan, A. A. (2014). The cycle of violence in context: Exploring the moderating roles of neighborhood disadvantage and cultural norms. *Criminology*, *51*, 217–249. doi:10.1111/1745-9125.12003

Chapter 5

Sociocultural Influences

Today's supervisors and supervisees are faced with perhaps the largest socio-culture diverse population of couples they have ever experienced. And these couples present for treatment with their own unique set of complexities and problems. The word socio-cultural as it is applied here stems from McIntosh's concept of multi-heritage. McIntosh et al. (2024) contended: "Multi-heritage couples encompass inherent differences in race, ethnicity, religion, gender, sexual orientation, national origin, and culture" (p. 611). A competent supervisor, especially when supervising supervisees with diverse couples, needs more than basic therapeutic skills. Having a multi-heritage perspective enhances the assessment, joining, and therapeutic processes as well as the supervisory process. The following factors should help supervisors address this issue with their supervisees:

Culture and Ethnicity

Culture and ethnicity are related but distinct concepts. Ethnicity refers to a couple's ancestry, history, and language. Culture refers to their learned behaviors, beliefs, values, and group customs. Immigrants come to the United States bringing with them both their ethnic and cultural heritage, and at times this can cause certain difficulties as they try to adjust to a new way of life – one that does not necessarily appreciate their differences. The Center for Immigration Studies reported there are 53.3 million foreign-born or immigrants living in the Unites States in 2025. This is 15.8% of the population – a new record high (Camarota & Zeigler, 2025). According to the U. S. Census Bureau (2013), there is approximately 11.4 million couples in the United States who consist of at least one foreign-born spouse. This figure represents 21% of all married couples.

Despite stressors such as language barriers, financial restraints, and stigma, foreign-born couples do seek psychotherapy when necessary. It is therefore essential for supervisors to develop the appropriate knowledge

DOI: 10.4324/9781003642732-5

and skills to help their supervisees do the same. Lee and Park (2013) defined a culturally competent therapist as one with the "awareness, knowledge, and skills to intervene effectively in the lives of culturally diverse backgrounds" (p. 6).

Although addressing cultural differences is especially challenging in couple therapy (Bhugra & De Silva, 2000), McDaniel (2008) claimed that marital therapy provides the best forum to do so. The American Association for Marriage and Family Therapy Association (*Code of Ethics* (2015)) requires therapists to conduct their practices in affirmative and inclusive ways. VandenBos (2015) offers a formal definition of cultural competence in the APA Dictionary of Psychology:

> The capacity to function effectively in cultural settings other than one's own. This usually involves a recognition of the diversity both between and within cultures, a capacity for cultural self-assessment, and a willingness to adapt personal behaviors and practice.
>
> (p. 273)

According to Vekaria et al. (2023): "Culturally responsive supervision assumes that culture permeates clinical practice and supervision. Culturally responsive supervisors promote the development of cultural competence in supervision, through modeling, reflective discussion and responsivity." (p. 1). Estrada (2008) supported this notion by emphasizing "the importance of giving voice in clinical supervision and the therapy room to the code of silence around issues of ethnicity, gender, spirituality, and socioeconomic struggles that plague many cross-cultural couples" (p. 17).

Marriage and family therapy supervisors in fact, are encouraged to "initiate conversations about power and privilege and sociocultural context and promote critical self-reflection and awareness" (Morrison et al., 2022, p. 4011). Clinical supervisees of different races and colors were found to be more satisfied with their supervision process and experienced a stronger working alliance when their supervisors were high in "cultural humility" and cultural comfort (Wilcox et al., 2023).

Initially defined by Tervalon and Murray-Garcia (1998), cultural humility includes: (1) continuously evaluating the self; (2) recognition of power imbalances between people and a willingness to fix these; and (3) the willingness to form fair and productive relations with various communities. According to Hook et al. (2016), cultural humility is an important feature in the clinical supervisory process for three reasons: (1) it promotes a strong working alliance between supervisors and supervisees, and can help alleviate issues of cultural difference and dissipate any microaggressions that may arise; (2) supervisors void of cultural humility may be limited in their ability to help supervisees in this context; and (3) supervisors with cultural humility will be more equipped to help supervisees to engage their clients with cultural humility.

Deangelis (2023) echoes some of the previous research by offering several recommendations to increase social awareness: (1) adjusting the supervisory power imbalance and increase transparency in the supervision process; (2) supervisors should possess a certain amount of vulnerability; (3) supervisors should become educated on social, economic, and power differentials between the privileged and the underprivileged; (4) supervisors should view culture as multidimensional and fluid; (5) supervisors should increase their own racial and cultural awareness; and (6) supervisors should take the lead in discussing sociocultural differences in the supervision process rather than put the burden on the supervisee. In this way, supervisors will train supervisees to likewise take the lead in discussing these issues with their clients.

Race

It would be helpful if supervisors and supervisees understand that Black couples have the highest divorce rate (30.8%) of all other racial groups, followed by Hispanic couples at 18.5%, and Whites at 15.1%. Asians have the lowest rate at 12.4% (Divorce.com, 2024). The many causes attributed to the high divorce rate for Black couples are: (1) systemic or institutional racism – these factors may limit educational and economical achievement; (2) low socioeconomic status and economic instability – these factors are typically major stressors on marriage; (3) divorce is more common and thus may contribute to a cycle of single-parent households – growing up in a single-parent household might make divorce a more acceptable solution to marital difficulty; and (4) Black women are much more likely to divorce than women of other racial groups (Global Statistics, 2025).

Statistically, Asian couples shy away from couple therapy. They tend to look to their close family structure to help them with problem-solving and seem to feel there is a stigma attached to attending couple treatment. I have experienced this with Far Eastern Asian couples such as those from China, Japan, and Korea. But I have had the honor of treating many Asian Indian American couples, most of which were in arranged marriages. As a result, they spent limited time together before marriage, were typically virgins when they married, and sexual issues were quite common.

Other contributing factors to the relational and sexual difficulties of this population include: (1) the cognitive dissonance stirred by loyalty to the traditions of their culture's patriarchal system; (2) the need to adapt to a more egalitarian society; and (3) the pressure exerted by parents and family members to return to their homeland at some point. In tune with these factors, Dupree et al. (2013) cited the following difficulties: "(a) the impact of intergenerational/extended family relationships on the marriage; (b) acculturation issues; and (c) the influence of gender roles on marital and parental patterns" (p. 311). Supervisors and their supervisees will need to empathize with the powerful forces pulling at these couples as they try to navigate a new and different environment.

Supervisors will also have to help the supervisee contend with the complexities of interracial marriage, which is on the rise. Rico et al. (2018), in a report for the United States Census, found the percentage of interracial and interethnic married-couple households grew from 7.4% in 2000 to 10.2% between 2012 and 2016. According to a Gallup poll conducted in 2021, interracial marriages are at an all-time high. Approximately 17% of new marriages are between interracial couples (McCarthy, 2021). Studies reported by the Pew Research Center found the biggest increases in intermarriage have occurred among Black newlyweds from 5% to 18%. The Center also found that Asian and Hispanic newlyweds are the most likely to intermarry each other (Livingston & Brown, 2017).

Thompson (2024) listed some of the most common issues facing interracial relationships, that supervisors and supervisees should consider: (1) societal pressure – the stress associated with racial stereotyping and critical judgement; (2) family disapproval – sometimes parents and other family members discriminate against the interracial couple; (3) an internal conflict about their identity or belonging – some interracial partners feel guilty about not marrying someone who shares their heritage; and (4) cultural misunderstanding – not understanding or being sensitive to their partner's norms, values, and traditions.

Religion

Both supervision and treatment will run more smoothly when supervisors and supervisees are familiar with a couple's religious beliefs and values. It is common knowledge that religion can have a powerful effect on the way people respond to life and its challenges. Religion, for example, can help to determine whether a couple feels comfortable seeking couple therapy, or seeking it with someone outside their religion. I have treated numerous Christian couples over the years, and they ask if I am a "Christian Counselor." Orthodox Jews have asked if I am "at least," Jewish. Even if the therapist they choose might have stellar credentials, if he or she is of a different religion the couple may feel as if they are taking too great a risk. The more religious the couple the more religion is a factor in the treatment process.

Some couples believe that secular therapists are more likely to encourage divorce, whereas other couples may feel that the therapist may challenge beliefs and values they hold dear. Regardless, the supervisor and supervisee should be empathic to their concerns, for they are very real to these couples. Passing judgment may be a quick route to pre-mature termination.

A young supervisee with a large caseload of orthodox Jews was frequently annoyed that the couples refused to shake his hand before and after treatment. He told me that he felt as if he was being used: "I'm good enough for them to want my help, but not good enough for them to shake my hand." The supervisee thought his clients did not like or respect him; he personalized what were simply the rules of their religion. I asked the supervisee two questions in response to his complaint: "What makes you think these people are not in conflict about shaking your hand? Is it not possible that they like you, but the pressure to conform to the rules of their religion is stronger?" Of course, the supervisee's reaction was a countertransference that merited attention – this will be addressed in the following chapter.

Not all religious messages from childhood lead to sexual dysfunction. But sex therapists have long warned how certain messages initially conveyed by parents, their surrounding communities, and their respective religious leaders can have a deleterious effect on a couple's sex life. For example, messages that condemn sexual desire, including masturbation, may lead to sexual guilt and shame which in turn, can result in a sexual desire or orgasmic disorder, among others.

Negative messages in the context of religion only complicates the lives for the sexually marginalized like the LGBTQ+ community. Killian et al. (2025) found that using religion to desecrate sexual minorities makes it more difficult for them to affirm their sexual orientation and to be open about this. Abbott et al. (2016) concluded that "high religious commitment and perception that God viewed sex negatively independently predicted lower sexual satisfaction, as related to moral judgment" (p. 1063). And Strati (2024) claimed that "Purity Culture" or the focus on sexual purity continues to tie self-worth to a person's sexual behavior which is especially damaging for women, and the LGBTQ+ community.

An experience I'll never forget occurred in my high school health class. The teacher asked the class: "How can you avoid teenage pregnancy?" Not waiting for any answers, he immediately held up a condom and dropped it in the trash can as he shouted "abstinence." He said if we couldn't abide by this tenant, we were "scum." There is a term used to describe experiencing an extreme form of religious indoctrination. It is referred to as Religious Trauma Syndrome (RTS) (Winell, 2011).

According to the Pew Research Center: Religious Landscape Study, approximately 26% of married couples consist of one spouse with a different religion: 7% of these couples who are Christian consist of one Christian from a different denomination such as a Catholic or Protestant; and 6% represent other pairings such as a Jew and a Catholic (Smith et al., 2025). And these couples have their share of problems. Tilahun et al. (2025) reported some of the problems that interfaith couples experience include: (1) pressure from family members; (2) social stigma; (3) difficulties in deciding how to raise the children; and (4) economic difficulties celebrating both religions.

The supervisor is responsible for checking his or her belief system to assess whether he or she can remain objective enough to provide supervision for couples from different religious backgrounds, and to make sure the supervisee can do the same. And while some may find it difficult to achieve, it is critical in treating inter-religious relationships.

Gender

Role Conflict

Pearlstein (2024) wrote: "Gender roles are social and cultural constructs that define the behaviors, expectations, and responsibilities typically assigned to men and women within a society" (p. 1). Feminine gender roles are stereotypically described as gentle, sensitive, and sympathetic. Masculine gender roles are described as dominant, leadership seeking, and goal-oriented (Mommersteeg et al., 2023).

According to Pearlstein (2024), "conflicts arise when the expectations of these roles are challenged or when individuals feel pressured to conform to traditional norms that may not align with their personal identities or aspirations" (p. 1). Gender role conflict (GRC) is specifically defined as a psychological state in which socialized gender roles have a negative impact on certain people. These conflicts happen when restrictive gender roles result in devaluation or degradation, often blocking individuals from fulfilling life objectives (O'Neill et al., 1995; O'Neill, 2008).

According to Khosravi et al. (2024), gender-role conflict is a predictor of marital issues, even divorce. Supervisors take gender-role conflicts seriously. To be a successful couple and sex therapist, supervisees must learn to join, engage, and empathize with members of the opposite sex. A male supervisee who makes light of a female client's concerns about her career being restricted by her male counterpart will most likely not fare well. A female supervisee who fails to consider a male client's fragile masculinity might not fare any better.

Bruk (2019) wrote: "The division of housework is one of the main sources of tension between cohabitating couples, one that even comes up as a reason for divorce" (p. 1). While society has warmed up to the concept of gender equality, inequities continue to exist that cause difficulties in couples. For example, according to data from the Pew Research Center, women are more educated than any other time in history. The number of young women with a bachelor's degree has increased 22% since 1995, from 25% to 47%. In comparison, men have seen a smaller increase from 25% to 37% (Hurst, 2024).

Women now make up 47% of the workforce. Yet women are still underrepresented in management positions, and a pay gap still exists that favors men, even when both sexes hold the same or similar positions (United States Government Accountability Office, 2023). According to *Harvard Business Review*, women earn 17% less than men on average (Bolotnyy & Emanuel, 2022).

And while men have begun to take on more domestic responsibilities, women still carry the bulk of the burden (Schaeffer, 2019). In a large study conducted by the Pew Research Center, 59% of the women claimed they did more of the work than their male counterparts, while only 6% claimed their male partners carried the bulk of the domestic chores (Barroso, 2021).

These statistics accentuate how important it is for supervisors to help their supervisees balance the couples they treat, especially if at least one partner is of the opposite sex of the supervisee. It is quite common for couples to prematurely terminate treatment if they felt the supervisee favored one partner over the other and in my experience the complaint is usually leveraged by the partner who is the opposite sex of the supervisee. Consider the following brief example.

Mazie complained in treatment that her husband of two years, Evan, did "nothing" around the house even though both had full-time jobs. Mazie took out the trash, did the laundry, cleaned the house, and took care of the couple's 2-year-old son, while Evan would only lend a hand when she threw a tantrum. Evan did not dispute Maize's accusations but claimed that because he made more money than she did, it was her job to take care of the rest.

Evan grew up in a traditional household where his father worked long hours, and his mother took care of all domestic chores. Evan said that was the way it is "supposed to be" and maintained that distribution of tasks leads to a more stable family life. A former female supervisee admitted to me that she was "disgusted" with Evan. And while we worked on her countertransference, she nevertheless lost her temper and told Evan to "grow up." This outburst led to a premature termination which even Mazie supported. The reality is, favoring one sex over the other will guarantee failure in couple therapy.

For those who supervise couple and sex therapy, one of the most common reported gender-role conflict regards a couple's sexual frequency and timing. Women in Maize's position have also complained that they are too tired to have sex given that they work full-time and do all or most of the chores. This is especially so if their partner desires sex late in the evening. The following example depicts this.

A female supervisee presented the case of Tina and Frank. Tina was the mother of three young children. She also worked part-time from home and did the bulk of the domestic chores. Her husband, Frank, did what he could when his career would allow for it, but he was required to work long hours. Frank did not have the same patriarchal attitude that Evan, from the previous case example did, but he expected sex when he wanted it, and this was usually late in the evening when Tina was spent. The couple fought over this until the supervisee convinced Frank that hiring a Nanny could possibly help with the couple's sex life. This took some time, but Frank acquiesced, and the couple were finally able to end their standoff.

The supervisee said that Frank did, at times, feel she was siding with his wife. But the supervisee claimed that while she did empathize more with Tina's plight, she also felt sorry for Frank because he seemed sincerely interested in rescuing his marriage to Tina, rather than simply trying to control her and have his way.

Identity and Diversity

Today's youth have stretched the concept of gender beyond the traditional male/female or binary perspective to include concepts such as cisgender (i.e., identifying with the sex you are assigned at birth), transgender (i.e., identifying differently from the sex you were assigned at birth), non-binary (i.e., not identifying as just a man or a woman), gender fluid (i.e., gender identity fluctuates), or genderqueer (i.e., identify as a mix of genders), to name a few. Anyone supervising or practicing in the current therapeutic climate should, at the very least, become familiar with some of these terms, the discrimination these individuals face, and the dynamics specific to them and their partners. Specialized knowledge notwithstanding, this familiarity will help form therapeutic alliances and enhance joining, increase empathy, and avoid discrimination.

The World Professional Association for Transgender Health (WPATH) advocates for a "gender affirming" approach to treatment, which would entail receiving specialized training in working with those who are unsure about their gender identity, experiencing gender dysphoria (a mismatch between one's gender identity and the sex they were assigned at birth), or other gender-related stressors.

Nichols (2019) warned against taking the view that variations in gender identity is a sign of mental health illness, and that gender affirming therapists should aid individuals in the exploration of their gender identity rather than be judged for and manipulated to change. WPATH, in its *Standards of Care for the Health of Transgender and Gender Diverse People (SOC8)* lists the following gender affirming general principles:

- Empower and be inclusive
- Reduce stigma and facilitate access to appropriate healthcare
- Respect gender diversity
- Respect all clients and all gender identities
- Avoid pathologizing differences in gender identity or expression
- Respect for the individual's right to autonomy and self-determination.
- Respect universal human rights including the right to bodily and mental integrity
- Freedom from discrimination
- Highest attainable standard of care

(Coleman et al., 2022, p. S17)

Based on WPATH's principles, The American Psychiatric Association (APA) also supports gender affirming treatment, and lists the following as its core interventions:

- Gender affirmation
- Space for processing and understanding
- Link to social support, legal services, health care providers
- Create a safe zone
- Allow for diversity
- Reflect and empathize

(American Psychiatric Association, 2025, p. 1)

Most pertinent to couple and sex therapy supervisors and supervisees, AAMFT and AASECT are also staunch supporters of gender affirming care. Contrary to one stereotype about the gender diverse, they can and do form lasting and satisfying relationships (Perez & Pepping, 2024). For example, Holt et al. (2023) found that 57% of transgender non-binary adults (TNB) were in a romantic relationship while Fuller & Riggs (2021) found 64% were in a romantic relationship.

While transgenders are less likely to be married than non-transgenders, they are twice more likely to be living with an unmarried partner than non-transgenders. A survey conducted in 2023 by the Kaiser Family

Foundation (KFF) found that 26% of transgender adults reported being married or partnered compared to 49% of non-trans adults and that 20% of transgender adults lived with an unmarried partner compared to 10% of non-trans adults (Dawson et al., 2023).

Although gender affirming care can be incorporated in the conflict theory supervision model proposed in this book, I tend to refer supervisees seeking to treat gender diverse couples to specialists in gender therapy. In the few cases I have taken, the supervisees were gender diverse, and I was therefore comfortable following their lead.

Sexual Orientation

According to the Statistical Research Department, Americans have grown more accepting of gays and lesbians. In 2001, 53% of respondents in a large study reported they believe that gay male or lesbian relations to be immoral, but by 2022 this was down to 25% (Fleck, 2025). Gays have made great strides in the social, political, and legal arenas of our society, but they still face a significant amount of discrimination (Lev & Nichols, 2015). This discrimination can be "external," coming from outside sources such as anti-gay individuals or institutions, or "internal," such as internalizing homophobia or self-hatred which is often propagated by external sources.

Gay couples suffer from many of the same problems heterosexual couples do, including money, intimacy, and family issues (American Association for Marriage and Family Therapy, 2025) but with the added consequence of the discrimination they face. When one or both partners possess an internalized self-loathing or a disproportionate internal feeling of shame, however, their problems are often exacerbated.

Supervisors must be on the lookout for both internal and external forms of discrimination exhibited in the work of their supervisees. They will need to be in touch with how these forms of discrimination might be connected to a couple's shared conflict and in turn, their sexual symptoms. Just as I trust that a gender diverse supervisee will have an edge on, for example, a cisgender heterosexual supervisee in treating diverse couples, most gay supervisees will be empathic and objective when treating gay couples. And while there is no guarantee of this, I believe that when the supervisee and couple do not match in this way, whether a straight supervisee with a gay couple, or a gay supervisee with a straight couple, the supervisee should be supervised more closely. In Chapter 10, I illustrate in detail how gay couples with sexual problems are supervised and treated using the conflict theory model.

References

Abbott, D. M., Harris, J. E., & Mollen, D. (2016). The impact of religious commitment on women's sexual self-esteem. *Sexuality & Culture: An Interdisciplinary Quarterly, 20*, 1063–1082. https://doi.org/10.1007/s12119-016-9374-x

American Association for Marriage and Family Therapy (2015). *Code of Ethics*. www.aamft.org/legal_Ethics/Code_of_Ethics.aspx

American Association for Marriage and Family Therapy (2025). Therapeutic issues for same-sex couples. www.aamft.org/AAMFT/Consumer_Updates/Therapeutic_Issues_for_Same-sex_Couples.aspx

American Psychiatric Association (2025). Gender-affirming therapy. www.psychiatry.org/psychiatrists/diversity/education/transgender-and-gender-nonconforming-patients/gender-affirming-therapy

Barroso, A. (2021). For American couples, gender gaps in sharing household responsibilities persist amid pandemic. Pew Research Center. www.pewresearch.org/short-reads/2021/01/25/for-american-couples-gender-gaps-in-sharing-household-responsibilities-persist-amid-pandemic/

Bhugra, D., & De Silva, P. (2000). Couple therapy across cultures. *Sexual and Relationship Therapy, 15*, 183–192. https://doi.org/10.1080/14681990050010763

Bolotnyy, V., & Emanuel, N. (2022). How unpredictable schedules widen the gender pay gap. Harvard Business Review. https://hbr.org/2022/07/how-unpredictable-schedules-widen-the-gender-pay-gap

Bruk, D. (2019). New study reveals how men and women perceive housework differently. BestLife. www.google.com/search?q=Bruk%2C+D.+(2019)+New+study+reveals+how+men+women+perceive+housework+differently.+BestLife

Camarota, S. A., & Zeigler, K. (2025). Foreign-born number and share of U.S, population at all-time highs in January 2025. *Center for Immigration Studies*. https://cis.org/Report/ForeignBorn-Number-and-Share-US-Population-AllTime-Highs-January-2025

Coleman, E., Radix, A. E., Bourman, W. P., Brown, A. L. C., de Vries, M. B., Deutsch. R., Ettner, L., Fraser, M., Goodman, J., Green, A. B., Hancock, T. W., Johnson, D. H., Karasic, G. A., Knudson, S. F., Leibowitz, H. F. L., Meyer-Bahlburg, S. J., Monstrey, J., Motmans, L., Nahata, T. O., Nieder, S. L. (...) Arcelus, J. (2022). Standards of care for the health of transgender and gender diverse people. Version 8. *International Journal of Transgender Health, 23*, S1–S259. https://doi.org/10.1080/26895269.2022.2100644

Dawson, L., Kates, J., Sparks, G., & Kirzinger, A. (2023). Trans-people in the U.S.: Identities, demographics, and wellbeing. KFF/Washington Post Survey. www.kff.org/other-health/trans-people-in-the-u-s-identities-demographics-and-wellbeing/

Deangelis, T. (2023). Continuing education: Increasing supervisor savvy around culture, race, and identity. *Monitor on Psychology, 54*, 35–39. American Psychological Association.

Divorce.com (2024, July 15). *51+ statistics in the U.S., including divorce rate, race, & marriage length*. https://divorce.com/blog/divorce-statistics/

Dupree, W. J., Bhakta, K. A., Patel, P., & Dupree, D. G. (2013). Developing culturally competent marriage and family therapists: Guidelines for working with Asian Indian American couples. *American Journal of Family Therapy*, *41*, 311–329. doi: 10.1080/01926187.2012.698213

Estrada, D. (2008). Supervision of cross-cultural couples therapy. *Journal of Family Psychotherapy*, *16*, 17–30. https://doi.org/10.1300/J085v16n04_03

Fleck, A. (2025). U.S. Support for same-sex marriage is strong, despite dip. www.statistica.com/chart/34478/us-adults-who-support-same-sex-marriages/

Fuller, K. A., & Riggs, D. W. (2021). Intimate relationship strengths and challenges amongst \sample of transgender people living in the United States. *Sexual and Relationship Therapy*, *36*, 399–412. https://doi.org/10.1080/14681994.2019.1679765

Global Statistics (2025). Divorce Rates by Race in the US (2025). https://www.theglobalstatistics.com/divorce-rates-by-race/

Holt, M., Broady, T., Callander, D., Pony, M., Duck-Chong, L., Cook, T., & Rosenberg, S. (2023). Sexual experience, relationships, and factors associated with sexual and romantic satisfaction in the first Australian Trans & Gender Diverse Sexual Health Survey. *International Journal of Transgender Health*, *24*, 38–48. https://doi.org/10.1080/26895269.2021.2016540

Hook, J. N., Watkins, C. E., Davis, D. D., Owen, J., van Tongeren, D. R., & Marciana, J. R. (2016). Cultural humility in psychotherapy supervision. *American Journal of Psychotherapy*, *70*, 149–231. https://doi.org/10.1176/appi.psychotherapy.2016.70.2.149

Hurst, K. (2024). Pew Research Center. U.S. women are outpacing men in college completion, including in every major racial and ethnic group. www.pewresearch.org/short-reads/2024/11/18/us-women-are-outpacing-men-in-college-completion-including-in-every-major-racial-and-ethnic-group/

Khosravi, F., Jamshid, J., Didehban, E., & Norouzi, Z. (2024). The moderating effect of gender role in relationship between emotional divorce and marital satisfaction: Comparison of partial least square (PLS) and consistent partial least square methods (PLSc) methods. *Journal of Family Reproductive Health*, *18*, 188–196. Doi://10.18502/jfrh.v18i3.16661

Killian, T., Fredrick, E. G., & Merenda II, F. (2025, June 27). From desecration to disconnection: Connecting negative religious beliefs about sexual minorities to social quality of life. *Pastoral Psychology*. https://doi.org/10.1007/s11089-025-01235-1

Lee, C., & Park, D. (2013). A conceptual framework for counseling across cultures. In C. Lee and D. Park (Eds.), *Multicultural issues in counseling: New approaches to diversity* (4th ed., pp. 3–12). American Counseling Association.

Lev, A., & Nichols, M. (2015). Sex therapy with lesbian and gay male couples. In K. Hertlein, G. Weeks, & N. Gambescia, N. (Eds.), *Systemic Sex Therapy* (2nd ed., 213–234). Routledge.

Livingston, G., & Brown, A. (2017, May 18). *Intermarriage in the U.S. 50 years after Loving v. Virginia*. Pew Research Center. www.pewresearch.org/social-trends/2017/05/18/intermarriage-in-the-u-s-50-years-after-loving-v-virginia/

McCarthy, J. (2021). U.S. approval of interracial marriage at new high of 94%. *Gallup*. https://news.gallup.com/poll/354638/approval-interracial-marriage-new-high.aspx
McDaniel, S. H. (2008). Marital therapy and the resolution of gender role conflict. *Journal of Family Psychotherapy*, *1*, 39–49. https://doi.org/10.1300/j085V01N03_03
McIntosh, D. L., & Wang, G. W. (2024). Assessments for multi-heritage couple therapy: A review of existing tools. *Journal of Marital and Family Therapy*, *50*, 611–629. https://doi.org/10.1111/jmft.12708
Mommersteeg, P. M. C., van Valkengoed, I., Loder, P., Juster, R. P., & Kupper, N. (2023). Gender roles and gender norms associated with psychological distress in women and men among the Dutch general population. *Journal of Health Psychology*, *29*, 797–810. https://doi.org/10.1177/13591053231207294
Morrison, T., Wayne, M. F., Harrison, T., Palmgren, E., & Knudson-Martin, C. (2022). Learning to embody a social justice perspective in couple and family therapy: A grounded theory analysis of MFTs in training, *Contemporary Family Therapy*, *44*, 408–421. doi: 10.1007/s10591-022-09635-8
Nichols, M. (2019). Supervision of therapists working with transgender clients. In J. C. Wadley & R. Siegel (Eds.), *The art of sex therapy supervision* (pp. 202–220). Routledge.
O'Neill, J. M. (2008). Summarizing 25 years of research on men's gender role conflict using the gender role conflict scale: New research paradigms and implication. *The Counseling Psychologist*, *36*, 358–445. doi: 10.1177/0011000008317057
O'Neill, J. M., Good, G. E., & Holmes, S. (1995). Fifteen years of theory and research on men's gender role conflict. In R. F. Levant & W. S. Pollack (Eds.), *The new psychology of men* (pp. 164–206). Basic Books.
Pearlstein, E. (2024). Gender roles and gender conflicts. *EBSCO*. www.ebsco.com/research-starters/health-and-medicine/gender-roles-and-gender-role-conflicts
Perez, J., & Pepping, C. A. (2024). Relationship experiences of transgender and non-binary adults: Exploring dating goals, relationship structures, minority stress, sexual fetishization, and relationship victimization. *International Journal of Transgender Health*, 1–20. https://doi.org/10.1080/26895269.2024.2316690
Rico, B., Kreider, R. M., & Anderson, L. (2018). *Growth in interracial and interethnic married- couple households*. www.census.gov/library/stories/2018/07/interracial-marriages.html
Schaeffer, K. (2019). Among U.S. couples, women do more cooking and grocery shopping than men. Pew Research Center. https://policycommons.net/artifacts/616594/among-us/1597277/
Smith, G. A., Cooperman, A., Alper, B. A., Mohamed, B., Rotolo, C., Tevington, J., Nortey, J., Kallo, A. Diament, J., & Fahmy, D. (2025, February 26). *Decline of Christianity in the U.S. has slowed, may have leveled off*. Pew Research Center: Religious Landscape Study. www.pewresearch.org/religion/2025/02/26/decline-of-christianity-in-the-us-has-slowed-may-have-leveled-off/
Starti, J. (2024, September 5). Purity culture and sexual shame: A closer look. *Council for Relationships*. Retrieved from https://councilforrelationships.org/purity-culture-and-sexual-and-shame/

Tervalon, M., & Murray-Garcia, J. (1998). Cultural humility versus cultural competence: A critical distinction in defining physician training outcomes in multicultural education. *Journal of Health Care for the Poor and Undeserved*, *9*, 117–125. https://dx.doi.org/10/1353/hpu.2010.0233

Thompson, M. (2024, May 12). Common problems in interracial relationships and how to address them. *Evolución Counseling*. Retrieved from https://evolucioncounseling.com/common-issues-in-interracial-relationships-and-how-to-address-them/

Tilahun, A. A., Gatisso, M. M., & Ali, A. M. (2025). Love beyond religious conviction: The challenges of interreligious marriage in South Wollo, Ethiopia. *Discover Global Society*, *3*, 1–26. https://doi.org/10.1007/s44282-025-00229-x

United States Census Bureau (2013). Census bureau reports 21 percent of married-couple households have at least one foreign-born spouse. *Married-couple households by nativity and citizenship*. www.census.gov/newsroom/archives/2013-pr/cb13-157.html

United States Government Accountability Office (2023). Women in the workforce: Underrepresentation in management positions persists, and the gender pay gap varies by industry and demographics. www.gao.gov/products/gao-23-106320

VandenBos, G. R. (Ed.). (2015). *APA dictionary of psychology* (2nd ed.). American Psychological Association.

Vekaria, B., Thomas, T., Phiri, P., & Ononaiye, M. (2023). Exploring the supervisory relationship in the context of culturally responsive supervision: A supervisee's perspective. *The Cognitive Behaviour Therapist*, *16*, e22. https://doi.org/10.1017/S1754470X23000168

Wilcox, M. M., Black, S. W., Farra, A., Zimmerman, D., Drinane, J. M., Tao, K. W., DeBlaere, C., Hook, J. N., Davis, D. E., Watkins, C. E., & Owen, J. (2023). Cultural humility, cultural comfort, and supervision processes and outcomes for BIPOC supervisees. *The Counseling Psychologist*, *51*, 1037–1058. https://doi.org/10.1177/00110000231188337

Winell, M. (2011, May). Religious Syndrome: It's time to recognize it. *Cognitive Behavioral Therapy Today*, *39*, 16–18.

Chapter 6

Therapeutic Approaches and Supervision

Many supervisors have long used use their preferred therapeutic approach as a framework for clinical supervision (Betchen, 1995). Smith (2009) referred to these as psychotherapy-based supervision models. The author wrote: "Psychotherapy-based models of supervision often feel like a natural extension of the therapy itself" (p.1).

A CBT therapist, for example, may use an ahistorical CBT-based approach in supervision. The clinical objectives are to set agendas, clarify objectives and goals, assign exercises or homework assignments, and help a supervisee recognize his or her own cognitive distortions and, in turn, the cognitive distortions of clients. Sudek (2021) of the Beck Institute contended that CBT supervision is most effective when using processes of CBT therapy.

In contrast to CBT, a psychoanalytic/psychodynamic therapist values a historical approach as a framework for a psychodynamic model of supervision. That is, he or she will consider any unconscious underlying conflicts responsible for client symptomatology. Affective reactions, defense mechanisms, and transference-countertransference are important concepts in the psychodynamic supervisory process. Norberg et al. (2016) found that not only did psychodynamic therapists utilize psychodynamic theories and techniques in the supervision process but gave negative feedback to those supervisees who failed to conform to psychodynamic principles in their work with clients.

A humanistic-existential therapeutic approach which focuses predominately on the client's personal growth and development is used in the supervision process by existential therapists to achieve the same results with their supervisees. That is, helping to increase both client and supervisee's self-awareness regarding their core values, beliefs, and biases are main objectives. Silva and Sousa (2022) wrote: "The eidetic dimensions, relationship and responsiveness arise in the existential approach as the foundational and promotional aspects of successful supervision" (p. 397).

DOI: 10.4324/9781003642732-6

A systems therapist might look for patterns of interaction between supervisors and supervisees, supervisees and clients, and between partners in the couple or family system to assess the impact these patterns are having on the supervisory and therapeutic process. In this sense, supervisors will utilize a circular rather than a linear or cause-effect approach in the supervision process. According to Holloway (2016), a systems-therapist developed model of supervision considers several systems that interact across different contexts.

And those who practice integrative psychotherapy use several different methods and models of treatment to suit a client's specific needs. Norcross and Popple (2017) wrote:

> The clinical reality is that no single psychotherapy proves effective for all patients and situations, no matter how good it is for some. That is the driving force behind integration, the modal theoretical orientation of psychotherapists in Western developed countries.
>
> (p. 5)

The authors further noted: "The cardinal principles of integrative therapy similarly apply to integrative supervision and working with trainees" (p. 7).

The supervision model presented in this book is, likewise, based on the conflict theory model I have been developing for many years and the model which I continue to write about, use clinically with couples, and employ in my supervision process (Betchen, 2010, 2022, 2024, 2025; Betchen & Davidson, 2018). The model is integrative on two levels: (1) Modalic Level – It combines psychoanalytic conflict theory and systems theory with the goal of determining the underlying, unconscious conflicts that may be behind a couple's interactive dynamic and their associated symptoms; and (2) Methodic Level – It also combines couple and sex therapy to seamlessly treat couples with sexual problems. As mentioned, while I focus on this model, many of the supervision concepts that will be discussed throughout the book are applicable to other supervision models, especially psychodynamic approaches.

In my model, conflict is not an external altercation. Rather, it is an unconscious, "internal duality" in which one part of a person desires one thing, and the other part desires the opposite. For example, if one partner is conflicted about being successful; one part of them wants to achieve and the other part is uncomfortable with success. Choosing one side over the other does not resolve the conflict because choosing one side means suffering the loss of the other side. As such, most people try to avoid this by holding onto both sides in the hope that the pain of the conflict will somehow subside. If, however, both two sides are integrated, the conflict can be balanced in a way that is tolerable and less likely to produce symptoms.

Internalized conflicts emanate from the family of origin and can be exacerbated by life experiences. That is, parents may verbally or behaviorally transmit conflict to their children who internalize them and carry them into their adult years. This "multigenerational transmission process" (Bowen, 1978) of internalized conflicts is an unconscious process which also directs an individual to choose a mate with a similar conflict or a "twin in conflict" (Betchen, 2010; Betchen & Davidson, 2018). This choice ensures that the couple's "shared conflict" lives, and the anxiety and depression that accompanies significant change is avoided. A tradeoff occurs between the discomfort that change brings versus the discomfort inherent in the symptoms of the unbalanced conflict.

Applying conflict theory to the supervision process can be a challenge, especially with couples. A couple's unbalanced conflict emanating from the family of origin (or from experience *via* the interaction with a parent or parents) may trigger a supervisee's shared conflict and *vice versa*. For example, a couple with a conflict about success may vacillate from success and failure in and out of the therapeutic setting and the supervisee may be provoked to do the same. If the supervisee and supervisor share the same conflict, the supervision process may vacillate between competent and incompetent supervision which may prevent both supervisor and supervisee from having to choose a side: succeed or fail.

There are many different combinations that could impact the supervisory process in both positive and negative ways. Although there are several different models of supervision, because my conflict model integrates both systemic and psychoanalytic conflict theory as well as couple and sex therapy, it can generally be described as an integrative approach to supervision.

While several institutes that I have trained and worked at required supervisees to have more than one supervisor at the same time (i.e., the supervisee has two individual sessions, one with each supervisor weekly or biweekly), several studies have found mixed results reported by supervisees with multiple supervisors. Dodds (1986) reported increase stress on supervisees. Nestler (1990) found conflicting guidance to be a problem. And Lane et al. (2024) found mixed results related to the following general themes: "making sense of multiple perspectives, orchestrating the process, supervisory relationship dynamics, and personal discrepancies and characteristics" (p. 24).

I have never been a fan of the multiple-supervisor approach – a common dynamic especially when one supervisor is operating within (internally) the supervisee's training institute or place of employment, and the other is hired by the supervisee to simultaneously operate outside (externally) those contexts (Smith, 2024). Being matched with two or more supervisors from different theoretical backgrounds might offer the supervisee different perspectives, but in agreement with the previous research cited I too fear this configuration may lead to theoretical and clinical confusion, control struggles, coalitions in the supervision process, and the potential for confidentiality breaches.

I take no issue with a supervisee being exposed to several supervisors from multi-theoretical backgrounds at different times in the supervisee's training. I believe this exposes the supervisee to the various models of practice that exist. I can also be convinced of the positive aspects of engaging more than one supervisor simultaneously if one is a generalist and the other is a specialist. In fact, if the situation calls for a special expertise in sexual issues, for example, some might consider it unethical to ignore the need to at the very least to consult a sex therapist.

Supervisors of different levels may also clash. A more experienced supervisor, for example, may become frustrated with a beginner supervisor for failing to intervene appropriately, adequately balance a couple, or to integrate the couple and their sexual issues. The beginning supervisor may also be less self-aware and therefore less skilled in the interpretation of transference-countertransference dynamics that may occur.

Difference in gender may also play a part. For example, a female supervisee may or may not favor a female supervisor and *vice versa*, and a male supervisor may or may not favor the male supervisee and *vice versa*. Also, when supervising sex therapy and discussing sexual issues there is also the potential for sexual feelings to be stirred up between supervisor and supervisees. In the end, it is the experienced, mature supervisor that has a better chance of remaining objective, setting and maintaining appropriate boundaries, and adapting to new and varied situations that may arise.

References

Betchen, S. (1995). An integrative, intersystemic approach to supervision of couple therapy. *American Journal of Family Therapy*, *23*, 48–58. https://doi.org/10.1080/01926189508251335

Betchen, S. (2010). *Magnetic partners: Discover how the hidden conflicts that once attracted* you to *each other is now driving you apart*. Free Press.

Betchen, S. (2022). *Couples in conflict: Clinical techniques for navigating sexual and relationship control struggles*. Routledge.

Betchen, S. (2024). *Unmet expectations in couple and sex therapy: Helping couples negotiate realistic relationships*. Routledge.

Betchen, S. (2025). *Commitment in couples therapy: A therapist's guide to assessing relationship durability*. Routledge.
Betchen, S., & Davidson, H. L. (2018). *Master conflict therapy: A new model for practicing couples and sex therapy*. Routledge.
Bowen, M. (1978). *Family therapy in clinical practice*. Aronson.
Dodds, J. B. (1986). Supervision of psychology trainees in field placements. *Professional Psychology: Research and Practice*, *17*, 296–300. https://doi.org/10.1037/0735-7028.17.4.296
Holloway, E. L. (2016). *Supervision essentials for a systems approach to supervision*. American Psychological Association. https://doi.org/10.1037/14942-000
Lane, W. B., Hakenewerth, T. J., Frank, C. D., Davis-Price, T. B., Kleist, D. M., & Moody, S. J. (2024). The more, the merrier? A phenomenological investigation of counselor-in-training simultaneous supervision. *The Professional Counselor*, *14*, 15–29. doi: 10.15241/wblj.14.1.15
Nestler, E. J. (1990). The case of double supervision: A resident's perspective on common problems in psychotherapy supervision. *Academic Psychiatry*, *14*, 129–136. https://doi.org/10.1007/BF03341284
Norberg, J., Axelsson, H., Barkman, N., & Hamrin, M. (2016). What psychodynamic supervisors say about supervision: Freedom within limits. *The Clinical Supervisor*, *35*, 268–286. doi: 10.1080/07325223.2016.1219896
Norcross, J. C., & Popple, L. M. (2017). *Supervision essentials for integrative psychotherapy*. American Psychological Association. https://dx.doi.org/10.1037/15967-001
Silva, S., & Sousa, D. (2022). Existential psychotherapy supervision: The supervisor's perspective. *Journal of Humanistic Psychology*, *62*, 397–417 https://doi.org/10.1177/0022167818802905
Smith, C. (2024). Internal vs. external clinical supervision: Which is best for your organization? *Motivo*, https://motivohealth.com/resources/for-your-organization/clincial-supervision-internal-external
Smith, K. (2009). *A brief summary of supervision models*. www.academia.edu/35618735/A_BRIEF_SUMMARY_OF_SUPERVISION_MODELS
Sudek, D. (2021). *Teaching and supervising CBT*. Beck Institute. https://beckinstitute.org/blog/teaching-and-supervising-cbt/

Chapter 7

Conflict Theory Supervision in Practice

Students and supervisees have said to me over the years that the conflict approach to treating couples is not that difficult to understand, but hard to put into practice. With this comment in mind, the basic steps to treat a couple *via* the conflict theory approach are highlighted and adapted to the supervision process. These include: 1) gathering data with the use of the genogram; 2) searching for contradictions in the family of origin and the couple's interactions; 3) uncovering the couple's shared conflict; 4) connecting this internal conflict to the couple's sexual problems; and 5) suggesting interventions. Detailed case examples of this process, including dialogue and specific clinical interventions, are presented in Chapter 10.

The Use of the Genogram

After the basic structure of supervision is set and formal supervision begins, I request that all supervisees construct a multi-generational genogram focusing on their partners, parents, and children (Bowen, 1978; DeMaria et al., 2017). I explain that understanding their personal histories and internal conflicts may help to better understand the "self" and the couples they will work with. This will enhance the supervision process as well. I do not, however, require that supervisees present their genograms in supervision unless I notice a chronic, potentially destructive pattern in treatment. In my experience, most supervisees value this process; some have even asked for help uncovering their personal conflicts. Supervisees who seek psychodynamic supervision are familiar with looking inwards or evaluating the self in the therapeutic and supervisory process.

Beyond their personal genogram, I also request that all supervisees make a small genogram for the couple they treat, beginning in the first session. These genograms can then be presented physically or verbally in supervision. The number of questions that supervisees are to ask and the emotional intensity this inquiry may cause can be quite exhausting for both

DOI: 10.4324/9781003642732-7

couples and supervisees. However, if supervisees control the structure of the therapy, they should be able to develop a therapeutic framework within two back-to-back treatment sessions.

The more experienced supervisees are, the less time they will need to complete a couple's genogram and to develop a framework. I tend to finish a working genogram on both partners in the first session. Allowing a couple to use most of the session arguing – something they can do at home for free – is a waste of time and money. While supervisees should sample the couple's interactional style, any unnecessary dedication to this dynamic might impede the supervisee's control of the therapeutic structure.

Because the focus of this supervision model is on the combining of couple and sex therapy, questions for the genogram reflect both disciplines. That is, supervisees are to ask each partner a series of general (nonsexual) and sexual questions with special focus on a couple's reported sexual difficulty. With such extensive information, supervisees will be better able to assess the link between the couple and sexual dynamics (Berman & Hof, 1987; DeMaria et al., 2017). Organic issues notwithstanding, a shared unconscious, internal conflict is deemed responsible for the couple dynamic, and in turn any sexual symptoms.

The following questions can be used by supervisees to construct genograms (Betchen, 2022, 2024; Betchen & Davidson, 2018). The supervisee can choose to leave out, or focus on, a certain line of questioning depending on his or her stage of development. I prefer that the beginner ask most of the questions below whereas the intermediate and advanced supervisee can focus on those questions that more closely reflect a couple's chief complaint.

Questions are asked of each partner. An asterisk after the question signifies that the question should be asked by the supervisee in individual sessions only (one per partner), which the supervisee is recommended to hold immediately after the first two conjoint sessions. Assume when reading all the following questions that a couple has presented the supervisee with a sexual issue:

Questions for the Genogram

How old are you?
What is your level of education?
What is your ethnicity?
How long did you date before you married, moved in, or decided to date exclusively?
Where and how did you meet?

What do you do for a living?
How long have you been at your present place of employment?
Were you ever engaged or married before, and for how long?
Does your current relationship remind you of any past relationships?
Did you two ever break up, separate, or divorce?
Have either of you had previous therapy, individually or together? If so, for what reason?
Do you trust your partner?*
Do you love- or are you in love with your partner?*
Do you or your partner use or abuse drugs or alcohol, or suffer from any addictive behavior?
How do you identify sexually?
When did you first experience this sexual issue?
Did you ever experience this issue in a previous relationship?
Can you give me a detailed description of your last sexual experience?
When did you lose your virginity?*
Do you masturbate?*
Do you fantasize?*
Do you watch porn? If so, what excites you most?
Do you have any paraphilias or fetishes?*
Did your parents talk about sex when you were a child?
Did you ever experience abuse of any kind?*
Are you physically attracted to your partner? If not, what type of individual typically attracts you?*
Are you sexually satisfied with your partner?*
To your knowledge, has there been any outside emotional or physical affairs?*
What is the most sexually risqué act you have ever done?*
Did you ever consider having sex with someone of the same sexual orientation?*
How often would you like to have sex?
Can you achieve orgasm? If so, under what conditions?
How many sexual relationships did you have before you met your partner?*
If you had a honeymoon, what was your experience like?
Do you and your partner share similar interests, politics, values, religious, and cultural backgrounds?
Do you take any medication? If so, for what condition?
Do you feel anxious or depressed?
Have you ever tried to harm yourself?
Are your parents still alive?
Did your parents approve of your relationship?

What did each of your parents do for a living?
Do your parents live nearby? If so, do you have contact with them?
Can you describe your parents' personalities?
Did your parents use or abuse drugs or alcohol, or suffer from any addictions?
How would you describe your parents' relationship?
Did your parents fight a lot? If so, was there a common issue that they fought over?
Did your parents ever separate or divorce?
Did either parent ever threaten to leave the other?
To the best of your knowledge, did either parent ever have an affair?
Did either of your parents discuss their sex life with you?
Were your parents polyamorous or swingers?
Would you consider either of your parents sexually provocative verbally or in dress?
Do you have any siblings?
Are you still in contact with your siblings?
Are your siblings married or in long-term relationships?
What do your siblings do for a living?
Do any of your siblings have the same problem you are reporting?
Do you have any children? If so, what are their ages and genders?
Do any of your children have any disabilities?

It is common knowledge that assessment is an ongoing process. But I believe that the supervisee will be much more effective and impressive if he or she has a framework from which to practice. I try to help supervisees to develop a framework as soon as possible by looking at or listening to the information they have recorded on the genogram as I will illustrate in the next section. I also demonstrate a way of mirroring how to cut through the massive amount of useless material a couple may try and confuse them with, consciously or unconsciously. I tend to see providing "too much" or unnecessary material as a form of resistance to avoid change.

Many supervisees, especially those that are behavioral-oriented, do not value the history of the couple. Others, however, prefer to wait in doing so for various reasons including the desire to first join with a couple (Weeks & Fife, 2014). This is especially true when it comes to asking sexual questions. These individuals find it uncomfortable to get that personal before adequately connecting with a couple (N. Gambescia, personal communication, November 9, 2016). While this is certainly understandable, I like my supervisees to get as much information as they can, as soon as they can, for three reasons: (1) The sooner they develop a framework for the treatment process the more confident they will feel, and the more impressed the couple will be. Supervisees have, in fact, told me that most of their couples expressed appreciation for the interest shown by them and the thoroughness of their approach; (2) Most couples who choose to see a couple and sex therapist will expect questions about their sex lives so there should be no need to worry about the joining process. The exception here are questions that may merit the privacy of an individual session such as those pertaining to affairs or sexual abuse that I highlighted previously with an asterisk; and (3) The more time that goes by, the harder it is for a therapist to go back and get information from a couple.

Once couples settle into their interactional cycle, emotions are usually high. Going back into an evaluative state may be seen as a therapeutic regression to them. The therapist may also feel pressure to deal with what is happening in the moment.

I still, however, have supervisees that resist taking a full history. This resistance is usually associated with anxiety about upsetting or losing a couple. Private practitioners, whose sole income might be dependent on a large caseload, tend to be even more concerned about losing couples.

Presenting Couple-Cases in Supervision

The next step in the supervisory process is for the supervisee to present a list of his or her couples and their sexual-related complaints. We go over these couples briefly and I keep the list for future reference. This way I can determine if the supervisee is underestimating the critical nature of a specific case. There is usually no need for a supervisee to present a genogram on these cases unless I deem it necessary. The supervisee is then given the opportunity to choose which specific couple he or she would like to discuss, but I usually request that they start with the most troublesome couple. If discussing one couple happens to take up an entire supervision session, so be it. But I try to get the supervisee to re-present troubling couples so that I have an idea how he or she is progressing. If the supervisee does not re-present a couple after two weeks, I will inquire as to the progress of the case.

While I expect the supervisee to have an extensive couple genogram, I usually ask what I think are some of the most important questions that they may have failed to consider. These questions focus specifically on questions related to the couple's presenting problem or chief complaint. For example, if a couple present with delayed ejaculation, I ask questions about control struggles in the family of origin. Many supervisees would not think to go in this direction. But in my experience people who withhold sex tend to withhold affection, feelings, and may even control finances.

If the presenting problem is one of low sexual desire, it would make perfect sense to focus on questions about affairs or hormonal issues – and

I would expect supervisees to do the same. But I might focus on the beginning of the couple's relationship: How did it form? Who pursued whom? How long did it take to consummate? Was there sex on the honeymoon? Was there sufficient physical attraction between the two? Who generally initiates sex? Is the couple engaged in any control struggles? I tend not to focus on material that bogs the process down or to throw me off track. Couples will often try and do this as a defense against what really may be happening, or because they think the real problem dwells in another area.

While some of my questions seem counterintuitive or even nonsensical to a supervisee, by asking these types of questions I accomplish several objectives:

- Demonstrate how the supervisee can cut through much of the confusion and massive amount of information the couple is conveying and get right to the matter. I witnessed a former supervisor do this and she was able to accurately diagnose a case in minutes.
- Teach the supervisee to broaden the context of sexual symptoms so that their couples can see the power and pervasiveness of their conflict in other (nonsexual) areas of their lives. Couples tend to focus on a specific sexual symptom when they present for treatment to the neglect of their process. With such a narrow view, if they do not accept what the supervisee is trying to convey to them in a sexual context, the couple might reject the treatment altogether.
- Help to increase a supervisee's independence. By teaching supervisees what to ask when they are on their own, they will be less dependent on me to analyze their cases. The first time supervisees accurately track the link between a couple and their sexual issues by asking counterintuitive questions is a revelatory and rewarding experience for them.
- Teach the supervisee to think outside of the box so-to-speak. The supervisee who fails to consider that even absurd behavior has an important meaning, may easily misunderstand the reason why some couples might behave or think the way they do. Our business is not always one that supports logic, but there is a reason for everything. With this perspective, a supervisee will be better able to empathize with a couple.
- Encourage the supervisee to rely on more than just facts. I want the supervisee to use "intuition." Shallcross (2016) defined intuition as "something that is known or understood without proof or evidence" (p. 1). I make it a habit of asking supervisees what they think of the couple, or of an individual partner? If they are hesitant to say without having enough background on the couple, I tell them to follow their gut. I often find their hunches or feelings are correct.

Another supervisory technique I use is to ask the supervisee to sum up the case using one descriptive word, or in one sentence. For example, in the case of delayed ejaculation the word might be "withhold" or the sentence could be "Fear of being all in." These few words are used metaphorically to give the supervisee a framework from which to work. While some supervisees find this exercise frivolous, descriptive words and the actions they represent may turn out to be clinically and theoretically prophetic.

I may also use a quote from literature, or a popular phrase or song to describe a couple's dynamic. One of my favorite lines, which to me describes the systemic dynamic of a complementary couple, is from the song, "You May be Right:"

> *You may be right*
> *I may be crazy*
> *Oh, but it just may be a lunatic you're looking for.*
>
> (Joel, 1980)

A third technique I use often is to have the supervisee look at the genograms they have constructed of a couple intently and to think of it as a portrait of the couple and each partner's family of origin. I then ask the supervisee to "visualize" the dynamic of the family system. In this sense, the genogram becomes a moving, theatrical drama projecting the roles of each member and symptoms they generate.

Contradiction, Conflict, and Symptom Connection

Teaching a supervisee to locate a couple's shared conflict in treatment is perhaps the most important, and challenging goal of my supervision process. Without revealing and understanding this, the sexual symptom cannot be alleviated. I make it a point to remind supervisees that when constructing the genogram if something confuses them or "makes them scratch their heads," to follow it because it will most likely lead to the couple's conflict. Conflicts are counterintuitive, presenting two conflicting messages.

To locate a couple's conflict, I instruct the supervisee to look out for contradictory messages on the couple's genogram. These messages were usually communicated by parents, verbally or behaviorally, during childhood. The supervisee is also instructed to look for contradictory messages demonstrated by the couple's interaction in real time – live in the office or *via* telehealth. The following are examples of each in the context of couples with sexual problems. Note that the contradictions do not have to be about sex to cause sexual symptoms.

Contradictory Messages from the Family of Origin

Example #1: *Hallie and Jack* – Hallie was upset because her husband Jack rarely, if, ever initiated sex with her. However, rather than challenge Jack to address his sexual issue she chose to have an affair. Jack was enraged with Hallie's behavior, but he still had difficulty initiating sex with her.

1. **Genogram:** A genogram exploration revealed that Jack was told by his parents his entire life that he was a "genius destined for great success." But as Jack aged, he realized that while he was a smart man, he was not a genius and therefore had to work hard to do well, especially in college. Jack admitted that he was both angry and depressed following his rude awakening and that he was ill-prepared to work hard for what he wanted. Hallie dreamt of being a great dancer. And she had the body-type, background training, drive, and discipline to give herself a chance. Even her mother, a former dancer of some repute, thought she had a good chance to make it. But rather than offer her positive reinforcement, her mother was hypercritical, competitive, and jealous of Hallie's talent. Hallie finally stopped her training and set her sight on becoming a nurse anesthetist. This decision enraged her mother.
2. **Contradiction:** Jack was told he was a genius and was going to be a great success in life. But because he believed this for most of his life, he refused to put much effort into anything, which often led to failure. Hallie was told by her mother that she had enormous talent but was simultaneously critiqued and humiliated.
3. **Conflict:** Jack wanted things to be handed to him, but as unrealistic as this was, he found it difficult to put the work in to succeed. Hallie's mother wanted Hallie to be a professional dancer, as did Hallie, but she simultaneously thwarted Hallie's development whenever she could. Rather than challenge her deflating mother, Hallie chose to leave dancing and pursue an entirely different career. Both Jack and Hallie shared a conflict about committing to, and working hard, to get what they wanted.
4. **Connection to the Sexual Symptom:** Because Jack was in conflict about having to work hard to get somewhere in life, he also put little to no work into his marriage and sex life. That is, he refused to do the work needed to satisfy his wife sexually. Hallie enabled Jack's behavior for a long time. But when it showed in their sex life, rather than make him confront his issue, she emotionally and physically left him, just as she did the field of dance.
5. **Suggesting Clinical Interventions:** The supervisee is to help the couple to make all the connections and integrate both sides of their conflict to better balance it and to alleviate their sexual symptoms.

Example #2: *Cheryl and Lucas* – Lucas presented with Delayed Ejaculation which he procrastinated treating for years. Lucas's wife, Cheryl, stopped trying to convince Lucas to get help. Instead, she started openly flirting with a former boyfriend on the internet.

1. **Genogram:** According to their genogram, Lucas's parents claimed to be open-minded and encouraged all their children to express their opinions about various subjects. But when they did express themselves, if it was something their parents disagreed with, they were usually chastised or shunned. Lucas's wife, Cheryl, was encouraged by her parents to aggressively defend herself against criticism. As an adult, however, she was both sensitive and cruel to anyone who disagreed with her.
2. **Contradiction:** Lucas's parents encouraged him to speak his mind but punished him for doing so. Cheryl's parents urged her to defend herself but as an adult she could not take even the slightest of criticism without retaliating viciously.
3. **Conflict:** Lucas and Cheryl both shared a conflict about openly expressing themselves appropriately.
4. **Connection to the Sexual Symptom:** Just as Lucas's voice was controlled as a child, he controlled his ejaculate. Just as Cheryl's voice was controlled as a child, she was overly sensitive and cruel in her reaction to Lucas's inability to meet her sexual needs.
5. **Suggesting Clinical Interventions:** The supervisee is to help the couple to make all the connections and integrate both sides of their conflict to better balance it and to alleviate their sexual symptoms.

Example #3: *Jenna and Trey* – Jenna and Trey saw themselves as counterculture types and agreed to an open marriage (as swingers). The "one" major rule they set for their sexual activity was to not swing behind each other's backs. Jenna, however, decided to break this rule by having a fling with a neighbor's husband. Trey only found out about the fling because his neighbor's wife alerted him. Trey was devastated.

1. **Genogram:** Trey's genogram indicated that he grew up in a military family that employed strict rules. But his father was also a severe alcoholic, and his mother a prototypical enabler, sometimes even getting drunk with her husband. For most of his youth Trey was always in trouble, having been suspended several times from school and having some minor scrapes with the law. Trey's father responded to Trey's delinquent behavior by kicking Trey out of the house when he was 16-years old, and before Trey could finish high school. Jenna was a "good girl" while growing up, especially compared to her delinquent younger

sister. Her father was a police officer, and her mother was a minister, who according to Jenna, ran their home like a "military barracks." But while her parents claimed to trust Jenna, whenever she made the smallest infraction, they would team up on her and overreact by calling her inappropriate names such as an "ingrate" or even a "whore." They would also threaten to kick her out of the home. To add insult to injury, as an adult, Jenna discovered that her parents made her chronically troubled younger sister in charge of their estate and left Jenna virtually nothing in their will.

2. **Contradiction:** Trey was told to always follow the rules, but his parents broke them repeatedly. Jenna thought she was making life easier on her parents by being the "good girl" of the family. But her parents failed to see her goodness and even favored her troubled sister.
3. **Conflict:** Trey and Jenna were in conflict about following versus breaking rules.
4. **Connection to the Sexual Symptom:** Trey and Jenna chose to rebel against traditional marriage norms to form an alternate relationship. But even though they set only one rule, one of them still managed to break it.
5. **Suggesting Clinical Interventions:** The supervisee is to help the couple to make all the connections and integrate both sides of their conflict to better balance it and to alleviate their sexual symptoms.

Contradictory Messages from the Couple Interaction

Example #4: *Greta and Lenny* – Greta suffered from Female Orgasmic Disorder (FOD); she gets close to orgasm with her husband but claims that "a wall comes down and blocks her." Lenny is frustrated with Greta. He thinks that she is not interested in experiencing passionate sex, and that she makes him feel inadequate. Greta claims that she is trying to achieve orgasm, and that she loves Lenny. But she also feels he pressures her to have sex and to orgasm, and this makes it harder for her to let go and experience pleasure.

1. **Genogram:** Greta admitted she was sexually abused as a child by a close relative. She claimed that she was too afraid to tell her parents for fear it would tear the family apart. Lenny came from a high-achieving family who felt pressure to succeed. He claimed that he never felt good enough, especially to his father. To exacerbate Lenny's poor self-worth, he lost his mother – his most supportive parent – in a car accident when he was only 11 years old. His father then remarried a woman who doted on her children from a previous marriage, which left Lenny feeling abandoned, neglected, and inferior.

2. **Contradiction:** Greta wanted to feel and function like an adult woman, but she had difficulty breaking the link between her childhood sexual abuse and the inhibited pleasure it caused her as an adult. Lenny wanted Greta to help him feel like an adequate male, but the pressure he put on her made it more difficult for her to orgasm and caused her to distance from him.
3. **Conflict:** Both Greta and Lenny were in conflict about being "adequate" adults. Parts of each wanted to feel competent, but the other parts had difficulty leaving behind the pain from their childhoods.
4. **Connection to the Sexual Symptom:** Greta's inability to orgasm made her feel less than an "adequate woman." Lenny wanted Greta to focus on his needs and to help him feel like an "adequate man," but the pressure he exerted exacerbated his own inadequacy.
5. **Suggesting Clinical Interventions:** The supervisee is to help the couple to make all the connections and integrate both sides of their conflict to better balance it and to alleviate their sexual symptoms.

Example #5: *Molly and Brent* – Brent suffered from Male Hypoactive Sexual Desire Disorder (MHSDD); his wife, Molly, was enraged with him.

1. **Genogram:** Molly complained in treatment that her husband Brent refused to engage her. She also said that he never initiated sex. Molly claimed that she would give anything if Brent showed some interest in her and their marriage. However, when Brent finally asserted himself, Molly immediately increased her verbal assault on him and shut him down. Molly would not let Brent speak unless he said something she agreed with. In turn, Brent allowed Molly to shut him down – he would resort to distancing.
2. **Contradiction:** Molly wanted Brent to engage her but prevented him from doing so. Brent wanted Molly to get off his back but rather than confront her, he allowed her to attack him so that he could use this as an excuse to distance from her.
3. **Conflict:** Molly and Brent had a conflict about closeness. They claimed they wanted to be more intimate but were creative in finding ways to maintain or increase the distance between them.
4. **Connection to the Sexual Symptom:** Brent was a distancer and used low sexual desire to distance from his wife. His wife consistently pushed him away.
5. **Suggesting Clinical Interventions:** The supervisee is to help the couple to make all the connections and integrate both sides of their conflict to better balance it and to alleviate their sexual symptoms.

Example #6: *Ruthie and Wayne* – Ruthie presented with Female Sexual Interest/Arousal Disorder (FSIAD). This contributed to her husband Wayne's jealousy of her past sexual experiences, which he felt she was more impressed by.

1. **Genogram:** Wayne complained that his wife Ruthie had better and more frequent sex with her past lovers and that with him the sex was rigid and lacking passion. Ruthie claimed that Wayne insisted on certain sexual activities that turned her off, but she participated because she did not want to fail him. Wayne refused to negotiate sexual activities that his wife could enjoy.
2. **Contradiction:** Wayne wanted Ruthie to be more involved in their sex life, but he insisted on certain activities that turned her off.
3. **Conflict:** Wayne unconsciously found a way to avoid getting what he claimed to want. Ruthie wanted to please Wayne, but not at the expense of her own needs.
4. **Connection to the Sexual Symptom:** Ruthie's arousal disorder was related to her disdain for the sexual activities that Wayne insisted she engage in.
5. **Suggesting Clinical Interventions:** The supervisee is to help the couple to make all the connections and integrate both sides of their conflict to better balance it and to alleviate their sexual symptoms.

Two additional components of couple and sex therapy merit consideration and elaboration: (1) transference-countertransference (and parallel process) and (2) premature termination and termination of supervision. Both are elaborated on in the next two chapters and play crucial roles in the process of supervision.

References

Berman, E., & Hof, L. (1987). The sexual genogram: Assessing family-of-origin factors in the treatment of sexual dysfunctions. In G. Weeks and L. Hof (Eds.), *Integrating sex & marital therapy: A clinical guide* (pp. 37–56). Brunner/Mazel.

Betchen, S. (2022). *Couples in conflict: Clinical techniques for navigating sexual and relationship control struggles*. Routledge.

Betchen, S. (2024). *Unmet expectations in couple and sex therapy: Helping couples negotiate realistic relationships*. Routledge.

Betchen, S., & Davidson, H. L. (2018). *Master conflict therapy: A new model for practicing couples and sex therapy*. Routledge.

Bowen, M. (1978). *Family therapy in clinical practice*. Aronson.

DeMaria, R., Weeks, G., & Twist, M. (2017). *Focused genograms: Intergenerational assessment of individuals, couples, and families* (2nd ed.). Routledge.

Joel, B. (1980). You May Be Right [Sound recording]. Glass Houses. Columbia Records.

Shallcross, L. (2016, July 24). *Embracing intuition: Counseling today*. Counseling Today. https://ct.counseling.org/2016/07/embracing-intuition/

Weeks, G., & Fife, S. (2014). *Couples in treatment: Effective approaches for effective practice* (3rd ed.). Routledge.

Chapter 8

Transference-Countertransference (and Parallel Process)

Transference

The concept of transference was perhaps one of Freud's most significant and enduring discoveries. In his paper, "The Dynamics of Transference," he wrote:

> It must be understood that each individual, through the combined combination of his innate disposition and the influences brought to bear on him during his early years, has acquired a specific method of his own in his conduct of his early life—that is, in the preconditions to falling in love which he lays down, in the instincts he satisfies and the aims he sets himself in the course of it. This produces what might be described as a stereotype plate (or several such), which is constantly repeated—constantly reprinted afresh—in the course of the person's life, so far as external circumstances and the nature of the love-objects accessible to him permit, and which is currently not entirely insusceptible to change in the face of recent experiences.
>
> (Freud, 1912/1958, pp. 99–100)

Given Freud's perspective, it makes sense that he thought it only natural that such repressed, unsatisfied desires would eventually be unconsciously transferred from patient to doctor/therapist, thus bridging the gap between fantasy and real life.

Transference may be positive, negative, or sexualized. Positive transferences occur if patients transfer positive feelings from early life experiences onto their therapists and see them in a positive light. In negative transference, the patients transfer feelings from past objects or experiences that are disappointing and painful onto their therapists thus casting them in a negative light. And sexualized transference occurs when the patients project intimate or sexual fantasies onto their therapists. According to Ladson and Welton (2007) there are two types of sexualized transference: (1)

DOI: 10.4324/9781003642732-8

erotic transference – positive sexual feelings towards therapists that the patients know are unrealistic and do not interfere with treatment; and (2) eroticized transference – where patients have irrational and intense erotic feelings towards their therapists.

Koo (2001) claimed that erotic transference may be a normal and manageable part of development. Bolognini (1994), however, found erotized transference to be a common phenomenon in severe personality disorders and psychotics. In tune with Bolognini, Freud described this type of patient as "a stubborn and rebellious spirit" who presented "a resistance under the guise of being in love" with the analyst (Freud, 1914/1958, p. 167).

Freud initially saw transference as "the most powerful resistance" to successful treatment (Freud, 1912/1958, p. 101). But he later decided it was something both therapists and patients needed to work together on to alleviate the patient's symptoms. He famously said about transference, "It is on that field that the victory must be won—the victim whose expression is the permanent cure of the neurosis" (Freud, 1912/1958, p. 108).

Working through transference is a difficult enough process for therapists who practice individual therapy. It is much harder for therapists, especially for the inexperienced supervisee without couple therapy training, to track transference and to interpret it accurately in couple therapy. Glausius (2024) commented: "The triangular setting of a couple therapy session can be as complex as 3D chess, because so many things are happening at once" (p. 184). The supervisee must pay close attention to transference between two partners, between each partner and the supervisee, and between the supervisee and the supervisor (**see Figure 8.1**).

Add to this the mutual blaming and emotional intensity most couples bring with them to treatment, it is easy to see how therapists can be startled by the volatility of a couple and distracted by one partner at the expense of the other. According to Glausius, "in the context of the intimate couple relationship, unresolved aspects of the past come alive and are repeated in the present with searing intensity" (p. 184). If the transference is *negative*, or if negative emotions such as anger and hostility are projected onto the therapist, the chances of a smooth therapeutic process and successful outcome are greatly reduced (Gelso et al., 2013).

Consider the following example and accompanying dialogue in which a young wife, Emma, feels like she is being picked on verbally by her emotionally and verbally abusive husband, Seth. The result is that she has lost all sexual desire for him and when he coerces her to have sex, according to Seth, "she lays there like a zombie." The supervisee in this case is Lena, a 32-year-old supervisee in a graduate program seeking a master's degree in marriage and family therapy. She already had previously completed a

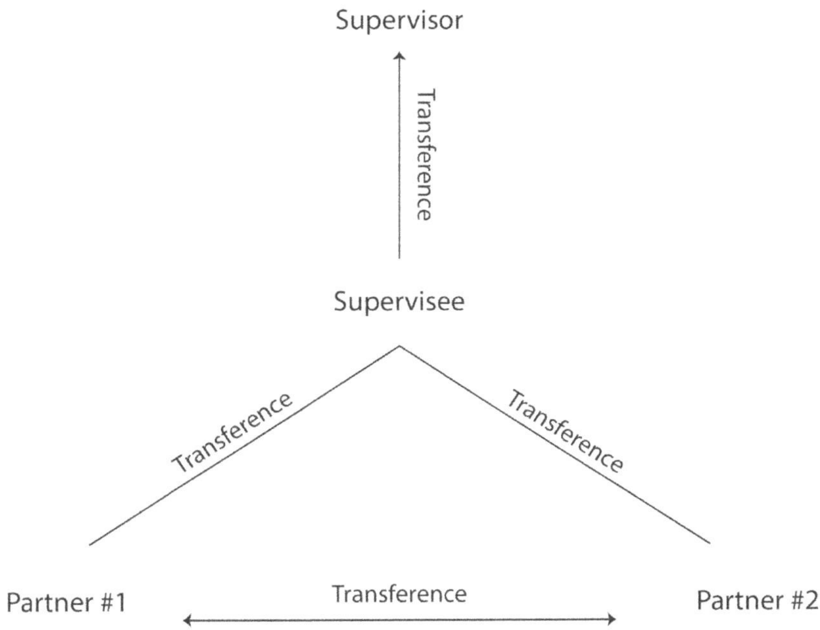

Figure 8.1 Transference in Couple Supervision

master's degree in counseling psychology. This case illustrates transference between partners of a couple and between the partners and the supervisee.

Lena was unsure how to intervene given that the husband, Seth, was constantly criticizing his wife, Emma. Emma made mild attempts to defend herself, but it was obvious to Lena that she was ill equipped to do so. Emma also feared that by confronting Seth, the situation would escalate. While Lena tried to calm Seth, he simply ignored her. The biggest surprise, however, was Emma's vicious attack on Lena after Lena valiantly tried but failed to help her. Lena was confused and hurt by this unanticipated response; she thought she would, at the very least Emma would credit her for coming to her rescue.

Supervisee: I am so confused. Instead of going after Seth, she unloaded on me. I didn't even think she was capable of so much anger.

Supervisor: Well, something you did or didn't do made her angry with you.

Supervisee: I can't think of anything.

Supervisor: As a rule, when you get stuck, you might want to re-visit the genogram. Do you see any conflict in her background that might explain her anger towards you?

Supervisee: Well, I know she had a very critical father who she wanted to please. That might help to explain why she married Seth and tolerates his behavior. But that's all I see.

Supervisor: Wasn't her mother somewhat passive?

Supervisee: Yes. She described her mother as a "sweet" person. I wonder if Emma is angry with her father for being so critical of her and unconsciously married Seth out of a fantasy that he would one day approve of her.

Supervisor: But Seth is not approving, and you were too weak, like her mother, to change that.

Supervisee: So, I also failed to save her from Seth. That explains her negative transference with me.

Supervisor: I suspect.

Supervisee: And so, Emma transferred her father's disapproving feelings onto Seth, and onto me for failing to change him.

Supervisor: That's my guess.

Supervisee: Got it. I think I'll bring this up with Emma in the next session. Do you think she'll come back?

Supervisor: I think her conflict will bring her back. She's an ambivalent pleaser with a high threshold for pain. Even though she lays in bed in passive protest, she still has sex with Seth. Anyway, I do think you have a choice. You can address the transference now, or you can try to re-establish some balance and challenge Seth a bit more. This may trigger something in him, but it's your decision.

The following week Lena reported that she challenged Seth, much to Emma's delight, about his abusive behavior. At first Seth tried to ignore her, but when she persisted, he turned towards her with anger.

Supervisee: I stepped-up my challenge on Seth's behavior. He ignored me at first, but when he saw I was not going to back down he then turned his rage towards me. I can't win.

Supervisor: Let's look at the genogram. What do you see?

Supervisee: I'm lost.

Supervisor: It's all right there in black and white. The genogram tells us that Seth's mother had a series of affairs. Perhaps Seth has a lot of negative feelings about this. I wonder if, she too, went through the motions in her marriage, or stopped having sex with Seth's father altogether. Maybe Seth feels that it is only fair that women should be punished. Perhaps when you tried to stop him from punishing Emma, he saw you as being unfair to him as well. Another significant woman doing something unfair.

Supervisee: A conflict about injustice. So, maybe he is transferring his anger onto Emma and me for being unfair to him even if I am trying to help him to get what he says he wants.

Supervisor: Unfair to him and his victimized father. It makes sense, doesn't it?

Supervisee: It does.

Supervisor: Welcome to couple therapy.

When a couple suffers from a more specific sexual disorder the treatment usually takes on an added complexity for both supervisee and supervisor. Sexual content must be integrated into the couple therapy in a way that makes sense to the couple. And the mere discussion of sexual material often triggers past sex-related traumas. This case depicts transference between the partners of a couple and between the couple and the supervisee.

The following example is about a young man in his early 30s, Peter, engaged to Kerstin, a woman in her late 20s. The supervisee, Julian, was a relatively experienced male supervisee with a PhD in psychology who wanted to specialize in couple and sex therapy. The supervision took place in my private practice.

Kerstin initiated treatment because Peter had delayed ejaculation (i.e., he cannot ejaculate inside Kerstin), which he developed soon after asking her to marry him. Peter claimed that he had a lot on his mind, but according to Kerstin, this was an excuse. Kerstin said that she wanted to someday marry Peter and to have a baby, but because of their sexual problem she grew skeptical and wondered whether she should stay with him. She thought that Peter might be having an affair, or that he no longer found her attractive. Peter claimed that he had no clue as to why he had delayed ejaculation. Julian had never treated delayed ejaculation before. He also thought that Peter might be having an affair.

Supervisee: I think Peter is having an affair, but he denies it. He even denied it in an individual session. I'm not sure what to do about him.

Supervisor: So, you agree with his girlfriend that he is hiding something?

Supervisee: What else can it be?

Supervisor: A lot of things. Let's look at the genogram before you jump to a conclusion. It looks like Kersten's father had a series of affairs. Perhaps she is transferring this onto Peter.

Supervisee: Maybe. But it is plausible he is having one, isn't it?

Supervisor: Yes, it is. But Peter was married before, wasn't he? Did he have the same problem with his ex-wife?

Supervisee: No. His genogram indicates that he first developed this issue soon after he proposed to Kerstin.

Supervisor: His genogram also shows that he loved his ex-wife but that she cheated on him and that this destroyed him emotionally. Do you think this may play a part in his symptoms?

Supervisee: He said he was depressed for two years after she cheated on him. And that she left him for her lover. I wonder if he is having an affair to protect himself from Kerstin doing the same thing to him that his ex-wife did?

Supervisor: Check it out.

After seeing the couple again, Julian reported that Peter was enraged that both he and Kerstin thought he was having an affair. He even swore at Julian in the session and threatened to terminate treatment. Julian pulled back and began to empathize with Peter, primarily because he thought Peter was sincerely angry. Julian had triggered an injustice transference which was anchored in Peter's family of origin.

Supervisee: Whew, that was a disaster. I almost lost them. But you thought he was having an affair too, didn't you?

Supervisor: No. But you sure got him upset. Let's search the genogram for conflict. Peter was the oldest of three siblings and his parents blamed him for everything. Peter also said he was the highest functioning sibling, and that his parents expected more from him. Peter worked incredibly hard his whole life and was expected to look after his parents and his siblings, one of which had developmental disabilities. Looks like a parentified pleaser to me?

Supervisee: Big time. So maybe my thinking he had an affair was perceived by him as being unfair. It was as if I was reminding him of his parents by blaming him for the delayed ejaculation. I triggered a negative transference.

Supervisor: That sounds right. Now see if you can uncover the cause of his delayed ejaculation.

The following example is about a couple in their mid-30s, Noah and Ruby. The supervisee, Mark, was a relatively experienced male supervisee with a PhD in psychology who wanted to specialize in couple and sex therapy. The supervision took place in my private practice. Transferences in this context can be triggered in a couple as well as in the supervisor and supervisee. The case example illustrates erotic transference.

Noah and Ruby were a very sexually active couple who were engaged in a cuckold–cuckoldress dynamic. That is, Noah was turned on when Ruby either flirted with or had sex with other men who they both perceived as better endowed than Noah. Sometimes the couple would advertise their desires in the personals, and other times they would meet other couples in chat rooms or by referral from like-minded couples. They also belong to a private sex club. The chief complaint was brought by Noah who felt that after becoming parents Ruby's desire to participate in these activities waned. Noah claimed that the couple's cuckold–cuckoldress dynamic is his chief form of excitement and that he married Ruby because she was "into it." Even though Ruby cut back on her activities with other men, both she and Noah developed an erotic transference with Mark that both confused and intimidated him.

Supervisee: Man, this is hard. Between Noah's pressure and Ruby's seductiveness I'm drowning.
Supervisor: So, you're getting it from both partners?
Supervisee: Yup. Initially Ruby kept her distance, but something pulled her into the game, and she is good at it.
Supervisor: Are they conscious of what they are doing with you?
Supervisee: It's hard to tell. Sometimes I think they are plotting to trap me. But Ruby seems to really have an attraction for me. She constantly compliments me on my looks and tells me how "buff" I am. She doesn't even hold back in front of Noah. Noah seems almost pleased by it.
Supervisor: Of course she doesn't hold back, that's the dynamic. Noah might even masturbate if, and when, he visualizes you with his wife. Their genogram shows that Ruby's father left her mother for another woman when she was 12-years old. And it looks like this other woman was in her early 20s.
Supervisee: You know, she usually only has affairs with married cuckolds. Maybe this is her way of competing with the "other women."
Supervisor: Also, controlling other men.
Supervisee: Oh right.
Supervisor: Noah was raised in a severe triangle. He might have had an unconscious need to rid himself of his mother but not lose her totally. You might inquire as to whether she was a seductive woman.
Supervisee: A conflict about keeping her.
Supervisor: Perhaps.
Supervisee: So, I'm just an object in this game?
Supervisor: Yes. If you give in and enable their erotic transference you will contribute to their problem rather than help them.

Supervisee: An erotic countertransference.
Supervisor: Yes. And I suspect there is a person vs. object conflict that underlies it.

Thus far, I have only presented examples of how couples, influenced by their shared conflicts, transfer their experiences between each other and onto the supervisee. This last case example on transference, however, will illustrate my handling of a supervisee's transference onto me – the supervisor.

Desiree was a 26-year-old supervisee with an MSW degree. She was assigned to me as part of her fulfillment of a master's degree in marriage and family therapy with a specialization in sex therapy. I saw her at the intermediate level developmentally, but a beginner in working with couples and their sexual issues.

I noticed a pattern in Desiree's work with couples: she tended to side with the female partners over their male counterparts; this made it difficult to join with a couple and cost her more than one premature termination. In the following case example Desiree presented a couple in their early 40s, Angelo and Marie, who were fighting over domestic responsibilities. Angelo was the sole breadwinner and Marie was a housewife. But with three children, Marie often felt overwhelmed and wanted help from Angelo. Angelo said he understood Marie's position but that he was a young lawyer whose firm demanded most of attention; he said he had nothing left to give the family, except on some weekends. This standoff had also negatively affected the couple's sex life in that Marie claims she is too tired to have sex with Angelo. She claimed that she is slowly losing her libido in general. Angelo was especially not happy about this turn of events.

Desiree did not understand Angelo's position. She felt he was a "typical man" trying to put all the domestic chores on his wife's shoulders while he went to football games and dinners with his clients. However, this was not an isolated position for Desiree to take in her couple cases. She was somewhat unaware of her prejudice against men. Rather, she saw herself as being an advocate for female justice. Eventually she saw me the same way she saw her male clients.

Supervisee: I can't believe this guy. He is out all day, and his wife is stuck inside taking care of three children and a big house.
Supervisor: Angelo is in a major law firm, and they can be very demanding, especially if he wants to make partner someday.
Supervisee: Are you defending him?
Supervisor: I am just trying to balance this out. I suspect they both work very hard at what they do.

Supervisee: Except he gets to have fun while she gets no break.
Supervisor: They are Italian. Does she have any family support?
Supervisee: What does that have to do with anything?
Supervisor: I am just thinking of possible ways to get them both some relief.
Supervisee: He doesn't need any relief, she does.
Supervisor: I think he needs relief from the stress she is transferring. You seem to think she is miserable, and he is a happy camper.
Supervisee: If the shoe fits...
Supervisor: You seem very hostile today.
Supervisee: You seem one-sided.
Supervisor: I am really trying to balance the couple. I've noticed that you are often unbalanced when working with heterosexual couples. And the art of couple therapy is "balance." Without it you lose couples, which you have, and you do damage to a marriage.
Supervisee: Well, I think men have been getting away with too much for too long. And this guy's upset because she too tired to have sex. I wouldn't have sex with a guy like that either.
Supervisor: Okay. Maybe we can balance our own relationship here. I agree with you that men have been getting away with too much. There is no dispute about that. Here we can join. But we need to put our own feelings and experiences aside and be as objective as possible for the good of the couple. Let's look at your genogram.
Supervisee: I don't need to. I know why I feel the way I feel. My father was a dominant bastard who ran my mother into the ground. She did everything for him and he demanded sex regularly, even when she was sick. He accepted no excuses no matter how legitimate they were. She died young and he tried to parentify me, but I left home. My younger brothers got the bulk of the work but they left as soon as they could also. I know my conflict. I feel guilty about abandoning my younger brothers, but I had to, to save my own life. Even in relationships I have always vacillated between commitment and freedom.
Supervisor: I am sorry. That sounds terrible. I can see why you perceive Marie as being trapped. But not all men are like your father. Some try hard to balance work and family and it's tough for them and their partners. Whether you are right about Angelo or not, these two individuals have chosen each other, and we shouldn't hate them for it. It is our job not to hate either one of them, but to help them find a viable solution to their

standoff. We need to locate the shared conflict that got them into this situation and subsequent standoff. Can we work together on this even if we both acknowledge that women have gotten a bad rap over the years. I am concerned this pattern will cost you in your career.

Supervisee: (Laughs Sarcastically) You're worried about me?

Supervisor: Yes, despite the transference, I am not your father. I don't want you to fail.

Countertransference

In his paper, "The Future Prospects of Psycho-Analytic Therapy," Freud said the following about countertransference:

> Other innovations in technique relate to the physician himself. We have become aware of the 'counter-transference', which arises in him as a result of the patient's influence on his unconscious feelings, and we are almost inclined to insist that he shall recognize the counter-transference in himself and overcome it.
>
> (Freud, 1910/1957, pp. 144–145)

Freud believed countertransference was an impediment to treatment and a sign that the analyst needed his or her own treatment. In his paper: "Observations on Transference-Love", he warned about reciprocating when a patient falls in love with the analyst:

> For the doctor the phenomenon signifies a valuable piece of enlightenment and useful warning against any tendency to a counter-transference which may be present in his own mind. He must recognize that the patient's falling in love is induced by the analytic situation and is not to be attributed to the charms of his own person; so that he has no grounds whatever for being proud of such a 'conquest', as it would be called outside analysis. And it is always well to be reminded of this.
>
> (Freud, 1914/1958, pp. 160–161)

Modern psychoanalysts view the concept of countertransference as a valuable tool to better understand the patient's unconscious conflicts, and it believed to be even more important in the context of couple and sex therapy. Given the practitioner of couple therapy must work with and balance two people simultaneously, there is an even greater chance for countertransference to be a factor in treatment (see **Figure 8.2**).

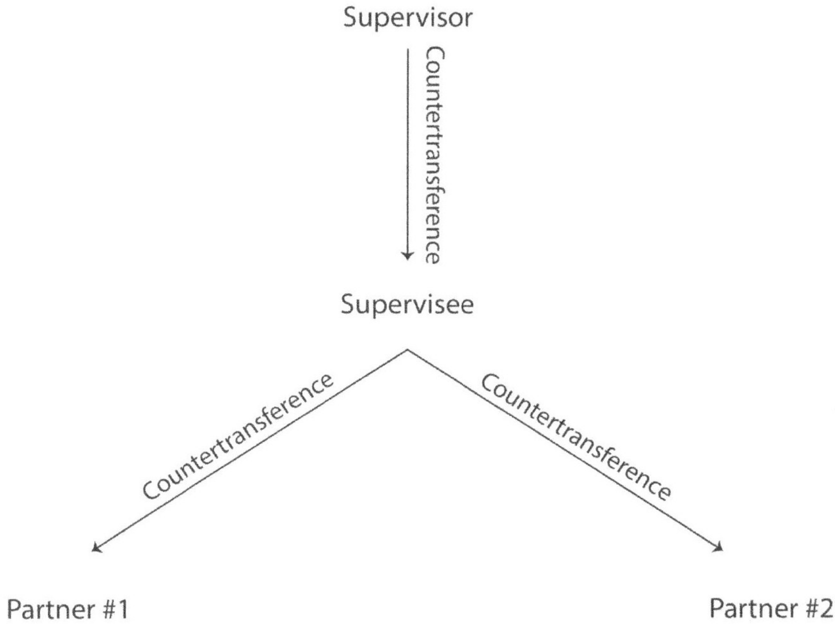

Figure 8.2 Countertransference in Couple Supervision

Vogel (1998) wrote:

> The issue of countertransference is, arguably, even more important in couples therapy than in individual treatment. The patient-couple is ever alert to the danger that the therapist might favor (or disfavor), or be more identified with, one of the two partners; the wise therapist will ever be alert to the same possibility.
>
> (p. 972)

The following example demonstrates a supervisee's countertransference with a couple. The supervisee is an experienced therapist, Derek, with an EdD in psychology who wished to become a specialist in couple and sex therapy. The couple presented with chronic fighting. The husband, William, had a PhD in engineering and his wife, Kathleen, had a master's degree in business administration (MBA).

William and Kathleen were the owners of their own computer consulting business and employed approximately 150 people. Most of their fighting was about how to run their business and who had the final say. And while their sex life suffered, this was not the main reason they presented for treatment. Derek said that he was leaning towards terminating treatment with the couple and referring them to a colleague. He hated treating them.

Supervisee: I dread it every time I see this couple on my schedule.
Supervisor: So, you've said.
Supervisee: They disgust me. And I feel a need to run away.
Supervisor: That's a strong reaction.
Supervisee: All they talk about every session is their business. I think they make a lot of money, and they still complain. No wonder they rarely have sex. I don't think it's that important to them. Money is the thing.
Supervisor: You don't think people should complain about anything if they make a lot of money? You think this couple should be focused on their sex life?
Supervisee: I know that sounds stupid.
Supervisor: How do you feel about "competition?"
Supervisee: With them or in general?
Supervisor: Either way.
Supervisee: That's interesting you ask that because it has always bothered me. My father was a very competitive person, and although I tried, I never felt I could keep up with him. He was a vice president of a pharmaceutical company and money was very important to him. It was disgusting. He was very upset with me when I chose to pursue psychology instead of majoring in business. I wanted to be me.
Supervisor: Partially.
Supervisee: What do you mean?
Supervisor: You said you tried to keep up with him.
Supervisee: Oh right, my conflict.
Supervisor: Anyway, it sounds like this couple are very interested in making a lot of money as well. They in fact chose to focus their professional lives on making money. But I don't think it is unbecoming of an engineer to seek a career as a successful entrepreneur. And one would expect this from an MBA. And yet like your father, they disgust you.
Supervisee: It sounds like you are annoyed with me.
Supervisor: No, I'm not. But just as you are, I am experiencing some countertransference. My father wanted me to be a lawyer and was disgusted with me when I chose psychology. He too, believed that being an attorney held more options and was potentially more lucrative. It looks like neither of us were

accepted for what suited us as individuals. But even more confounding, do you think our fathers were "all" wrong about our chosen careers? I don't.

Supervisee: So, we have the same conflict?

Supervisor: Looks like it. We both wanted to please our fathers but wanted to be our own unique selves as well.

The next example focuses on a married couple who suffered from a difficult sexual disorder. Joyce, 35, and her husband Ian, 37, presented for couple therapy because Joyce was diagnosed with the Genito-Pelvic Pain/Penetration Disorder (Vaginismus). The supervisee, Dina, was an experienced PhD in psychology who was also certified as a sex therapist, but this was her first vaginismus case. Note the erotic countertransference exhibited.

While the couple had unsatisfactory, sporadic sex during the dating process, almost immediately after marriage Joyce would not allow Ian to penetrate her in part, because she said it was much too painful. Ian did not know what to do. It was all a mystery to him. He considered divorce, but he is very attracted to Joyce and saw her as his best friend. Dina was clearly angry and frustrated with Joyce. She joined with Ian in her thinking that Joyce knew she had sexual problems before the couple formed and yet did not seek any help. She felt Joyce scammed Ian.

Supervisee: I can't stand this woman. She knew she had problems and still trapped this great guy into a sexless relationship. I can't get her to try dilator treatment, and she is unwilling to take any medication to help relax her vaginal muscles. If Ian ever gets the guts to leave her, I feel she deserves it. He needs to be with someone who can take care of his needs. Heck, I wouldn't mind meeting his needs.

Supervisor: He did marry her suspecting that their sex life wasn't going to immediately thrive. I think you know this, Dina.

Supervisee: I guess. There's just something sneaky about the way she did this.

Supervisor: You're also assuming she was conscious of her actions and motivations. What is going on with you? It's not like you to unbalance a couple so blatantly and to have such strong negative feelings towards one partner. You might want to look at your personal genogram.

Supervisee: I don't think I need to. My mother married my father and yet never really loved him. Although he tried to please her in every way, nothing worked. It was pathetic. I even think my mother had affairs and my father knew about them, but he could not let go of her. She finally left us when I was in high school. My father was a great guy. I get emotional just thinking about it.

Supervisor: So, you have a positive countertransference with Ian courtesy of your father and a negative one with Joyce courtesy of your mother.

Supervisee: I guess. What a mess.

Supervisor: Can you say more about your feelings for your father?

Supervisee: Like what?

Supervisor: I know you were upset with your mother but what about your father's weakness?

Supervisee: Yeah. I did get angry with him for not being able to stand up to her. There's a conflict.

Supervisor: Yes, and perhaps you have lost sight of that side of your conflict in working with this couple. But let's take this a little further. Is there anything else happening?

Supervisee: What do you mean?

Supervisor: Well, you did say that Ian was such a great guy that you "wouldn't mind meeting his needs." Sounds like an erotic countertransference to me.

Supervisee: So, you want to know if I have a crush on Ian?

Supervisor: Do you?

Supervisee: I do wish I had a guy like him. Some people just don't appreciate a good guy when they have one.

Supervisor: Like your mother?

Supervisee: I see your point.

Supervisor: It would certainly unbalance the couple if you don't get a handle on this. Not to mention the other problems that could occur. Remember, he married her because, like it or not, he was drawn to her. Let's not pathologize her and idolize him. I doubt meeting his needs would turn him on at this point.

While I touched on my countertransference to a supervisee (Derek) in the first case example, the following example will demonstrate how I manage countertransference in greater detail.

Marta was a 55-year-old experienced therapist with PhD in marriage and family therapy. She had a significant amount of experience in treating couples and families but was short on experience treating sex disorders. She was seen in my private practice as partial fulfillment for her AASECT certification.

Marta carried a full caseload but chose to present a young married couple, Liam and Sophia, suffering from Liam's acquired ED. The couple had an active sex life prior to marrying but as soon as they married Liam began having difficulty. He could get an erection during foreplay but as soon as he entered Sophia he lost his erection. Sophia was hurt and angry about this and believed that Liam was trying to avoid sex. Liam claimed he did not understand what was happening to him and that he was still very attracted to Sophia. If he had any complaints, it was Sophia's incessant push for him to get help, which took two years. Liam saw a urologist who cleared him of any organic issues and prescribed a PDE5 medication for his ED. Nevertheless, both partners preferred couple and sex therapy over medication.

Even though Marta sought out my supervision, she did not seem to appreciate what I had to offer her. She was resistant in doing her own genogram – which was an option anyway – and preferred to use her own model of couple's work – which I was okay with. However, when it came to integrating the two, she was very argumentative and resistant to my input, which triggered something from my past that I had to control to avoid an unproductive supervision experience.

Supervisee: I'm going to prescribe Sensate Focus 1 exercises for this couple.
Supervisor: Why?
Supervisee: To bring them closer together. And to reduce Liam's performance anxiety so he can maintain an erection.
Supervisor: But you didn't take a sex history yet.
Supervisee: I have enough information to go on.
Supervisor: I am not sure performance anxiety is the problem here.
Supervisee: I read that it usually is when it comes to ED.
Supervisor: It can be. But Liam never experienced this problem before.
Supervisee: You don't have all the answers.
Supervisor: I never said I did. But there is something about penetrating Sophia that is bothering Liam. Remember, he gets and holds a good erection during foreplay.
Supervisee: I know. But Sophia is pressuring me for sex exercises.
Supervisor: I get it. That happens a lot. And you can prescribe Sensate Focus 1. But I don't think it's going to work.

After two weeks the supervisee reported that while the couple enjoyed Sensate Focus I there was no change in Liam's ED.

Supervisee: The exercises went well but there was no change in Liam.
Supervisor: The couple have no children. Do you know why?
Supervisee: What does that matter. Maybe it's because Liam can't get it up.

Supervisor: Maybe. Or maybe he can't get it up because he doesn't want any.
Supervisee: That's a guess.
Supervisor: Yes, but an educated one. Check it out.

The following week the supervisee did not ask the couple about having children, and I got annoyed with her.

Supervisor: So, what about children?
Supervisee: I didn't ask.
Supervisor: You come here seeking my help and do not listen to a word I say. What's up?
Supervisee: You're angry.
Supervisor: I think you've come here to fight me, and I don't know why because you won't even construct a genogram. Why seek supervision with me at all and waste your money? Unless it's worth it to you to simply fight.
Supervisee: (Softer) I don't want to fight you.
Supervisor: Look, I can own my own countertransference to both you and the couple. My parents made a lot of bad decisions in their lives and parentified me to take charge. But they never took my advice and things got worse for them. I used to blame myself for their dilemmas, but I eventually realized that I know what I'm talking about and that my advice is usually solid. This is what I think is what's bothering me about our supervision.
Supervisee: Okay. I get you're trying to help me and that I'm not letting you do that. My husband complains to me about the same thing. I'll examine my transference with you, and my countertransference with my couple, and get back to you. It's only fair that if you take responsibility, I should too.

Parallel Process

As mentioned earlier in the book, in the context of supervision, parallel process occurs when the supervisee mirrors the same dynamic in supervision that he or she is experiencing as a treating therapist (Koltz et al., 2012; Mothersole, 1999). According to Prasko et al. (2024):

> The parallel process is a psychological phenomenon where the relationship dynamics between the therapist and the client are repeated in the supervisory relationship between the therapist and the supervisor. The

> concept of the parallel process can be a useful tool for understanding and solving problems in therapy. However, it can induce supervision drift or block the supervision process.
>
> (p. 107)

Searles (1955) initially referred to parallel process as the "reflection process." He wrote: "the processes at work currently in the relationship between patient and therapist are often reflected the relationship between therapist and supervisor" (p. 135). Ekstein and Wallerstein (1958) are credited with naming the dynamic *parallel process*. The authors defined it as the unconscious transfer of a therapist's conflicts from the treatment to the supervision process.

The following vignette and dialogue illustrate parallel process with a young supervisee, Gail, a PhD in Social Work. Gail was treating an older married couple in the institute in which we were both affiliated. The husband, Ted, was a 62-year-old judge, and his wife, Mary, was a 59-year-old housewife. Notice in the following example that the supervisee often challenges me. This is consistent with Grey and Fiscalini (1987) who found parallel process to be the result of unresolved issues about authority and dependency.

Gail was concerned because she was getting into repeated control struggles with the husband of the couple, Ted, and eventually these struggles were replicated with me in supervision. Gail seemed very oppositional to authority figures, but not quite conscious of her role in the dynamic.

Supervisee: This guy is a pain in the neck. He even wants me to call him Judge Theodore in the sessions. I'm not doing that. He's just another client to me. Besides, that will elevate him above his wife and me.
Supervisor: That may be what he wants.
Supervisee: Well, that's not happening. I don't know who he thinks he is.
Supervisor: You're very angry with him.
Supervisee: I can't stand people like him. They're always telling people what to do.
Supervisor: It sounds like he is getting to you.
Supervisee: Not really. I just don't like him.
Supervisor: Do you like his wife?
Supervisee: Yes. She's great.
Supervisor: So, you're a bit off balance.
Supervisee: I wouldn't say that. And I don't want to check my genogram. I'm human. And humans don't have to like everybody.

Supervisor: That's interesting, I didn't even ask you to check your genogram. Sounds like you are taking me on as well. Maybe you think I'm trying to push you around. Look, my job is to supervise, and sometimes that might feel as if I'm pushing you around. But pushing you around is not my intent. I want what's best for you.

The supervisee was indeed oppositional with the judge and me for some time. But when the judge threatened to call the institute to report the supervisee for being "unnecessarily difficult," and for treating him "unfairly," the supervisee became frightened and more open to examining her role in both the treatment and the supervision.

The next example is that of a young, newly married couple in their middle 20s, John, and his wife Traci. The couple dated for two years and have been married for approximately six months. The supervisee, Ken, a male, marriage and family therapist, was in supervision as part of a post-graduate training program.

John is frustrated with Traci because she stopped having sex with him as soon as the couple married. John said Traci lost sexual desire right after the wedding ceremony and wouldn't even have sex on their honeymoon. Traci's OB-GYN diagnosed her with Female Sexual Interest Arousal Disorder (FSIAD), but John was suspicious. John also said he was mad but did not mention ending the relationship.

Traci did not seem to understand why John was so mad. She said that he constantly chides her about not having sex, and sometimes does this in public when they are with friends. Ken claimed that Traci and John were noncompliant with the treatment. Traci would not allow him to take a family history and John would not follow his recommendations to stop harassing Traci to have sex with him and to curb his anger. Traci would say, "the past is the past" and "it has nothing to do with what is currently going on."

When Ken asked Traci if she thought it was alright to withhold sex from her husband, she defiantly said it was her body, and she could do or not do whatever she wanted with it. When Ken asked Traci if there was a triggering event that might have led to her FSIAD she, again, told him to deal with the present. Ken said that he found treatment with this couple to be a waste of time.

Ironically, in the supervision process I began to feel the same way about Ken. He would sometimes fail to bring the couple's chart with him and instead would make up information about the couple as he went along. Because his information was often contradictory, I began to doubt that Ken had collected information about the couple at all. The following dialogue illustrates my attempt to show Ken there was a parallel process operating: The couple blocked him from treating them and he blocked me from supervising him.

Supervisee: This couple is very difficult, and I do not think Traci is even interested in therapy. I think she only agreed to give it a try to get John off her back. This is a waste of my time.
Supervisor: Traci is especially withholding. Do you know if she ever experienced any sexual abuse in her past?
Supervisee: I did not ask that question. But I should. I do think it would fit with her behavior.
Supervisor: That's an important question and one that should have already been recorded on the couple's genogram.
Supervisee: I thought it was too soon in the therapy to ask, but I'll get to it.
Supervisor: You know, I believe you have been giving me conflicting information about this couple, and I only recently figured this out. I think you're making things up for some reason. Were you going to tell me about this?
Supervisee: I've been scattered lately.
Supervisor: I understand, but you didn't answer my question. I get a sense that you're engaged in a parallel process. Like the one you experience working with Traci. I, too, feel as if I am in the dark because you withhold information from me. I also get a sense that you are fighting me the way the couple is fighting you. I am not sure you even drew up a genogram on the couple. It might be useful to examine if there is an internalized conflict about control in your early life.

Transference-countertransference, and parallel process are multidirectional concepts that are independent, yet usually interact with one another. A client's transference may trigger a therapist's countertransference, which may further impact the client's transference, and the cycle can continue until processed therapeutically. If the therapist is in supervision, he or she can unconsciously bring the same cycle into the supervision process, culminating in a parallel process. Zetzer et al. (2020) describes a similar dynamic:

> The general pattern that emerged from the analysis of the supervisors' reports was that clients behaved unusually in session, therapists "got hooked" by this change, therapists enacted the client's behavior in supervision, supervisors "got hooked," supervisors reflected on their reactions and intervened in a different way; reported outcomes

were mostly positive (e.g., enhanced growth or understanding for the therapist.

(p. 252)

McNeil and Worthen (1989) claimed that although parallel process merits more investigative study, the authors concluded that parallel process interventions in supervision can make a very powerful impact on both supervision and therapy. But not all scholars are convinced of this. Watkins (2016), for example, cited many problems conducted in the research on parallel process. The author recommended ways to make improvements in this area such as providing case commentary that clarifies how the interpreter arrived at his or her interpretations. I believe I have done so *via* the case examples.

In the supervision process, the concepts of transference, countertransference, and parallel process are always operating to various degrees and levels of intensity. These concepts will be better utilized if supervisors are mindful of and prepared to address the many layers that present themselves in the supervision process.

References

Bolognini, S. (1994). Transference: Erotised, erotic, loving, affectionate. *International Journal of Psychoanalysis*, *75*, 73–86.

Ekstein, R., & Wallerstein, R. (1958). *The teaching and learning of psychotherapy*. International University press.

Freud, S. (1910/1957). The future prospects of psycho-analytic therapy. In J. Strachey (Ed. & Trans.), *The standard edition of the complete psychological works of Sigmund Freud:* Vol. 11. *Five lectures on psycho-analysis, Leonardo da Vinci, and other works* (pp. 139–151). Hogarth Press and the Institute for Psychoanalysis.

Freud, S. (1912/1958). The dynamics of transference. In J. Strachey (Ed. and Trans.), *The standard edition of the complete psychological works of Sigmund Freud:* Vol. 12. *The case of Schreber, papers on technique, and other works* (pp. 99–108). Hogarth Press and the Institute for Psychoanalysis.

Freud, S. (1914/1958). Observations on transference-love. In J. Strachey (Ed. and Trans.), *The standard edition of the complete psychological works of Sigmund Freud:* Vol. 12. *The case of Schreber, papers on technique, and other works* (pp. 159–171). Hogarth Press and the Institute for Psychoanalysis.

Gelso, C., Bathia, A., & Palma, B. (2013). Attachment theory as a guide to understanding and working with transference and the real relationship in psychotherapy. *Journal of Clinical Psychology*, *69*, 1160–1171. https://doi.org/10.1002/jclp.22043

Glausius, K. (2024). Transference and Countertransference in couples therapy. *Couple and Family Psychoanalysis*, *14*, 180–193.

Grey, A. L., & Fiscalini, J. (1987). Parallel process in transference-countertransference interaction. *Psychoanalytic Psychology*, *4*, 131–144. https://doi.org/10.1037/h0079131

Koltz, R. L., Odegard, M. A., Feit, S. S., Provost, K., & Smith, T. (2012). Parallel process and isomorphism: A model for decision making in the supervisory triad. *The Family Journal: Counseling and Therapy for Couples and Families*, *20*, 233–238.

Koo, M. (2001). Erotized transference in the male patient-female therapist dyad. *Journal of Psychotherapy Practice Research*, *10*, 28–36. PMID: 11121005.

Ladson, D., & Welton, R. (2007). Recognizing and managing erotic and eroticized transferences. *Psychiatry*, *4*, 47–50. PMID: 20711328

McNeil, B. W., & Worthen, V. (1989). The parallel process in psychotherapy supervision. *Professional Psychology: Research and Practice*, *20*, 329–333.

Mothersole, G. (1999). Parallel process: A review. *The Clinical Supervisor*, *18*, 107–121. https://doi.org/10.1300/J001v18n02_08

Prasko, J., Liska, R., Krone, I., Vanek, J., Abetina, M., Sollar, T., Gecaite-Stonciene, Jurisova, E., Juskiene, A., Bite, I., & Ociskova, M. (2024). Parallel process as a tool for supervision and therapy: A cognitive behavioral and schema therapy perspective. *Neuro Endocrinology Letters*, *45*, 107–126. PMID: 38583187

Searles, H. (1955). The informational value of the supervisor's emotional experiences. *Psychiatry*, *18*, 135–146. https://doi.org/10.1080/00332747.1955.11023001

Vogel, W. (1998). Countertransference in couples therapy. *Psychiatric Services*, *49*, 972–978. https://psychiatryonline.org/doi/full/10.1176/ps.49.7.972

Watkins, C. E. (2016). Reconsidering parallel process in psychotherapy supervision: On parsimony, rival hypotheses, and alternate explanations. *Psychoanalytic Psychology*, *34*, 506–515. doi: 10.1037/pap0000127

Zetzer, H. A., Hill, C. E., Hopsicker, R. J., Krasno, A M., Montojo, P., Plumb, E. I. W., Hoffman, M. A., & Donahue, M. T. (2020). Parallel process in psychodynamic supervision: The supervisor's perspective. *Psychotherapy*, *57*, 252–262. doi: 10.1037/pst0000274

Chapter 9

Premature Termination and Termination of Supervision

Premature Termination

When a couple prematurely terminate treatment, it should be processed with the supervisee. The supervisee may not be primarily responsible for the termination but may collude in it consciously or unconsciously. For example, a couple may not be ready to hear anything that strikes them as disturbing no matter how careful the supervisee presents it. But in some cases, the supervisee may dislike one or both partners or find their presenting problem too disturbing, such as the remnants of childhood sexual abuse and thus directly and openly sabotage the treatment. The most complex situation, however, arises when the supervisee unconsciously sabotages the treatment. Here the supervisee may be aware that a couple is troubling, but unaware how it is impacting the clinical work, or the supervisee may be totally unaware that he or she is troubled and taking it out on a couple.

I have found that the supervisee's unresolved conflict from the family of origin is often responsible for most supervisee sabotages and collusions – usually by way of a negative countertransference – and the exposure of this conflict may lead to a great teaching moment in the supervision process. I generally ask the following questions of supervisees to determine whether they are primarily responsible for the premature termination, the couple is the sole culprit, or how all three participants may have colluded in the termination, all in the context of sexual issues:

Q: Did you know that one or both partners were upset with you or the treatment?

The supervisee must be in touch with a couple's feelings. If not, they may not realize that a couple has been offended and enroute to premature termination. There are times, however, when couples use their sensitivity to control the treatment process or to prematurely terminate treatment. In the following example, the supervisee is held primarily responsible for the premature termination of the case.

DOI: 10.4324/9781003642732-9

A male supervisee was treating a Jewish couple for the wife's Female Sexual Interest/Arousal Disorder (FSIAD). The supervisee saw the couple as "cool and having a good sense of humor," however, during one of the sessions the wife tried to soften a sexual insult that her husband hurled at her by saying that he wasn't so bad because he was a great guy in other ways. The supervisee countered with: "Well, dog lovers can do bad things," meaning that the client should not excuse her husband for doing something terrible simply because he wasn't all bad. But the wife of the couple saw the supervisee as "disrespectful" and "flippant" and failed to return to treatment.

In retrospect, the supervisee reported that the wife reminded him of his manipulative, overly sensitive mother who he was always conflicted about. He loved and hated her at the same time. He believed it was this conflict that led to a sabotaging countertransference.

Q: Were you paying close attention to each partner's body language?

Not all communication is verbalized. The supervisee should look for non-verbal signs that he or she is losing the couple. Sighs, eye rolling, little to no eye contact, or certain hand gestures may be signals that the supervisee is not holding a couple's interest or that a couple has little trust in the supervisee or the therapeutic process. When a partner is sexually shut down, they may fold their arms to cover their body, use a pillow for the same purpose, sit with tightly crossed legs, or sit with their back facing the partner. Granted the supervisee may not be able to join with or hold an ambivalent couple in treatment no matter how observant he or she is. But noticing and calling attention to these signs as soon as possible gives the supervisee a chance to prevent premature termination. In the following example the supervisee noticed the signals but because of her own conflict, lost her composure which led to immediate termination.

A female supervisee reported that a married woman in her late 70s rolled her eyes at every intervention she offered, as if to dismiss the supervisee's interventions. The woman's husband wanted to have sex with her, but given their ages, she saw this as annoying and immature. She told her husband that she wanted to be left alone.

Although the woman's husband tried to mediate between his wife and the supervisee, who admittedly was becoming more frustrated, he was too afraid to risk getting on his wife's bad side and pushing her even further away – at least she would masturbate him when he complained too much. But the supervisee finally reached her limit and asked the woman: "Why are you here? You are not listening to a word I say." With that, the woman said nothing more but refused to make another appointment when her session was over. Processing this in supervision, the supervisor felt ashamed of herself and stated that in her family of origin nobody ever seemed to pay attention to her. She admitted that she was ambivalent about her family: she both wanted to be a part of them, but she was also angry with them for making it so difficult for her. She believed that her negative countertransference was influenced by her ambivalence.

Q: Which partner was dominant in the relationship?

The supervisee must make a concerted effort to join with the dominant partner. It is these partners who usually initiate treatment and may be most invested in the treatment process. If the dominant partner is not satisfied, he or she is more likely to terminate treatment with the passive partner following suit. In the next example, the supervisee made a grave error and attempted to defend who she perceived as the victim of the couple – a passive, weak husband. While the wife was indeed difficult and controlling, this one is on the supervisee for not joining with the right partner.

A female supervisee presented a middle-aged married couple that she lost within two sessions. Apparently, she believed that the wife of this couple was "bullying" and "emasculating" her husband by insisting that he have sex with her every day. The supervisee thought the husband was trying his best to sexually satisfy his wife and that her demands were narcissistic and unrealistic. She believed the husband needed protection from his wife. However, this was a gross misjudgment on the supervisee's part because the wife, a clearly dominant woman, held the power to end treatment and that if not for her, the couple would never have been in therapy. The supervisee said to me: "I thought I was helping the husband and believed he would appreciate that. Instead, he sat back in silence as his wife turned on me."

In supervision, it was eventually revealed that the supervisee's father was an alcoholic who relentlessly picked on his wife. The supervisee claimed that she often got in between her parents primarily to protect her mother who she saw as a victim of her father's persecution. The supervisee came to believe that her negative countertransference with the wife was influenced by this past injustice.

Q: Did the couple seem especially uncomfortable discussing sexual issues?

If a couple demonstrates or expresses significant discomfort discussing certain issues such as sex, the supervisee must deal with this immediately. Politely telling a couple there is nothing to worry about will not necessarily allay their anxiety enough to avoid a premature termination. The supervisee should spend as much time as needed to make couples feel safe.

If the supervisee tries to push through this, they may scare the couple off. In some cases, the supervisee will need to offer sexually skittish partners an individual session to achieve this. The following case is that of a non-compliant partner who was sexually avoidant with her husband, and in the treatment. Her offense seemed to be her best defense. That is, she was always on the attack to avoid looking at herself.

A male supervisee presented a couple in which the wife had not had sex with her husband for two years. The wife insisted, however, that she did not have a sexual problem but that she has been angry with him for sabotaging his business – the sole support of the family. She added that sex was fine before her husband began to make business blunders that put the family in financial jeopardy. She claimed that the husband probably had ADHD or some other neurological problem because his judgement has been poor. She said that he has avoided ADHD testing and that he tells her all would be fine if she would start having sex again. The husband countered that his business is not doing that badly, and that his wife uses it as an excuse to avoid having sex. He also said that sex was never that regular and that his wife always controlled it.

The supervisee admitted to being "scared" of the wife. He said she was intimidating and that challenging her would only lead to premature termination. He recognized that she was the boss, and that he had to get along with her to keep the case alive. Therefore, the supervisee urged the husband to seek testing for ADHD and to get a consultation from a psychiatrist. Reluctantly, the husband did so and after he was cleared of any issues, he said to his wife: "See, I'm fine. Now let's look at what's wrong with you. Let's talk about your promiscuous background." Note that the supervisee did take a sex history, but the wife failed to mention her numerous lovers and made the husband promise he would not bring it up in treatment. I urged the supervisee to discuss the couple's collusion, but he chose to let the topic pass and spent most of his time siding with the wife, out of fear.

The supervisee's plan backfired. When the husband exposed his wife's sexual past she refused to return to treatment. Both husband and wife were angry with the supervisee: the husband was angry because he felt the supervisee was on his wife's side; the wife was upset because she felt the supervisee should have gone after her husband harder and focused on his sexual desire problem and its underlying causes.

The supervisee was somewhat relieved when the case was over and eventually revealed to me that he had mediated his parents' problems growing up. He added that trying to force each of them to take responsibility for their behaviors only seemed to escalate their dynamic. He was in conflict; he wanted to help, but he also wanted to run away. He believed that his negative countertransference, born out of his conflict with mediating led to his unbalancing and losing the couple.

Q: Did you feel uncomfortable discussing sex with the couple?

A supervisee that is uncomfortable discussing sexual issues with a couple may avoid asking pertinent questions about sex, make the couple feel equally uncomfortable discussing the topic, and lower the couple's confidence that they can be helped. To work with sexual issues, it is imperative that the supervisee normalizes the topic or take what I call a "matter of fact" approach to treating it. The more anxiety attached to the subject the greater the chance of premature termination. I will often recommend a supervisee to attend a Sexual Attitude Re-assessment (SAR) – an experiential process-oriented seminar, for this very reason, and to process and realign any sexual prejudices or sexual stereotypes the supervisee may hold. I recommend the SAR for supervisees even if a supervisee is not interested in becoming a certified sex therapist. The following case example depicts a female supervisee who is uncomfortable asking a couple about their sex life even though they presented with a sexual problem.

A female supervisee with years of experience treating a wide variety of psychological problems in her private practice decided to seek supervision to better learn how to integrate couple and sex therapy. However, while the supervisee consistently took general histories of her couples, even using the recommended genogram, she demonstrated a significant amount of ambivalence in doing so. When I questioned her about this, she said that she did not mind taking a sex history, but it was too uncomfortable to do so before she and the couple were better joined. She also told me she had every intention of going back to the couple for information at some later point in the treatment. However, I soon found that the supervisee never did go back to ask about sex and was losing couples because of her avoidance. I told the supervisee that she had a lot of talent and that if she wanted to continue supervision with me, she would need to attend a SAR or to find a way to better understand her discomfort with sex.

Eventually the supervisee admitted she was not sexually abused as a child in the traditional sense, but that her father would consistently make inappropriate remarks and embarrass her, even in front of her friends. The supervisee was in conflict: She liked sex, but she also found it distasteful, which seemed to be at the root of her ambivalence. She decided to seek therapy, and her supervision continued, ultimately with successful results.

Q: Are you having any trouble prescribing sexual exercises?

Prescribing or refusing to prescribe sex exercises when appropriate can lead to premature termination. Some couples who suffer from a sexual disorder may demand exercises, while others refuse them even if the therapist can make a good case for their use. Some of those who demand them, nonetheless, sabotage them. The following are examples of each.

A male supervisee reported that the live-in boyfriend of a couple was having intermittent Erectile Disorder (ED), and his girlfriend was furious. The girlfriend demanded a quick cure and wanted the supervisee to "skip the history taking" and prescribe some of the exercises she read about on the internet. Rather than accommodate the girlfriend, the supervisee insisted on focusing on the couple dynamic and how it may be related to the ED. The girlfriend refused to return for treatment after the third session. The supervisee's genogram revealed that she felt pressured by her parents growing up, and that she often rebelled. She eventually came to realize that she had a conformity vs. rebellion conflict that was interfering with her work.

Another female supervisee prescribed dilator exercises for a wife's vaginismus in the second session of treatment. Although I warned her that she was moving too fast, she decided the couple had suffered long enough and were ready to advance. To her surprise, however, each partner took turns sabotaging the exercises. The wife refused to lubricate the dilators and soon stopped inserting them altogether because of pain. The husband started altercations about unrelated issues just before the couple were to use the dilators. But the supervisee pressed on until the couple disappeared.

The supervisee admitted that she was too afraid the couple would end up childless and divorced. These are fears she projected onto them out of fear that she would never find someone to settle down with. When asked what the source of this belief was, the supervisee claimed that she had a hypercritical father who she wanted to please. Her fears about being inadequate led her to pressure the couple before they were ready and in turn, led to a premature termination.

Q: Did the couple complain about the fee, the poor proximity of the office to their home, or other troubling logistics on more than one occasion?

The supervisee should be aware that when a couple consistently complains about the same thing, it either means they are truly upset about it and would like it addressed, or it is being used as a distraction for something more clinically significant.

A male supervisee, for example, told me that the husband of a couple he was treating incessantly complained about the fee in every session. The supervisee admitted that he was getting very angry with the husband and even suggested that he seek cheaper treatment. When I found out about this, I recommended that the supervisee and I examine both the husband's and the supervisee's genograms for answers. I suspected that the complaints were an avenue for the husband to avoid treatment. It happened that the fee was simply the husband's way of communicating that he did not think he was worth being helped. He was adopted by one parent who desperately wanted him and one that did not.

As a defensive strategy against facing this, the husband always seemed to find a way to get himself thrown out of places or metaphorically, to be put up for adoption again. The supervisee, on the other hand, was severely parentified as a child and felt he was never appreciated for his efforts. The husband's incessant claim that the fee was too high triggered the supervisee's conflict about his self-worth and in turn, his negative countertransference.

Q: How do you feel about each partner?

The supervisee who does not like one or both partners may sabotage the treatment. This can be done both consciously and unconsciously.

A female supervisee admitted that she did not like the husband of a couple she was seeing. She thought he was "a manipulative liar and that his low sexual desire for his wife was because he was most likely having an affair." When I asked for proof of this, she just said that she had a "gut feeling." She did not insist on transferring the case to another therapist, but she did unbalance the treatment by siding with the wife.

I suggested to the supervisee that she might be sabotaging the treatment because of her dislike of the husband – a notion the supervisee admitted was a possibility. But what soon followed shocked the supervisee: The wife of the couple became angry with her and terminated the treatment. She said that the supervisee was not being fair to her husband in treatment. The wife felt that the supervisee was ruining her marriage. In exploring the supervisee's behavior, it turned out that she had always wanted her mother to leave her gambling father, but this never happened. The supervisee was unconsciously trying to bring about a premature termination – an obvious countertransference.

Q: Did one or both partners do anything specific to aggravate you?

Some couples can be rude or belittle the supervisee and in turn, provoke anger. This behavior may be born out of anxiety and used to block or prematurely end treatment. Rather than react to the couple's behavior, the supervisee should gently confront it and attempt to find out what is behind it.

A supervisee told me of an incident that annoyed him: Rather than wait for him in the waiting room as other couples routinely did, the husband of a couple decided to enter the supervisee's office without permission, leaving his wife in the waiting room – and this was before the supervisee had even met the couple. When the supervisee asked the man why he took this liberty he laughed and said that he didn't feel like waiting in the waiting room. This behavior set the tone for what eventually became a series of control struggles that ended with the husband taking control and terminating the treatment.

The supervisee admitted that he disliked the husband who he saw as somewhat sadistic to both he and the man's wife. "Indeed, he was," I said. "And you were engaged in a power struggle with a man who, given the data from his genogram, was fond of BDSM. He was used to power and control struggles."

When we looked at the supervisee's genogram, we also discovered that he always felt his personal boundaries were disrespected by his mother. He told me that he often found her snooping in his bedroom and listening to his telephone conversations with his girlfriend. This experience served as the point of origin of his countertransference reaction to the husband.

Q: Did any control struggles develop between you and the couple right before termination?

Locking into a struggle with one or both partners, especially the dominant one, might end in premature termination. The supervisee should avoid gridlock with a couple. He or she would do better to respectfully acknowledge a couple's perspective and offer an alternative view rather than criticize it. If this does not work, the supervisee should pull back and wait until a couple can better digest what they are trying to tell them.

A female supervisee reported that the wife of a couple whose husband had stopped having sex with her challenged her on almost every intervention. According to the supervisee, the woman would say something like: "I could have thought of that," or "That's not it."

In our supervisory sessions the supervisee was quite frustrated. She claimed that she almost got into an argument with the wife because she felt pressured by her into giving her an immediate diagnosis. Rather than encourage the husband to answer this question, however, the supervisee took a big gamble and told the wife that her husband was reacting to her need for control – which was "massive." The wife promptly responded by firing the supervisee and her husband did nothing to stop the abrupt termination. In exploring the supervisee's genogram, it was evident that she was reacting in real time, to the control struggles she often had with her deeply religious parents who loved her but left her little freedom as a child and adolescent.

Q: How did the couple find you?

While some couples find a supervisee through a trusted referral or the internet, others may be sent by a frustrated therapist who wanted to unload them as soon as possible. In this case the couple may already be hurt and angry, and ready to take these feelings out on the unsuspecting supervisee.

A female supervisee was referred a couple suffering from delayed ejaculation. At first, the supervisee was excited because the couple were smart, professional, and anxious to please each other and the supervisee. But soon they teamed up to criticize everything the supervisee said and were quite cruel about it. When the supervisee asked the couple why they were picking on her, they gave no answer. When she offered a referral, they refused to take it. And when I recommend that the supervisee offer empathy to the couple because they were unceremoniously dumped by their previous therapist, they got even angrier and increased their attacks on the supervisee.

The supervisee was paralyzed until I told her that she needed to explain to the couple that they were wasting their time and money and that the treatment was failing – and with this they finally left. The supervisee was very relieved. We eventually determined, by way of her genogram, that her high tolerance level might be attributed to her parents, who stayed in a long-term abusive marriage even though they seemed to hate each other. Thus, her conflict was to oblige herself to someone or something even when she wanted to escape.

One of the most common questions supervisees ask me is whether to call a client back if they have suddenly and unexpectantly ended treatment without warning. Being "ghosted" upsets most supervisees and they often take this act personally given most therapists are sensitive individuals. They tend to blame themselves first and foremost and believe that closure can alleviate their anxiety. Swift and Greenberg (2015), claimed in this context most therapists will feel a sense of failure, demoralization, or rejection. Patterson et al. (2018) contended that some experience a sense of loss. And according to Piselli et al. (2011), others experience confusion, disappointment, and shame. I, however, stand by the adage "do not pursue a distancer." This is especially applicable to those couples who suffer from sexual problems given their potential for embarrassment. Couples have many reasons to prematurely terminate, some of which I have already discussed. They also have a reason to disappear. These reasons may not be healthy, but they usually fit with their relational dynamic or life patterns.

I tell supervisees that if a couple wants to stay in treatment they would; and if they want you to contact them, they would not have left the way they did. Whenever I pursued a couple – in my younger days – they were not impressed. In fact, I was usually made to feel like a "salesman" trying to regain business. For some I was a reminder of that shameful sexual problem they were trying to forget. These were not only uncomfortable feelings, but I felt a slight on my integrity.

I recommend that the supervisees only pursue if he or she feels the client or couple is in danger (e.g., domestic violence; risk of suicide), and sexual issues usually do not qualify. Again, if the supervisee is supervised in an institute, he or she will be regulated by policy. I once supervised in a clinic that, prior to any official case closing, demanded the supervisee write a letter to the client warning that the case would soon be closed unless heard from by a specific time; all letters had to be approved and signed by the supervisee's respective supervisor.

Termination of Supervision

"Ending the supervisory relationship is just as important as beginning it and the supervisor should devote attention to it" (NASW, 2025, p. 27). The date of the termination of supervision is usually clearly stated in the supervision contract signed and dated by both supervisor and supervisee prior to the beginning of supervision. Often, however, this can be amended either way: the supervisee may wish to terminate supervision early, or to extend it.

I have been lucky enough to experience the latter far more often than the former. In fact, because most of my supervisees have the goal of accumulating enough clinical supervisory hours to achieve licensing in marriage and family therapy or certification in sex therapy, or both, premature termination is rare. This has been my experience whether I am supervising at an institute or in my private practice. Many of my former supervisees also continue supervision well after they have achieved their initially stated professional goals. This may be partially reflective of the shortage of supervisors skilled and certified in both couple and sex therapy, especially in less populated areas. When first certified as an AASECT supervisor, I remember reading that I was only one of 69 others who had achieved that status. I counted on one hand the number of those who achieved supervision status in both marriage and family therapy through AAMFT, and in sex therapy through AASECT.

For those who are close to reaching their goals in supervision, I begin to discuss the ending of the supervisory relationship and ask if there is anything they need that we did not cover. While this is an ongoing question throughout the supervision process, I offer it at the end of the contract because I have found that the supervisee always seems to appreciate it. I will also sum up the supervisee's strengths and weaknesses and will make appropriate recommendations. I ask what their post-supervision plans are and offer to help to fill out supervision applications at no charge should they need it; most accept my offer thankfully. I also let them know I will be available for future consultation, and I usually recommend that they continue to seek supervision throughout their careers, not necessarily with me. Nevertheless, these are the relatively peaceful, pleasant terminations. There are less pleasant ones as well.

One issue I have found frustrating, post-supervision, is more harmful to the supervisee than to me. That is, after having completed all the requirements for certification or licensing some former supervisees procrastinate in applying for these credentials, and for many years. Before a supervisee formally terminates treatment, I urge them not to hesitate. I remind them that some certifying organizations have time limits and may ask them to repeat coursework or to obtain more supervision. Organizations also change their requirements, and a supervisee who may have once qualified for certification may no longer be so. Despite my warnings, however, some of my supervisees who were well qualified following supervision allowed so much time to pass that they simply gave up. Others contacted me years later for help with putting together an application package; an overwhelming task for both me and the supervisee.

There are times when a supervisor has no choice but to continue to supervise a budding therapist who is noncompliant. If the supervision is in the supervisor's private practice, the supervisor or supervisee may choose to terminate the relationship citing a mismatch, or that the process is doing neither participant any good. In an institute, however, this flexibility may not exist. My first choice is to try and work through whatever issues may be blocking the supervision process, and this has often worked. But I have also experienced premature termination of the supervisory process over the years, primarily for noncompliance. Consider the following brief examples:

Jane, a middle-aged woman I supervised at an institute presented a couple in which a woman, Ceila, was chronically, verbally abused by her angry husband, Oliver. Jane was a caring, gentle supervisee with approximately five years of clinical experience but very little with couples. And while she was generally considered comforting to most of her clients, after three years of treatment with Ceila and Oliver, their destructive dynamic was still in place: the husband remained angry and abusive, and his wife could not set firm limits with his behavior.

When I offered Jane my interpretation of the couple's dynamic, that was clearly anchored in each partner's respective families of origin, she bristled. Jane accused me of being "too harsh," especially to the wife whom she perceived as having no responsibility in the relationship dynamic. Even my attempt to discuss the obvious transference-countertransference issues in this case was met with formidable resistance.

While it was clear that Jane and I were different personalities, thrown together in a post-graduate program, we were able to continue the supervision with me tempering my interventions to fit her softer personality. In fairness to Jane, she admitted that her case had not progressed and that perhaps being a bit more challenging might bring greater therapeutic success. She agreed to examine her family of origin for answers. It is not as if the tension between us completely disappeared, but we did agree that we could learn something from each other.

Serina was a young therapist who I supervised in private practice. She presented two partners who continued to feed each other's anxiety in various ways, and Serina had no idea how to break this dynamic. Although I had a feeling this would stir up anxiety in Serina, I had to tell her that I noticed a pattern: she was clinically and emotionally paralyzed when treating anxious clients. I did not recommend that she go to therapy, but I did tell her that therapists can only take clients as deep as they can go themselves, and that I believed that her anxiety was making it difficult to successfully treat several clients. I was very willing to work through this with Serina, who I liked. But I suspect her anxiety was too great to handle my confrontation and it caused her to end supervision in anger. Perhaps another supervisor could have been even more gentle with Serina, but some relationships cannot be salvaged.

Levendosky and Hopwood (2017) wrote: "Although clinical supervision is considered the backbone of most mental health training programs, it gets little theoretical or empirical attention. The termination of supervision has received even less attention" (p. 37). According to *Best Practice Standards in Social Work Supervision*, focusing on the termination process will not only help to smooth the supervisor–supervisee termination transition, but the supervisee–client termination as well (NASW, 2025).

While differences in supervisor and supervisee can complicate termination of the supervisory process, I find these can be overcome if both participants are flexible and demonstrate a willingness to grow. Sharing similar therapeutic and supervisory models makes this process even easier for both supervisor, supervisee, and client-couples. The next chapter will demonstrate, with the use of a wide variety of case studies, the conflict model approach to supervision in the context of couple and sex therapy.

References

Levendosky, A. A., & Hopwood, C. J. (2017). Terminating supervision. *Psychotherapy*, *54*, 37–46. doi: 10.1037/pst0000096

National Association of Social Workers (2025). *Best practice standards in social work supervision*. www.socialworkers.org/practice/nasw-practice-standards-guidelines/best-practice-standards-in-social-work-supervision

Patterson, J., Williams, L., Edwards, T. M., Chamow, L., & Grauf-Grounds, C. (2018). *Essential skills in family therapy: From the first interview to termination*. Guilford.

Piselli, A., Halgin, R. P., & MacEwan, G. H. (2011). What went wrong? Therapists' reflections on their role in premature termination. *Psychotherapy Research, 21*, 400–415. https://doi.org/10.1080/10503307.2011.573819

Swift, J., & Greenberg, R. (2015). *Premature termination in psychotherapy: Strategies for engaging clients and improving outcomes*. American Psychological Association.

Chapter 10

Supervision Case Studies

The integrative conflict model of supervision highlighted in this book will now be demonstrated in its entirety across six diverse couple-cases and their respective supervisees (see Figure 10.1). This six-step approach includes (1) structuring supervision; (2) presenting data from the family of origin; (3) searching for contradictions; (4) uncovering the shared internal conflict; (5) connecting conflict to the sexual symptom; and (6) suggesting interventions.

The sexual symptoms presented by the couples include a variety of male and female sexual issues such as delayed ejaculation, erectile disorder (ED), male hypoactive sexual desire disorder (MHSDD), and genito-pelvic pain/penetration disorder (GPPPD) (Vaginismus), and female sexual interest/arousal disorder (FSIAD). A case of a couple in an open relationship is also included.

Each of the six cases is presented in detail with dialogue and includes managing transference, countertransference, and parallel process. Progress notes and the one-way-mirror serve as the primary methods of evaluation. The confidentiality of all supervisees and couples is protected by using composites made up of two to three couples and supervisees. To further protect all participants, names, ages, and professions are fictitious as well.

Supervisee #1 (Kelly) with Peter and Michael – Disagreement over Open Relationship

Kelly, a gay, white, female supervisee in her early-30s, contacted me for private supervision on the recommendation of a colleague. Her goals for supervision were to learn couple and sex therapy and to ultimately complete her supervision hours as part of the requirements to become an AASECT-certified sex therapist. Kelly held a PsyD in Clinical Psychology. From this point she will be referred to as the supervisee.

DOI: 10.4324/9781003642732-10

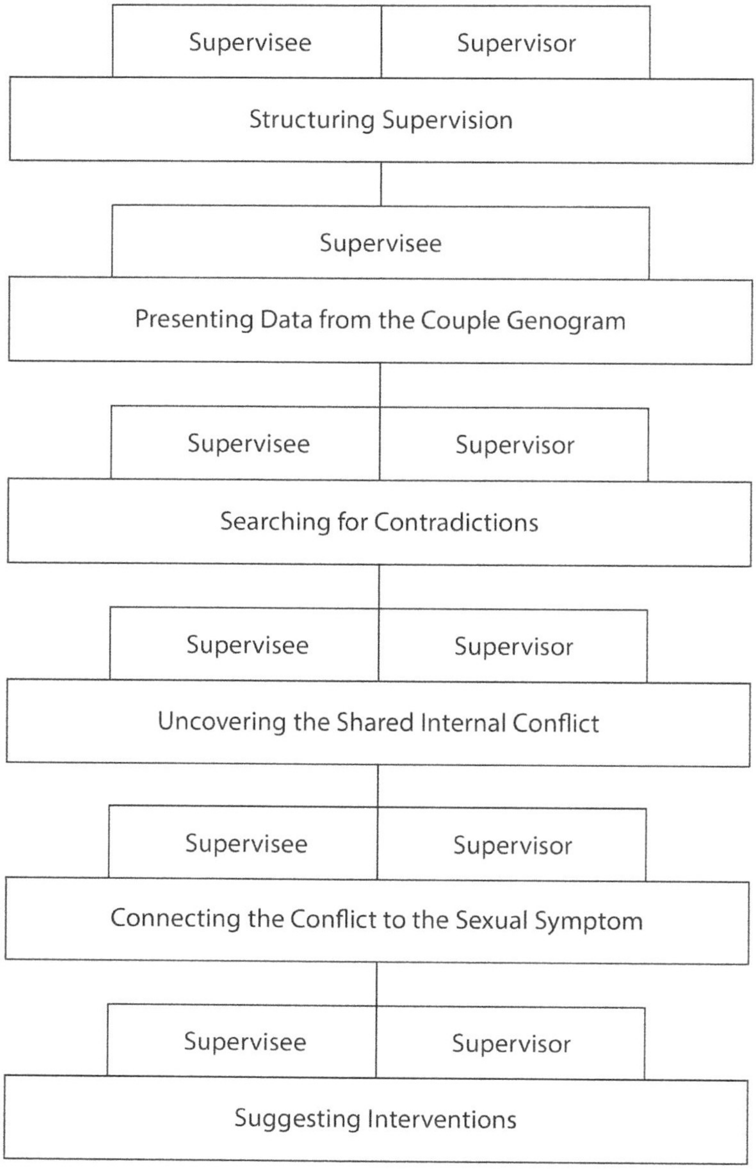

Figure 10.1 Six-Step Supervision Process

Step 1. Structuring Supervision

The supervision took place in my office, 55 minutes per session on a bi-weekly basis. The modality was one-on-one. The supervisee presented case notes from her private practice.

The supervisee and I connected almost immediately. Despite our age difference, I found her easy to get along with, mature, open-minded, and to have a good sense of humor. She also appeared to truly care about her clients and with a real desire to learn. I saw her at the intermediate developmental level primarily because of her experience in treating individuals; she was far less experienced treating couples. She was also knowledgeable about sexual issues having taken several courses over the years but less so in applying them to working with couples.

The supervisee was compliant with the contracting process, and we agreed and put into a writing that I was only to be responsible for the couple and sex therapy cases that she presented in supervision. It was her responsibility to let me know immediately if there was a crisis looming in any of the cases I was responsible for.

In our first session, the supervisee gave me a brief sketch of the 15 cases in her practice. Seven of the cases were couples with sexual problems and eight were individuals with sexual issues. She chose, however, to first spend some time on Peter and Michael, a couple she liked but felt confused by. She also said that she found herself siding with one of the partners over the other.

According to the supervisee, Peter and Michael were a gay male couple in their 40s who had been living together for several years; they were childless. The couple sought therapy because they disagreed about allowing a third person into their sex life. Peter wanted this and Michael did not.

Step 2. Presenting Data from the Couple Genogram

It took the supervisee a few supervision sessions of coaxing to ask the kinds of questions I wanted her to ask of Peter and Michael, and to record them on a genogram. She was never required to take a detailed general and sexual history before. I find this to be a common occurrence in supervisees who were trained in behavioral or ahistorical models of therapy such as Cognitive Behavioral Therapy (CBT).

The supervisee's initial history of each partner was helpful but somewhat basic, and I found that there was little follow-up to the answers. In such a situation I serve as a role model by asking the supervisee the questions that I think she should ask the couple. If my reasons for asking certain questions are not obvious to the supervisee, I will readily explain them. The less time it takes for the supervisee to copy my style, the smoother and more efficient the supervision process will go.

According to the information gathered by the supervisee's genogram, Peter, a 44-year-old engineer, was raised in a middle-class family. His father was also an engineer; his mother was a housewife. Peter had an older brother who left home to attend law school, leaving Peter to cope with his parents' marital difficulties.

Peter's father had an affair which lasted for many years. Peter was in high school when it began but despite his knowing about it his father refused to terminate it until his lover passed. Peter's mother also knew of the affair, but instead of divorcing her husband she enlisted Peter as her commiserator and confidante. Both parents used Peter as a mediator.

Peter reported that he was depressed as an adolescent primarily because he felt trapped. He said he felt bad for both his parents, especially his dependent mother, but longed to have his own life. Peter came out before he enrolled in college and reported that his parents were fine with it. He said his parents seemed more afraid of him leaving home than having a gay son. Nevertheless, they were generally supportive. For example, both father and mother would tell Peter that he could accomplish anything he wanted if he put his mind to it. His father was especially proud that Peter secured a prestigious engineering position.

According to the genogram, Peter began to suspect he was gay at 13 years of age. He admitted that he had a crush on a couple of boys around that time, but he did not have his first sexual experience until he completed college. After college Peter reported having numerous affairs. He said that once he broke free of his parents, he "went wild," only settling down when he met Michael, who he was emotionally and physically attracted to. He reported that he never suffered from any sexual dysfunctions.

Michael was a 47-year-old PhD in physics, employed by a large engineering corporation. He was raised in an upper-middle-class home by two college professors. His father held a PhD in chemistry, and his mother had a PhD in biology. Michael had two younger siblings and claimed that he was considered by his parents to be the most reliable of all their children. His grades throughout his academic career were stellar and he never exhibited any behavioral issues. Michael said his parents touted him as their "perfect child." Like Peter, he too was showered with praise and positive reinforcement in his formative years.

Michael claimed that both his parents were perfectionists, somewhat rigid in their beliefs, and very religious. He said the topic of sex never came up and that it was especially important to his mother to present as a traditional, highly educated, and cultivated family. He added that given he was the oldest, it was his job to make sure his siblings followed this conservative path of living. "My parents would blame me if my siblings got out of order. And when I couldn't handle a situation, they expressed deep disappointment in me. I remember feeling a lot of pressure." Peter made it a point to say that his parents could not handle stress. "It was ironic that they handled my being gay but could not tolerate my brother getting into a fight at school," he said.

Michael claimed that he was diagnosed with high blood pressure in high school after having passed out. He said the family doctor told him he was under too much pressure and recommended family therapy, but Michael's parents would not hear it. The supervisee suggested that it probably made the family feel "imperfect."

Michael came out much later in part because he feared disappointing his family. But when he did tell his parents about Peter they were surprisingly accepting. Michael said despite their reaction he felt bad that he let his parents down. He claimed that he was a "good boy" his entire life, but he was gay and "that was that." He could not deny his gayness any longer.

Unlike Peter, Michael was attracted to other boys in his early youth but did not think much of it. He said that he simply chose to limit his sexual activity to girls. But he also claimed he was never really satisfied with his straight experiences. With Peter, Michal experienced his first gay sexual experience.

I suggested that the supervisee ask Peter and Michael the following questions so that I could get a better understanding of the couple and their chief complaint. Sometimes a supervisee will already know the answers to my questions but forget to put them on the genogram.

Supervisor: You really gathered a lot of data about the couple. That's great! I just have a few more questions that you might already know the answers to. First, I think we know what Peter's sex drive is like, but do you happen to know about Michael's drive?

Supervisee: It's not as high. That's why they bicker. Peter wants more sex than Michael.

Supervisor: I see. Is there any sexual abuse in either partner's past? I ask this because it could help to explain Michael's sexual inhibitions.

Supervisee: None.

Supervisor: Are they on any medication? And has Michael been checked by a urologist.

Supervisee: No medication.

Supervisor: Any testosterone issues?

Supervisee: I didn't check. I'll ask.

Supervisor: So, does Peter want to include a third party in their relationship because he feels shorted by Michael sexually?
Supervisee: I'm not sure. I think so.
Supervisor: Why don't you check that out. The distinction might be very important. He was severely parentified and did say he felt "trapped." He could be feeling restricted by Michael.
Supervisee: Okay, I'll check it out.
Supervisor: What about Michael? He comes from a traditional, conservative family. Do you think he may be somewhat homophobic?
Supervisee: I don't know.
Supervisor: You might want to check that out as well. He is a perfectionist. We need to know what is at the bottom of Peter's request for a third person, and if Michael is inhibited in any way.

The supervisee reported back in two weeks with the information I requested. She said that Peter did feel angry and hurt by Michael's unwillingness to initiate sex and to express as much passion in the relationship as he did. And he often fantasized about being "free," even though he loves Michael. Michael admitted he came from a conservative background where sex was never talked about, but he insisted that he was not homophobic. Rather he saw himself as somewhat shy. He also admitted that his sex drive was never as high as Michael's.

I told the supervisee that I still suspected that Michael's perfectionism was an important factor in the couple's sex life. I then introduced the supervisee to the concept of "contradiction," and the role I believe it was serving in this case.

Step 3. Searching for Contradictions

Supervisee: (Laughs). I'm still lost.
Supervisor: Okay, let's start with Peter. Is there anything about him or his family of origin that strikes you as odd? Perhaps contradictory?
Supervisee: Not really. It sounds like he had a lot of responsibility.
Supervisor: Yes. And how did he feel about that?
Supervisee: Upset. It seems like he wanted to be free to live his own life.
Supervisor: Yes. Remember, his parents told him he could accomplish anything he wanted to if he only tried?
Supervisee: Yes.
Supervisor: Is that true?
Supervisee: What do you mean?
Supervisor: Could he accomplish anything he put his mind to?
Supervisee: He did become a successful engineer.

Supervisor: Yes. But was he able to help his parents? Could he end his father's affair? Could he alleviate his mother's depression? And could he set himself free?

Supervisee: So, he received double messages. They told him he was wonderful but would not allow him to fix anything.

Supervisor: Something like that. And what about Michael? Anything strike you as contradictory in his background?

Supervisee: When I think about it in this way, Michael did have to be perfect. But I think the fact that he was gay might have contradicted that in his mind.

Supervisor: We don't think that way, but he might, and that's important. I also wonder how successful he was at keeping his siblings in line. He was under a lot of pressure most of his life to be the perfect son. Do you see a similar contradiction in Michael and his life?

Supervisee: Like Peter, he was not free to live his own life.

Step 4. Uncovering the Shared Internal Conflict

Supervisee: What is so important about pointing out contradictions?

Supervisor: They often lead to internal conflicts, which we can then connect to a couple's symptoms. For example, both partners loved their parents and felt a strong sense of responsibility to please them and to meet their needs. But…?

Supervisee: But, both longed to be free to live their own lives.

Supervisor: You got it. It's as if they have a shared self vs. other conflict. Do I please the self or give up my life for others?

Supervisee: (Laughs). But what do I do with that?

Step 5. Connecting the Conflict to the Sexual Symptom

Supervisor: Do you see any possible connection between the conflict we've identified and the couple's sexual symptom?

Supervisee: Not really.

Supervisor: Well, they were both trapped. I suspect Peter feels trapped by Michael's sexual inhibitions and that opening his relationship solves two problems: It buys him sexual freedom but allows him to hold onto Michael at the same time.

Supervisee: That fits Peter but what about Michael. His conflict is not as clear to me.

Supervisor: That's right. One partner's conflict is usually more obvious. This might be interesting to study, but I haven't thought much about it. I do think, however, Michael also felt trapped in his perfection, and now feels trapped and controlled by Peter's sexual needs. I suspect he is unconsciously rebelling against this and his need to be a perfect partner.

Supervisee: So, is this all unconscious?

Supervisor: Most of it. They might be conscious about being trapped, and a desire to be free. But they probably do not connect it to their behavior in real time. Now you need to try the conflict out on the couple and see if it has any merit.

Step 6. Suggesting Interventions

Supervisee: I'm not so sure where to take the conflict. Do I just bring it up?

Supervision: You have options. But I would recommend you start by gently pointing out that both Peter and Michael had great responsibilities when growing up in their respective families of origin. Peter was parentified, especially by his mother, and served as a mediator; Michael felt that he needed to be perfect to please his demanding parents. This way you will send the message that the partners have something important in common. This will help you join them, and to create mutual empathy.

Supervisee: I can do that. But how do I introduce the conflict?

Supervisor: If they agree that they both had major responsibilities – which they should, you can then ask each of them how they felt about it. We already know that they were burdened but it's important to build on this issue.

Supervisee: So, I need to get them to talk about their feelings of being trapped?

Supervisor: Yes. And what controls them.

Two weeks later the supervisee reported back about her experience introducing the self vs. others conflict to the couple.

Supervisee: I thought Michael was impressed. But Peter was more interested in focusing on the sexual issue. He said they came to see me to talk sex, not relationship dynamics. He was annoyed with me.

Supervisor: How did you feel?

Supervisee: I saw him trying to sabotage the treatment and it annoyed me. If I'm honest with you, he has been annoying me the whole time. I don't like the fact that he wants an open marriage. It's against my values. I think it gives gay people a bad reputation.

Supervisor: How so?

Supervisee: I grew up in a conservative Christian family and, even though I'm gay, I want one partner. I think we gays get discriminated against enough without causing our own problems. I certainly do not have a problem with Michael and Peter being gay. I'm not homophobic. In fact, I really like Michael. And if gays prefer to serial date that's okay with me. I just don't like it when they give others the ammunition to attack them.

Supervisor: It's not unusual for a male gay couple to include a third individual in their relationship. In this case, however, I suspect that Peter was experiencing the same transference with you that he experiences with Michael. That is, he sees both of you as limiting him. Your countertransference (i.e., siding with Michael against Peter) has unbalanced the couple. You might want to process this with them and regain your balance. We can't judge everybody from a heteronormative perspective.

Supervisee: I know. And if I look at it from a mutual conflict perspective, it helps me.

Supervisor: I should have told you this sooner and I apologize for not doing so, but when integrating couple and sex therapy, unless you can show the couple you have not forgotten about their sexual symptom, they might get upset with you. In fact, a good colleague of mine made this mistake and was instantly fired by a couple. When Peter attacks you because he feels you are limiting him, you can empathize with his need to be both obligated and free, and by connecting this conflict to his sexual needs. In this case, it would be his desire for a third person, which represents freedom, because he is obligated to a sexually unsatisfying relationship. Eventually you will have to confront Michael about his inhibited desire and sexual control, which I strongly suspect represents freedom from the pressures of his own perfectionism and the sexual pressure Peter is exerting. This explains his transference to Peter.

The supervisee did a terrific job with this case, eventually helping this couple to understand their shared conflict about pleasing the self vs. pleasing others. This in turn enabled them to openly discuss their mutual concerns about feeling both obligated and trapped and to empathize with each other. Eventually their sexual differences were resolved with Peter giving up the idea of including a third individual in the relationship, and Michael slowly opening to Peter sexually.

Supervisee #2 (Raymond) with Melanie and Larry – Larry's MHSDD

Raymond was a white, 48-year-old, advanced family therapist interested in learning more about couple and sex therapy. He held an MSW with post-graduate training in marriage and family therapy. He has been in private practice for many years. From this point forward, Raymond will be referred to as the supervisee.

Step 1. Structuring Supervision

The supervision took place *via* telesupervision, 55 minutes per session on a bi-weekly basis. The modality was one-on-one, and the supervisee used his case notes. The supervisee had read some of my writings and told me he was interested in learning my psychodynamic couple and sex therapy model. He had experience in couple therapy, but his specialty was family therapy. He told me that his individual and family therapy cases were being supervised by another supervisor.

Because of the supervisee's experience, the contracting process went smoothly, and there were no control struggles. The supervisee and I had a mutual respect that was evident from the beginning of supervision. I was confident that he would immediately bring any crisis up in our work together.

In our first session the supervisee gave me a brief sketch of the five cases he wished to be supervised in treating. He carried a caseload of approximately 25 clients. He decided, however, to first spend some time on Melissa and Larry, a couple in their late 40s with three children. Melissa insisted that Larry go to therapy with her because the couple had not had sex for approximately two years. And, even before the sex stopped, Melissa said that Larry was never the initiator. She believed that he was either having an affair or no longer attracted to her.

The previous therapist – a sex therapist – that saw Larry in individual therapy diagnosed Larry as having MHSDD (Situational), but beyond that, he couldn't get anywhere with Larry. Eventually Melissa pressured Larry to go to couple therapy with someone who also knows sex therapy. She said that this is her last attempt to salvage the marriage.

Step 2. Presenting Data from the Couple Genogram

As in the previous case, this supervisee had some difficulty getting used to taking a complete general and sexual history. This was due in part to his ahistorical training. He primarily assessed his couples and families systemically in real time. In fact, it took the supervisee approximately two months to consistently gather what I considered enough information on a couple and their sexual issues. When he finally began to use a genogram and to take a sexual history, it was gratifying to both of us, and more helpful to his couples. As part of the supervisory process, however, I continued to pepper the supervisee with more questions about his couples.

According to the supervisee's genogram, Larry was a 45-year-old owner of a small furniture restoration business that he inherited from his father. While at one time the business was thriving, it had slowed considerably, and Larry was struggling to maintain it. He was under tremendous financial pressure. Larry was the oldest male sibling of two sisters. He claimed that he had always got along with both siblings and does so to this day. "I always looked out for them. I am their big brother."

Larry claimed that family life was peaceful because in part, his parents were conflict-avoidant. But he said both stressed that he should protect his sisters and "not take any crap from anybody." When Larry had a problem, he kept it to himself but would often serve as a confidante for his sisters. He said that his father worked a lot in his furniture shop and his mother, a housewife, focused on domestic issues.

Larry had many friends as a child and adolescent and enjoyed playing sports. He had only a couple of long-term relationships with women and lost his virginity to his first girlfriend, a high-school class mate. He claimed that he never had a sexual problem until a couple of years ago, and that his urologist cleared him of any physical issues.

Larry rarely complained about anything in treatment and in fact did not think the couple needed professional help. Ironically, he did agree that he no longer had sexual desire for his wife and was totally baffled by this. He acted as if it had simply disappeared with no idea where it went. He did claim to have a general sex drive and that his regular usage of porn and masturbation supported this. The only thing Larry seemed to worry about was the state of his business.

The supervisee said that he doubted very much that Larry would have taken the initiative to enter treatment had Melissa not threatened him. While Larry agreed he worried about his business and was especially concerned because he lacked a college degree, he denied any significant anxiety or depression. He said he had some trouble sleeping but he said that this had been a lifelong problem. Larry denied any abuse in his past and was not on any medications. Neither partner reported any affairs or separations.

Melissa was a 46-year-old housewife who appeared far more outgoing and dominant than her husband. According to the supervisee, Melissa could take over a session with her complaints about her lack of sex life. The supervisee claimed it was obvious that she was hurt and angry with Larry for not having sex with her. She didn't know what was wrong with

Larry, but she did not think she had anything to do with it. She believed she was a very attractive woman who rarely struggled to find boyfriends.

Melissa grew up in a Catholic home and was the youngest of four siblings. According to the supervisee, Melissa's father was a truck driver and her mother worked as a school secretary. She described her father as "dominant when he was at home." She added that he was ex-military and claimed that he tried to teach all the siblings to be tough but subservient to him. Melissa claimed her mother was quiet and passive.

According to the supervisee, Melissa's family struggled financially, and that money was always a source of tension. Her mother was not a big spender, but whenever she did spend money, an argument ensued with Melissa's father. Melissa saw her father as unfair because he bought whatever he wanted. She said that he had "toys" that the family did not really need such as a motorcycle and a small boat. But her mother was too meek to challenge him.

Melissa was not on any medication, and she denied any type of abuse in her childhood. She had a few long-term boyfriends and reported never having any sexual difficulty in these relationships. She was orgasmic and claimed to masturbate primarily because Larry would not have sex with her. She used movie stars in her sexual fantasies. There was no substance use or abuse in her family, except for an uncle on her father's side, who was an alcoholic. The following are some added questions I wanted the supervisee to ask about.

Supervisor: What does Larry do with his anger?

Supervisee: I don't' think he allows himself to get angry. But I'll ask. He always seems so pleasant.

Supervisor: I ask this because it usually goes somewhere. I wonder if he's withholding sex from Melissa for good reason.

Supervisee: I'll check. But I know he'll say that he has no complaints other than his business issues.

Supervisor: So, he's not angry with Melissa?

Supervisee: If he is, he won't admit it.

Supervisor: Ask him if anyone has ever angered him, like his father or mother, or a good friend. Then ask what he did with this feeling.

Supervisee: Okay. What about asking about disappointment?

Supervisor: Good. And I would have an individual session with each partner. With Larry, I would like you to check out Melissa's beliefs that he is having an affair or has lost his attraction to her. With Melissa, ask her if she knows what tends to upset Larry.

Supervisee: I know what to do if Larry is having an affair. But what if he has lost attraction to her?

Supervisor: Let's hope we won't have to go there.

Step 3. Searching for Contradictions

The supervisee said, "this is a very tough case." Larry said he rarely if ever gets angry, and his low sexual drive is probably related to his business woes. The supervisee thought Larry might be right, and so he asked me about sending Larry for a medical evaluation. I told him that I did not think that was necessary at this point, but that we should keep an eye on him. To expedite matters, I asked the supervisee to get permission from Melissa to see Larry alone under the guise that he needed to get to the bottom of Larry's issue. Melissa readily agreed.

Supervisee: Something important came out. I think I found a contradiction. Larry said that his father always told him to protect his sisters and not to let anybody push him around. But his parents were otherwise passive and conflict-avoidant. Larry recalled a physical fight he got into in high school with a bully, and when both sets of parents were called into the principal's office, Larry's parents quietly let the bully's parents take over the meeting. In other words, his parents didn't defend him. In terms of an affair Larry said, "no way." And he claimed to still be attracted to Melissa. So, nothing unusual there.

Supervisor: No worries. But you certainly discovered a contradictory message. Nice work. How about Melissa?

Supervisee: The only thing I noticed in her history is that she was told to be both tough and subservient.

Supervisor: I think that's something we can build on.

Step 4. Uncovering the Shared Conflict

Supervisor: So, given the contradictions you have found in the couple's families of origin, how would you describe their shared conflict?

Supervisee: (Laughs). Are they connected?

Supervisor: Think about it. How would you feel if you received these double messages?

Supervisee: Confused.

Supervisor: Right. On the one hand, Larry's parents told him to be "tough," but they also told him to be a wimp. Melissa's parents, especially her father, told her to speak up and challenge others, but not him. And she saw her mother comply. Both partners were trained to be simultaneously powerful and passive.

Step 5. Connecting the Conflict to the Sexual Symptom

Supervisor: Do you see a possible connection between the conflict and the couple's low drive?
Supervisee: The only thing I can think of is Melissa doesn't want to be a wimp like her mother and be dominated by a man, so she has taken control of the marriage.
Supervisor: She is trying isn't she. But I am not so sure she's in control.
Supervisee: Oh right. Because she can't get the sex she wants.
Supervisor: Right. Perhaps Larry wants to confront her but can't. He wants to be powerful but acts powerless, or at least he thinks he is.
Supervisee: But by withholding sex from Melissa, he is exerting power in a covert way.
Supervision: And how is Melissa's conflict manifesting?
Supervisee: Well, that's harder to figure out.
Supervisor: Often one partner's conflict is a bit easier to see but remember the conflict is shared but may manifest differently in each partner.
Supervisee: Okay. I would say that her power is in her constant belittling of Larry, and yet it might make her powerless in that it probably enables his withholding sex.
Supervisor: I would agree.

Between supervision sessions the supervisee called me on the telephone. He said that he got Larry to agree to initiate sex with Melissa but that she rejected him. He said she made up an excuse about not feeling well. The supervisee said he could not believe that after complaining of about a lack of sex for years, she rejected it.

Step 6. Suggesting Interventions

Supervisor: So, you assumed Melissa wanted sex.
Supervisee: Of course. That is what she has been clamoring for.
Supervisor: Welcome to the paradoxical world of conflict.
Supervisee: (Laughs). What do you mean?
Supervisor: If she wasn't in conflict about her power she would have already figured out a way to get sex. If Larry wasn't in conflict about his power, he would have probably offered it already.

Supervisee: How can I tell them their sexual issue is related to a power conflict and that part of them may not want sex? They'll fire me.

Supervisor: (Laugh). Right. The trick to good couple and sex therapy is to keep the context of sex and the process of relationship dynamics close throughout the therapeutic process. So, I would recommend that you start by asking Larry how he felt about being rejected. He will probably tell you he was as surprised as you were. You might then re-frame his answer to reflect a disempowerment of sorts. From there you can ask him if he might try to initiate sex again soon. I'll bet he will most likely say "no way." You can re-frame this as a power move to protect himself against anymore rejection. Now you can turn to Melissa to interpret her rejection as a power move that will only result in her being rejected sexually by Larry. It's a start.

Supervisee: I see how you're doing this, but I also see how I can really get fired.

Supervisor: That's the second time you mentioned being fired. Certainly, we can all be fired but isn't it hard to work in fear. How can you freely practice your art?

Supervisee: I never thought about it that way.

Supervisor: Have you considered that you too might be coming from a place of powerlessness?

Supervisee: (Laughs). I think I have the same conflict that they have. I say this because sometimes I feel very confident and powerful and other times I'm scared.

Supervisor: What about supervision? How is it playing out?

Supervisee: As an old family therapist, I should have recognized the parallel process. I was afraid to tell you about encouraging Larry to approach Melissa for sex, especially because it was a disaster. While I do feel confident in my marriage and family therapy knowledge and skills, I feel somewhat lost when it comes to sex therapy and the integration of couple and sex therapy.

Supervisor: So, your power vacillates in supervision the way it does in treatment.

Working through the supervisee's countertransference and the parallel process helped to free him in the therapeutic and supervisory processes. That is, he became less afraid of the couple and the supervisory process and was better able to manage his vacillating power vs. passivity conflict.

Supervisee #3 (Latisha) with – Shameka and Tyrone – Shameka's GPPPD (Vaginismus)

Latisha is a 34-year-old Black female, with a PhD in Psychology and post-graduate training in marriage and family therapy. The supervisee was referred to me by a colleague because she was interested in focusing her practice on the integration of couple and sex therapy and was looking for a more intense supervision experience in this area. She was also interested in becoming an AASECT-certified sex therapist. From this point forward she will be referred to as the supervisee.

Step 1. Structuring Supervision

The contracting process went very smoothly. We joined well and I found her to be open and with a good sense of humor. The supervision was to take place weekly, one-on-one, and in my office.

During the contracting phase, the supervisee did say that she wanted to make sure I had sufficient experience treating Black couples given most of her caseload was Black. I told her that I did but was always open to learning more about their struggles. She seemed pleased with this answer. I told her that in the next meeting I would expect a brief overview of her couple cases and that she should decide which ones she wanted to present. She told me that she had genograms on all her cases and that she was prepared to present any or all of them. I considered this supervisee to be at the advanced stage of development in the field of marriage and family therapy but the beginner stages in sex therapy and the integration of couple and sex therapy. She used her practice notes in supervision.

In our first formal session, the supervisee gave me a quick overview of her five cases. She then chose to present the case of Shameka and Tyrone, a Black couple in their mid-30s with three children: two daughters together and a son from Tyrone's previous relationship. Shameka was employed full-time as a pharmaceutical sales representative, and Tyrone was a jazz musician with intermittent employment. Shameka was experiencing pain upon intercourse.

Step 2. Presenting Data from the Couple Genogram

According to the supervisee's genogram, Shameka was a very hard-working young woman with a strict persona. She was raised by her mother in a single-parent family and, as the oldest, she was given a lot of responsibility especially for her three younger siblings. Both Shameka and her mother worked full-time to support their family and continued to do so through Shameka's college years. Shameka made it clear that she role-modeled her mother and was proud of her work ethic. She said it was the only thing that saved her and her siblings. In this sense, Shameka was a second mother to her siblings and as her mother aged, she began to take over the family, running it with an iron fist. Shameka's siblings resented her at times, but they also knew Shameka had their mother's support and they did not wish to challenge their mother.

Shameka was introduced to Tyrone by a girlfriend while they were at a jazz club; Tyrone was one of the musicians. Shameka said she thought he was "shy, but really nice, and extremely talented." When she had a chance to talk to Tyrone more intimately, she also found him to be driven and ambitious. She said that he had all the qualities she looked for in a man; not an angry, lazy man like her father, who had left the family when Shameka was 12 years old, never to be seen again.

Shameka had one boyfriend who she met in high school, but she told the supervisee that she had no time for relationships given all her responsibilities. She said there were times that she wished she had an average childhood, but those thoughts would quickly leave her. She said she mostly thought about surviving. She admitted that she could be tough, and still is, but that is what it takes, especially for a Black family.

Shameka claimed she was a virgin until she met Tyrone. She mostly feared getting pregnant and ending up like her mother, so she stayed away from boys. She denied any physical or sexual abuse and claimed that she knew of nobody in her family that took drugs or abused alcohol. She did say in her first session with the supervisee, however, that she was thinking of taking prescriptionanti-anxiety medication.

Tyrone also grew up in a single-parent home. His mother was never married to his father but did have two other sons with a man she dated prior to becoming involved with Tyrone's father. Tyrone's father left when Tyrone was 5 years old. Tyrone would see his father "around town now and then," but they never spoke. His father had remarried and divorced. Tyrone does not have a relationship with his two half-brothers.

A high-school music teacher took an interest in Tyrone and gave him some private lessons on the saxophone. This mentor of sorts also encouraged Tyrone's mother to do what she could to support her son's music. After graduating high school, Tyrone received a full scholarship to college to study music. He was the first individual to graduate college in his family.

While Tyrone was initially ambitious, because he studied jazz, it was especially difficult for him to find regular work. Shameka said he "started out like a ball of fire but slowly the fire dimmed." She claimed that he got depressed and started to hang out with his friends. "As usual, I had to take over. And I'm still caring for my mother and siblings," she said.

Tyrone was a "ladies' man," and after college he moved in with a girl he knew from high school. They soon had a son together, but the mother eventually developed a serious drug problem and Tyrone moved out. Soon thereafter she died of a drug overdose and Tyrone found himself a single father with all the responsibilities. Tyrone sidelined his dream of becoming a jazz great and reluctantly got a job at a music school to make ends meet, but he hated it. He eventually stopped teaching soon after it was evident Shameka could support the family.

The couple always reported an adequate sex life, that is, when Shameka wasn't too tired and Tyrone wasn't too depressed. But after watching Tyrone waste his days with his friends and seemingly give up on his dream, Shameka developed vaginismus (as diagnosed by her OB-GYN), and Tyrone was threatening to leave. Shameka did not want to lose Tyrone, but she was angry, overworked, and had "lost her respect for him as a man."

The supervisee did a great job with the general and sexual history, and I had a lot to work with. I did, however, request that she ask a few more questions:

Supervisor: How has Shameka reacted to having to care for Tyrone's son, especially with him under-functioning at this point?

Supervisee: She loves the boy, but she does remind Tyrone quite often that he isn't doing his part. She doesn't take it out on the boy if that is what you're asking.

Supervisor: Good. She is to be admired, isn't she?

Supervisee: Yes, she is. But she did get herself into this mess.

Supervisor: Say more.

Supervisee: (Laughs). After all, she married a musician.

Supervisor: Hmmm. What's your gut take on this case so far?

Supervisee: I think she got herself parentified again, and he has given up.

Supervisor: Okay. How does she feel about her vaginismus?

Supervisee: Helpless. She has no idea where it comes from or what to do about it.

Step 3. Searching for Contradictions

Supervisor: I think you've got a good idea as to what is going on in this case. Do you see any contradictions?

Supervisee: (Laughs). I thought you would help me with that.

Supervisor: Think about it. You're close.

Supervisee: Well, if I had to guess I would say they both want to be in charge. But she feels overwhelmed by this responsibility and he feels powerless.

Step 4. Uncovering the Shared Internal Conflict

Supervisor: Shameka was put in charge of her family of origin but was overwhelmed by the responsibilities. She then marries a man she sees as competent, disregarding how hard it is to make it in his field. He tries to fulfill his dream, but not too hard. He then completely gives up and re-parentifies his wife by quitting, because unconsciously he wants to be taken care of. Does this sound right to you?

Supervisee: I think so. But what is it a conflict about? Is it about adequacy?

Supervisor: I don't think so because she is still very adequate. I'd say it's like a power vs. powerless conflict. That is, they both want and don't want power.

Step 5. Connecting the Conflict to the Sexual Symptom

Supervisor: Can you connect this conflict to the vaginismus?

Supervisee: (Laughs). No way.

Supervisor: Well, Shameka is a competent caretaker and a part of her seeks this out consciously and unconsciously. But while she can tolerate her mother and younger siblings being somewhat helpless, she cannot tolerate this from Tyrone.

Supervisee: So, she's withholding sex because she's mad at him for not being helpful.

Supervisor: Well, part of her wants to be in charge and part of her doesn't. And part of him wants to be the "man" and part of him wants to be the "prince" he was in his family of origin.

Step 6. Suggesting Interventions

Supervisee: It's one thing to tell someone they want to be in charge but it's another to tell them they want to be taken care of, especially a Black man.

Supervisor: Why a Black man?

Supervisee: I think there is a cultural piece here. Respect is very important to Black men, and Black women do not like wimpy men. Shameka doesn't think of Tyrone as a man anymore, and that's especially bad for a Black couple.

Supervisor: Got it. So how can we use that sociocultural piece in the context of their shared conflict?

Supervisee: We know Shameka is angry and overwhelmed so no need to go there. I would start by asking Tyrone how he went from high hopes to giving up on his dream.

Supervisor: Great. If he can see his conflict that might motivate him to do something with his life and in turn de-parentify Shameka. What about Shameka?

Supervisee: I'm not sure.

Supervisor: How about telling her that for someone who is overwhelmed by responsibility she sure knows how to find it?

Supervisee: Then I can help her to set limits.

Supervisor: Yes. If he can share in the responsibility and she can give some up, she might then give up control of her vaginal muscles. If her OB-GYN isn't helping her with her vaginismus, you can integrate pelvic floor exercises *via* dilators into our treatment.

Supervisee: I think her OB-GYN is leaving this to us.

Supervisor: Okay. Can you then ask Shameka to get a prescription from her OB-GYN for dilators? You can explain that they are used to stretch her vaginal muscles – which she can do at home. Also, please tell her that we will not be using them right away. I like to loosen the couple's defenses with therapy before I start with dilators. I find that if the therapist moves too fast, he or she can scare the client, especially those who were previously sexually abused. It's best to lower the client's anxiety and to let the couple know that they can decide how to insert the dilators. Meaning, Shameka might want to insert them herself, or she may want Tyrone to do it. When the time comes, instruct the couple to put a water-based lubricant on the dilator to make it easier to insert.

Whoever is inserting can then insert with a slight, gentle twist. Dilators usually come in a pack of four ranging in size from small to large or penis size. After Shameka successfully inserts the first dilator without pain – which may take a week or two (practicing 2–3 times per week) – she may then move onto the second dilator but before inserting it, she should prep by inserting the first dilator again. When she is ready for the third dilator, she should prep with the first and second ones. When she is ready for the last dilator, she should prep with the first, second, and third dilators. You'll get the hang of it. The tough part is the integration of it into the couple's therapy and the defenses you will encounter.

Supervisee: Wow! I have never treated vaginismus before.

Supervisor: You'll be fine. For now, continue to point out the contradictions in each partner's family of origin, connect them to the couple's shared conflict, which in this case is about power, and then to the couple's sexual symptom – the vaginismus.

One thing you should warn the couple about: Usually by the third dilator one or both partners may sabotage the treatment. This is because the couple is getting close to controlling the conflict, which will unconsciously trigger it to fight back in the service of maintaining the couple's dysfunctional homeostasis. In my experience, this strikes the couple as counterintuitive, and they may not believe you. But if, or when, they do try to sabotage it, at least you will be prepared.

Supervisee: That sounds crazy.

Supervisor: Yes, defenses work in mysterious ways.

The supervisee reported that she found that Shameka was so worn out that she was almost begging Tyrone for help. This triggered a countertransference in the supervisee who admitted to me that her father was both "macho and lazy." She said he expected that she and her sisters to do all the chores. According to the supervisee, her father would say, "Chores are women's work." The supervisor and I processed this, and it helped her to have more empathy for Tyrone, who unlike her father, she saw as a "sad man with broken dreams." Tyrone might not have been as enthralled with therapy, but he wanted his sex life back so according to the supervisee he was hanging in there. Nevertheless, the supervisee and I agreed that the couple understood their conflict and were ready for dilators.

Supervisor: Okay how did the first exercise go?

Supervisee: Good. Shameka wanted Tyrone to insert the first dilator in part because she wanted to involve him in the exercise. He felt honored by this request.

Supervisor: I assume Shameka is not a masturbator.

Supervisee: No way. How did you know?

Supervisor: Some women who do not like masturbating, do not want to insert the dilators themselves. Any pain with the first dilator?

Supervisee: No, the lubricant and twisting helped. Should I go to the next one?

Supervisor: Let them decide.

Supervisee: Okay.

After three insertion exercises with the first dilator Shameka moved onto the second dilator. Shameka acknowledged that her vaginismus was connected to her conflict about power and in turn, her withholding sex from Tyrone for not helping her. According to the supervisee, she cried in several sessions while Tyrone expressed guilt. The supervisee skillfully got Tyrone to focus on how he felt about failing to fulfill his dream of becoming a jazz great and this caused him great sadness. He apparently told Shameka that he already felt less of a man without her help.

Supervisor: How did the second dilator exercise go?
Supervisee: So far so good. Tyrone moved too fast on one exercise and Shameka temporarily stopped the exercise. I think it was a potential sabotage, but we processed it and the couple tried again, successfully.
Supervisor: There will be more to come.

After using the third dilator for three weeks, Shameka decided to try the fourth and final dilator. The supervisee reported that Shameka was excited, but Tyrone began to distance. The supervisee remembered that this was a critical time in the exercise and so she brought it up again. Tyrone typically resisted saying that he was tired of waiting. But the supervisee was ready to challenge him.

Supervisee: That was weird. They were almost there, and Tyrone started to act out.
Supervisor: I know, it's one of the most fascinating things about our work. What did you do?
Supervisee: I told him that he was doing such good work. I told him that he was contributing to the chores and helping more with the children. And that Shameka was excited about having sex with him again because in part, she felt supported by him. He was also now giving saxophone lessons and playing gigs more on weekends. I mentioned that doing well might be uncomfortable, and worthy of sabotage. I asked if it is possible that his conflict is threatening to make him powerless again?
Supervisor: How did that go?
Supervisee: He seemed to feel challenged by me. Like I was challenging his masculinity and ability to tolerate success. This brought him around.
Supervisor: Great. You're getting them there.

The couple got through the fourth dilator with no pain and began to have intercourse twice per week. While Shameka was not ready to achieve orgasm, she was very happy with Tyrone's general contribution and her sex life. The supervisee offered to send her to a psychiatrist for anxiety medication to help her enjoy sex even more, but she wanted to do it on her own. Tyrone reported that he disliked himself for giving up, and that he felt bad for burdening Shameka who he said was a "great woman."

Not all supervisors who practice couple and sex therapy integrate sex therapy exercises into their couple work. But I believe they should at least be versed in them, especially for vaginismus. Clinical treatment notwithstanding, couples have greater access to the treatment methods for sexual disorders *via* the Internet and expect the therapist to be at least equally knowledgeable. Some couples will have self-diagnosed their sexual issues before they even present for treatment.

Supervisee #4 (Jane) with Indira and Ram – Ram's Delayed Ejaculation

Jane was a white, 42-year-old female with an EdD in Psychology. She also had post-graduate training in family therapy and sex therapy, which suggested she is between the intermediate to advanced stages of development. She has been in private practice for many years and holds a part-time academic adjunct position at a local university. Jane sought supervision primarily to learn couples therapy and to integrate couple and sex therapy. From this point forward she will be referred to as the supervisee.

Step 1. Structuring Supervision

The supervision was conducted through telesupervision on a weekly basis. The modality was one-on-one. The supervisee presented her case notes.

The supervisee and I joined instantly. She claimed that she had a large caseload and at times felt overwhelmed; she believed regular supervision would be helpful. The contracting process went very smoothly, and she agreed to contact me immediately if she had a clinical emergency.

The supervisee said that her caseload was too big to give me a synopsis of all her cases. But she agreed to present all new couples and to report any cases that gave her difficulty. Given that she was an experienced clinician, I agreed to those terms, and it turned out to be the right decision. The supervisee proved to be both detailed and organized. She gathered extensive data (including genograms) on all her couples, and I suspect it was her family therapy training in Bowen Theory that served her well in this context.

The supervisee chose to present Indira and Ram, an unmarried Hindu couple in their early 30s. The couple were born and raised in India but met each other in graduate/professional school after immigrating the United States. Ram was suffering from delayed ejaculation, which both partners claimed stopped them from enjoying sex and marrying. The supervisee suspected that sociocultural factors were significant in this case. She also admitted that she had never treated delayed ejaculation before, despite her training in sex therapy. "All I know about Delayed Ejaculation is what I've read in a book," she said.

Step 2. Presenting Data from the Couple Genogram

The supervisee was instantly able to provide a detailed general and sexual history of each partner. According to the supervisee's genogram, Ram was an engineer working at a small branch of a large company. He had one younger brother. Indira held a PhD in biomedical engineering and worked in a large pharmaceutical company. She had two younger sisters.

Ram and Indira were mutually attracted to each other. Indira thought Ram was smart, kind, and open. She did not want a man who would dominate her, and she did not think Ram would want to. Ram thought Indira was smart, and "refreshingly outspoken." He said Indira was an activist for women's causes and this intrigued him. The couple reported that, initially, both sets of parents were happy to hear of the relationship, especially since Ram and Indira were from a similar caste. While Ram's father preferred an arranged marriage, they thought their son may have chosen the right woman without their help. Neither set of parents knew that Ram and Indira were having premarital sex.

Ram's parents were traditional Hindus. His father was a successful engineer who unilaterally made the decisions for the family and demanded that they follow the rules of their culture. Ram's mother was quiet and passive and rarely challenged her husband's authority. Ram was a "good boy," who tried hard to please his parents. He did well in school, accepted their customs, and became the engineer his father wanted him to be. At this point in his life, however, Ram's parents expected him to be married and have children.

Indira's parents were also traditional but less so than Ram's parents. Indira's father was a physician (surgeon) and her mother was a computer scientist. While they accepted most of their countries' cultural norms, they prioritized their daughters' happiness. Indira's father told her that he thought Ram would be a good match for her but ultimately it was up to her who she married. Indira said that despite their traditional approach to life in India, they encouraged their daughters to "have a voice."

Ram and Indira were virgins before they met and were generally inexperienced when it came to sexual matters. But they reported their sex life as "good," until Ram began having difficulty ejaculating. "We want to marry and have children, but Ram can only ejaculate when I stroke him manually," said Indira. "Also, sex is no fun. Our parents are getting frustrated with us because they want us to marry and give them grandchildren," she added. Ram was at a loss. He said he has always needed a lot of stimulation but not being able to ejaculate was very frustrating. He said the more trouble he has, the more pressure he feels, which only makes it harder for him to ejaculate.

Neither partner reported any physical or sexual abuse in their past nor took any medication. Ram said that the couple's foreplay was adequate and that Indira tries hard to make him ejaculate to no avail. Neither partner masturbates.

Jane conducted a comprehensive evaluation of the couple. But because I suspected Ram was ambivalent about his commitment to Indira, I recommended that the supervisee ask the couple if they were having any difficulty with anything other than their sex life. The following week the supervisee reported back with some important information:

Supervisee: Well, I asked about other difficulties and Ram said that Indira and his parents have grown apart. He said his father thinks he should "act like a man" and forbid Indira from arguing with him all the time, especially in public. I asked what she argues about, and Ram said "everything." Indira interjected that it was mostly about sexist men, and his parents influence over Ram. She also admitted she likes to argue politics, but Ram's family forbids this.

Supervisor: So, Indira stands up to Ram's parents, but he doesn't?

Supervisee: I think so. But I have to say Ram is not a push over either. It's a little confusing. I think he has great loyalty to his parents and doesn't appreciate Indira disrespecting them.

Supervisor: Does Indira think she is disrespecting them?

Supervisee: She understands their position, but she basically thinks she is standing up for herself and her husband.

Supervisor: Okay. Maybe if we find their shared conflict it might shed more light on the couple.

Step 3. Searching for Contradictions

Supervisee: The only contradiction I can come up with is that Indira's dating a traditional guy and she's not traditional.

Supervisor: I think you're on target. I suspect Indira really wants Ram, but she also wants equality in the relationship.

Supervisee: And Ram appreciates an intelligent, outspoken, women but he is a traditional guy from a patriarchal culture.

Supervisor: If we're right, it shouldn't be too hard to locate their shared conflict.

Step 4. Uncovering the Shared Internal Conflict

Supervisor: Have you considered that Ram might be in conflict about committing further to a woman who fights his tradition and his parents?

Supervisee: The father did tell him to "be a man."

Supervisor: Right. But I suspect that Ram really respects Indira. He even said that he admires her assertiveness and intelligence.

Supervisee: So, the conflict is that he loves her independence, but also finds her too independent and outspoken, which clashes with his family's traditional values. It is if he must choose between what he wants for himself and what others want of him.

Supervisor: Yes. Something like that.

Supervisee: But I can't see Indira's conflict.

Supervisor: I think it's the same – a self vs. others conflict. She really likes Ram, and she thinks deep down he is an open, nice guy. But he is caught between allowing her to have her say and the traditions of his parents and culture. If she gives in, she will not be true to herself and the way her parents raised her. She might even feel that she is disappointing her parents.

Supervisee: How does the couple's delayed ejaculation fit in?

Supervisor: Check this out with the couple first, and then we'll talk about the sexual issue.

Step 5. Connecting the Conflict to the Sexual Symptom

Supervisee: I didn't ask about ambivalence. I think I'm too afraid I will upset them. I might have to split them up to ask this kind of question.

Supervisor: You can split them if you want. But I would first recommend that to better balance the couple you pose the question to both. This way they might not suspect that you are accusing one of ambivalence.

Supervisee: I can do that.

The supervisee asked the couple about ambivalence, and she was able to get an answer without splitting the couple. In fact, Ram was direct with her and Indira. He stated that he loved Indira but that the cost of alienating his parents might be too much of a price to pay:

Supervisee: Well, it looks like Ram is unsure about marrying Indira. But not because he doesn't really want her. He is caught between

Indira and his parents. It looks like we have a bigger problem than delayed ejaculation.

Supervisor: It's all related. I have seen cases in which a man who cannot fully commit to his partner will withhold a part of himself to maintain distance. Do you know what I am getting at?

Supervisee: You mean by withholding sex he is withholding commitment?

Supervisor: Yes, unconsciously. It is possible that because of his ambivalence, Ram is withholding his ejaculate from Indira.

Supervisee: How do you get to that?

Supervisor: Ram and Indira are smart, outspoken people. I don't think it will be that difficult.

Step 6. Suggesting Interventions

Supervisor: Now that Ram has admitted his ambivalence, he has done most of the work for you. I would stay with this and ask how he feels when he is about to have sex, or during it. Ask him what he is thinking about, if anything.

Supervisee: Do you think his sexual desire is low because of the conflict?

Supervisor: Possibly. Something is blocking him, and I am just trying to understand how this works and what he is conscious of.

Supervisee: Suppose he says that he doesn't think of anything?

Supervisor: I would then offer the hypothesis that his delayed ejaculation might be a symptom of his ambivalence. I really doubt you are going to get the resistance you are anticipating. These are two very smart people, even if they are sexually inexperienced.

Supervisee: Okay I'll try it.

Supervisor: Do you have a choice?

Supervisee: (Laughs).

The supervisee reported back the following week and the results were promising. She moved Ram one step closer to differentiating from his parents:

Supervisee: Ram said that he wasn't aware of the direct connection between his sexual problem and his ambivalence, but that he is somewhat guilty about having sex. He said he feels as if he is betraying his parents and encouraging Indira when he is not sure he wants to marry her. He doesn't want to lead her on.

Supervisor: How did you respond?

Supervisee: I asked Indira how she felt about what he said. She said she sees the connection and that it makes sense because Ram often seems distant during sex. She reiterated that she loves Ram, but that he must choose between her and his parents.

Supervisor: Not necessarily.

Supervisee: Don't you think Ram needs to differentiate?

Supervisor: Yes. But perhaps there is a way to do so without giving everything up. Can you think of any alternatives?

Supervisee: I think it's Ram's job to control his parents. I think they interfere too much in his relationships.

Supervisor: Hmmm. I sense some countertransference. Consider the couple's cultural context. We can't just tell these two individuals to completely abandon their cultural heritage and ignore their parents' wishes. In time this wouldn't be good for anyone involved.

Supervisee: Maybe I'm reacting to my intrusive parents. They shunned me when I went against their wishes. God knows how many boyfriends they made me break up with.

Supervisor: Well, I admit that you have sparked a countertransference reaction from me. I think sometimes kids don't listen enough to their parents. I've had that experience with my kids from time to time and it would really annoy me.

Supervisee: (Laughs). I could tell.

Supervisor: I do think that if you could process Indira's need to be outspoken – find out where it comes from beyond living in an open-minded family – perhaps you might help her to tone it down somewhat so that she would not clash with others with a different point of view. I suspect that she might have witnessed injustice somewhere. If, however, it is not there, check to see if her assertiveness has cost her any losses in her life and connect it to the potential loss of Ram and his family. We'll get to Ram after you do this.

At our next meeting the supervisee presented with some useful information about Indira and her past relationships with men:

Supervisee: Indira could not identify any injustices. She claimed that she was simply role modeling her parents, especially her mother. But she did say that her behavior has scared boyfriends off in the past. In fact, there was one young man she lost which depressed her for several months. "I thought we were going to marry. He was perfect for me and my parents loved him," she said, "It was sad." When I asked Indira about the possibility of losing Ram, she teared up and said: "I love Ram, but I have to be true to myself." Ram softened when he heard this.

Supervisor: Great work. What about posing to them a potential compromise in which nobody loses?

Supervisee: Let me guess: Indira picks her battles, and Ram sets some limits with his parents when possible.

Supervisor: Let's see how that goes. If it works, I suspect the delayed ejaculation will dissipate. If not, we can help the couple to increase sexual stimulation. In some cases, I would add the stimulation while I am in the process of revealing and challenging the couple's conflict, but here the couple is in crisis, and I doubt we would get very far with sexual exercises.

This supervisee did a nice job and helped the couple to save their relationship and move toward marriage. Specifically, she fostered mutual empathy in the couple, emphasized the attraction and natural desire each partner had for the other, and pointed out the potential losses the couple had and will continue to suffer if their shared conflict was allowed to remain in control. In the end, Indira was able to choose her fights more judiciously and with less intensity without feeling as if she was being disloyal to herself and her way of life. And Ram was able to gently set limits with his parents without feeling guilty. His parents weren't necessarily happy about this, but they did not want to lose their son. As predicted, the delayed ejaculation dissipated.

Supervisee #5 (Kristen) with Sarah and Steven – Steven's ED

Kristen was a white, 32-year-old female with an MSW. She was receiving supervision as part of her post-graduate program in sex therapy. I assessed her at the intermediate level primarily because of her experience with individual therapy. From this point forward she will be referred to as the supervisee.

Step 1. Structuring Supervision

The supervisee was enrolled in a post-graduate training program for sex therapy. She agreed to present her case notes at each meeting and participate in the use of the one-way mirror. The supervision took place on a weekly basis and was conducted one-on-one. The supervisee's main goals were to learn how to integrate couple and sex therapy and to complete the requirements to become an AASECT-certified sex therapist.

In our first session, the supervisee offered a brief synopsis of her cases and chose to focus on a Jewish married couple, Steven and Sarah. After developing a genogram of the couple, the supervisee reported that Steven suffered from ED. The supervisee claimed that Steven was cleared of any organic issues by a urologist (e.g., normal testosterone levels, good blood flow) who suggested he seek couple and sex therapy. She said she felt pressure to help the couple but did not know where to start. She also said she was anxious to help the couple because they were both professionals, and probably "smarter than she was."

Step 2. Presenting Data from the Couple Genogram

The supervisee was generally prepared to present Steven and Sarah but left out many questions in the couple's genogram that I felt might help to understand the couple and their ED.

According to the genogram, Steven was a 52-year-old physician (general surgeon) married for approximately 12 years to Sarah, a 49-year-old physician (rheumatologist). The couple had two children, both in college. The couple met in medical school and were lucky enough to do their residencies at the same school, so they were never apart.

Steven was raised in an upper-middle-class household in the suburbs. His father was an accountant in a large firm, and his mother was a homemaker. Steven was the oldest of two brothers – his youngest brother, to whom he was close, was a practicing dentist.

Steven described his father as a quiet, distant man who preferred to stay in his study and read in his spare time. He otherwise worked very hard and virtually disappeared during tax season. Steven said his father was not involved in his activities and only seemed to get mad if Steven's grades were substandard.

Despite the distance, however, Steven did not hold any animosity toward his father, who he said was neither abusive nor hypercritical. "He was okay. He did the best he could," Steven said. On the other hand, Steven's mother was portrayed by both partners as demanding and intrusive. Steven said she was a "Tiger Mom." He saw her as controlling with very high standards. She not only wanted her two sons to become professionals, but she strongly encouraged them to marry the right women, which from Steven's perspective meant pretty, smart, Jewish women.

Sarah was raised in a middle-class family. She described her father as a "nice man who worked hard." Apparently, he was employed for many years in the garment industry and dreamed of having professional children. Sarah described her mother as unsophisticated but very nice. She worked part-time in a dress shop and took care of the family's domestic responsibilities. Sarah said her mother wanted to please her father, and so she rarely disagreed with him even when it was clear he was wrong. Sarah said that she sometimes felt sorry for her mother because she had no sense of self. I believe my mother thought she was put on the earth to please my father and her children. She once told me that family was the most important thing in life.

Sarah was the oldest of two sisters. Her younger sister married immediately out of high school to a local dentist, and together they had three children. She claimed that she was close to her sister but wanted a bit more for herself. Nevertheless, she shared her mother and sister's perspective that family was very important.

According to the genogram, there was no emotional or sexual abuse, and neither sets of parents used or abused drugs that weren't prescribed by a physician. The topic of sex was rarely mentioned in either partners' family of origin. Steven had sex with only one other women prior to meeting Sarah. He said studying took precedence over everything. Sarah had two previous boyfriends that she had sex before meeting Steven. She claimed to have a strong sex drive but little confidence in her attractiveness to men.

Steven said that he first noticed his ED after marrying Sarah. He said it was an intermittent issue, but he had never experienced it with his previous girlfriend. Despite taking medication from his urologist, his difficulty persisted. Apparently, Sarah is worried about this development. In the past, she attributed his ED to stress over his grades and work. Now, however, she worries that he has some underlying medical condition that the urologist might have missed.

I had many questions for the supervisee in part, because she was not yet skilled in taking a sexual history. Some of the questions were as follows: (1) Can you get Steven to be specific about his ED? (2) Does he have trouble getting erect or does he get erect and lose it once he is inside Sarah? (3) Does Steven masturbate? (4) Does Steven fantasize, and if so, what are his fantasies? (5) Was there an incident that might have made his ED worse? (6) Is Steven upset with Sarah? (7) Is he physically attracted to Sarah? (8) If he had to remarry, would he choose Sarah again? (9) Did he ever have an affair? (10) Did he ever fantasize about leaving Sarah? (11) Is he satisfied with Sarah's sexual technique? (12) How is the couple's foreplay prior to having intercourse? (13) Does he take his ED medication correctly?

The supervisee said she was overwhelmed by the number of questions and could not see herself asking many of them in front of Sarah. I agreed and recommended that she split the couple up for one session each to ask any the questions she felt merited a modicum of confidentiality. She then asked what she should ask Sarah in her individual session. I recommended she try and determine whether Sarah felt loved and desired by Steven. But I also recommended that she warn the partners that whatever is said in their individual sessions is protected by confidentiality and to avoid revealing anything one partner has said about the other:

Supervisee: Well, I split the couple. Steven said that he has trouble achieving erection even during foreplay, and that he does wait at least an hour after taking his medication to attempt sex. He was adamant, however, about being attracted to Sarah.

Supervisor: Do you believe him?

Supervisee: No.

Supervisor: Let's look for contradictions while you tell me what else they said in their individual sessions.

Step 3. Searching for Contradictions

Supervisee: The first contradiction I noticed is that while Steven clearly seemed to be upset about his ED, he didn't seem invested in solving the problem. He was very uncomfortable in the session. I think he wanted to jump out of the window of my office to escape.

Supervisor: I'll bet. What about the other questions?

Supervisee: Same result. Steven denied having any affairs, which I believe. He said that he did not fantasize and that he rarely masturbates, which I also believe. He said that he would probably marry Sarah again and that her sexual technique was fine, which I'm not sure of. And claimed there was no incident that he thinks led to his ED, which is reasonable.

Supervisor: So, you're not sure about the attraction.

Supervisee: Or whether he is in love with Sarah. I think he likes her enough to live with, but I doubt he is satisfied living with her. Another contradiction.

Supervisor: How about Sarah's session?

Supervisee: That was worse. She is in total denial. She just thinks Steven's ED is a medical issue.

Supervisor: And did you ask her if she felt loved by Steven?

Supervisee: She said he could treat her better, but it was good enough. She added that nobody gets everything they want in a marriage. I found this contradictory in that she almost teared up when she said it but refused to allow me to follow up on her reaction. She was even more uncomfortable in the individual session than Steven was.

Supervisor: I think you're on to something.

Supervisee: I can guess their conflict at this point. But they would never admit it. I don't think I'll ever get them to see it.

Supervisor: (Laughs) Don't guess. This isn't a game show. But this might be a good time to start using the one-way-mirror.
Supervisee: Okay. I'll schedule the room for next week.
Supervisor: And don't forget to get the proper consent form signed by both partners. You can tell them that your supervisor will be the only one watching and that they will receive added help free of charge.
Supervisee: Okay. But this is going to be hard.
Supervisor: Every case is hard, if you know what you're doing.

Step 4. Uncovering the Shared Internal Conflict

Before the supervisee entered the one-way-mirror room, I told her to relax and that I would only intervene if I felt it was important. I told her if she treats it like any other session the couple will relax as well. The supervisee asked me where she should begin to locate the couple's conflict. I told her not to mention the individual sessions and to begin with each partner's family of origin. I recommended that she starts by pointing out to Steven that his mother seemed to be in charge when he was young and if he agrees, ask him how he felt about it. She could then ask if he ever rejected her advice and if there were consequences. I said she could also ask if Steven ever regretted taking her advice about anything? And if his father ever intervened to help him with his mother? She then asked about Sarah. I said she could talk to Sarah in more detail about feeling sorry for her mother. She might want to get into her feelings for her father. I then told the supervisee that at the end of the session she should let the couple know she would like to continue using the one-way mirror. The following took place in the one-way-mirror room:

Supervisee: Steven, from the looks of your genogram, your mother was the boss of the family.
Steven: Yes. Mom was in charge.
Sarah: She still is.
Steven: That's true. But it wasn't so bad.
Supervisee: Was it ever bad?
Sarah: Oh yeah. Tell him how your mother felt about the girl you dated before me.
Steven: She didn't like her.
Supervisee: So how did you deal with it.
Sarah: I'll tell you how he dealt with it. He broke up with her.
Supervisee: Didn't you like her?
Steven: Yes. I thought I was going to marry her.

Supervisee: So, your mom has that kind of power.
Steven: I guess.
Supervisee: So how did she feel about Sarah?
Steven: She loved her from the start. She started putting pressure on me from the beginning to propose to Sarah. She was smart, from a good family, and Jewish.
Supervisee: And you did marry her.
Steven: I did.
Supervisee: So, is it safe to say whether you're in love or not, you listen to your mother?
Steven: That's not good.

At this point the session ended, and the supervisee said she was relieved that it was over because she was increasingly uncomfortable about closing in on the couple's underlying issue. She said this scared her because it might mean the end of the couple's marriage. I told her that I thought she was doing a great job but recommended that we look at her genogram to explain what looks like a countertransference. The supervisee discovered that her parents were always on the edge of divorce and that she served as a mediator between them. Getting to the core of their problem might have pushed them over, something that the supervisee greatly feared. When they finally divorced, she said she felt guilty for having failed them.

The supervisee was sad, but she knew that she had to continue to uncover the couple's conflict because like her parents, the couple was no better off lying to themselves. She then asked me how she should start the next session. I recommended that she ask Steven how he could tell if he or his mother is choosing a mate for him:

Supervisee: Picking up from last week's session Steven, how do you know whether you're picking a partner or your mother is doing it for you? It sounds like she has so much influence.
Sarah: I think he picks, but his mother has veto power.
Supervisee: So, Sarah, how do you know that Steven would have chosen you if his mother didn't sanction you?
Sarah: I know he would not have married me if his mother told him not to.
Supervisee: That's not what I asked.
Sarah: How do I know if he really loves me?
Supervisee: Yes.
Sarah: I never thought he loved me that much.
Steven: So why did you marry me?
Sarah: I liked you.

Steven: That's it?
Sarah: Well, why did you marry me?
Steven: I thought I loved you, but now I'm wondering whether I loved you because my mother loved you.
Sarah: (Sarcastically). Great.
Supervisee: Steven, perhaps you're in a conflict between being true to your needs versus being true to your mother.

The supervisee was on target with Steven's conflict. But she told me that she did not see Sarah's conflict. I recommended we re-check the genogram because it was right in front of her. The supervisee sheepishly guessed that Sarah had been trained to maintain the family at the expense of her own personal desires. "I see it. It's a self vs. others conflict," she said, "Now I need to get Sarah to see it."

Supervisee: Sarah, I don't think you and Steven are so different. In fact, I think you two are very much alike.
Steven: How so?
Supervisee: Sarah, your genogram suggests that you were a mediator in your parents' marriage. And that your mother was selfless in her marriage. Perhaps you too are also selfless in your marriage. But not necessarily without ambivalence. That is, like your mother, maybe you put family first regardless of your own feelings.
Sarah: (Crying). I always have, and what do I get for it?
Supervisee: In this sense both of you give someone or something else precedence over your own desires.

Step 5. Connecting the Conflict to the Sexual Symptom

The supervisee told me that she understands the connection between the couple's shared conflict and their sexual symptoms, but getting the couple to see it will be hard. I then asked her what she thought the connection was and she said, "Steven felt that he had to marry Sarah, someone he wasn't attracted to, because his mother wanted him to. He is caught between what he wants and what his mother wants." I agreed with her and recommended that she might want to start the next session by asking Sarah why she thinks Steven doesn't love her:

Supervisee: Sarah, you said you don't think Steven loves you, and that he would not have married you if not for his mother. What makes you say that?

Sarah: I just never felt love coming from him. Our relationship has always felt more like a business arrangement. There has never been much affection, and I know he didn't have erection issues with his old girlfriend.
Supervisee: So, you feel unloved.
Sarah: Pathetic, aren't I? I don't know why I put up with this all this time.
Steven: I love you.
Sarah: Come on Steven. I wish it were true. But we're spending good money here. I think you're still in love with your old girlfriend.
Steven: (Tears up). I don't want to hurt you.
Sarah: And you don't want to disappoint your mother. Your penis isn't lying.

Step 6. Suggesting Interventions

Thus far, I felt no need to intervene in the treatment process. I thought that the supervisee stayed on track and was doing a good job with the couple under stressful conditions. But during this phase, which took place a week later, I had to get her back on track as the couple regressed to defend against their underlying anxiety about differentiating:

Steven: I think I want Sarah more than she thinks. I don't want to split up our family.
Sarah: Then why don't you act like it?
Steven: I'll try harder.

At this point I called the supervisee out of the room and recommended that she go back to each partner's family of origin. I recommended that she approach Steven about his feelings for both his parents. I told the supervisee to explore his relationship with his father who I believed served as a weak role model for Steven. I also suggested that the supervisee ask Sarah what she thinks it would be like to feel loved:

Supervisee: Steven, you described your father as a passive man.
Steven: Yes. He was a good man but distant. He let my mother be in charge.
Supervisee: Was there ever a time you wanted him to intervene?
Steven: Many times. But I knew he wouldn't.
Supervisee: It just seems that he gets a pass, and your mother gets all the credit or blame.

Sarah:	He was a wimp.
Steven:	Yes. I guess he wasn't very supportive.

At his point I interrupted the session again because the supervisee froze. I told her that she was doing a great job, but she must help Steven to make the connection between his weak father and his inability to make his own decisions in life. The supervisee admitted that in her countertransference over being unable to help her parents, she froze with fear.

Supervisee:	Steven, do you see any similarity between you and your father?
Steven:	Not really.
Sarah:	I think she's trying to tell you that you're too afraid to be truthful about our relationship.
Steven:	(Angry Tears). I know, I know. But I didn't come here for a divorce. I came to fix my erection.
Sarah:	(Crying). I know honey. But we have both been living a lie, and our sex life is telling us that. I now realize I have been living like my mother for years. Maybe if we face the truth, we can give ourselves a real chance to be happy. I know Steven thinks the therapy has hurt us. But we would've never had the guts to get there by ourselves, and we would have wasted years. I think we can still be close even if it's not in marriage.
Steven:	I'm sorry, Sarah.

I thought the supervisee practiced skillfully with minimal intervention from me. I only recommended that she continued to work on her fear of losing couples to divorce – a common fear among couple therapists but especially triggering for her given her parent's divorce. I told her that if she chose to work with couples, she would no doubt experience this again in part, because divorce was part of the job. I also told her that divorce does not mean that the treatment was a failure. Many couples like Steven and Sarah are in fact helped despite their eventual dissolution.

Supervisees #6 (Leigh and Lori) with Ashley and Cody – Ashley's FSIAD

Leigh and Lori were licensed clinical social workers (LCSW) employed by the same mental health agency. And while they both were provided with clinical supervision neither of their supervisors were AAMFT or AASECT certified and could help them to qualify for AASECT sex therapy certification. Because both supervisees did have experience in conducting individual therapy, I considered them to be at the intermediate level of clinical development. The supervisees were friends in their early 40s.

Step 1. Structuring Supervision

This case illustrates the one-on-two supervision modality. The supervision took place in my private office for 55 minutes on a weekly basis. During the contracting process I suggested that it might be more productive to double that time, but they rejected this notion claiming they could not afford it; they preferred to take turns presenting their cases. The supervisees also requested that they be allowed to comment on each other's cases to enhance the supervision process, which we all agreed to.

The rest of the contracting process went smoothly, and I was especially careful to specifically delineate which cases I would supervise, and which ones would be the sole responsibility of their individual supervisors. The supervisees and their supervisors were fine with this arrangement. One supervisor said: "The more supervision the merrier." The other was relieved she did not have to deal with sexual issues in supervision. Both supervisors were LCSWs and their models were eclectic in nature and were not wedded to any one model of treatment and supervision.

Leigh chose a couple in their 30s, Cody and Ashley. Ashley and Cody were a white couple who were married for 5 years and had a 2-year-old boy. The couple sought treatment because although they once had "very good sex," over the past two years Ashley lost interest. While they each claimed to be attracted to each other, Cody claimed that Ashley found numerous excuses to avoid him. He ruled out Ashley having an affair, but feels angry, lost, and lonely. Ashley has no idea where her sexual appetite went, and she was just as confused and lost as Cody. The couple both agreed that her desire soon began to wane after the birth of their son and has gotten progressively worse with time.

Step 2. Presenting Data from the Couple Genogram

Leigh was very efficient and timely when it came to creating a genogram for the couple. She told me that she was trained to use a genogram that she found helpful providing some direction in in her clinical work.

According to the couple's genogram, Ashley works as a computer programmer at a large company. She has a college degree in mathematics and a master's degree in computer science. She described herself as a "good girl" who did the right thing even when many of friends were getting into trouble. She was a long-distance runner on the cross-country team in high school and was relatively popular.

Ashley reported two significant relationships prior to meeting Cody. Her first was in high school with a boy she said was extremely jealous of her. She said he was from a good family, but he was insecure. She broke up with him after two years of dating. Her next boyfriend came at the beginning of college. She described him as easy going but boring. She said that she lost her virginity to this boy but more so because she felt she was getting too old to be a virgin, not because she was attracted to him. She said she quickly lost interest in him and only had sex a couple times before she began to distance from the relationship.

Ashley eventually met Cody at a college party and decided to leave her current boyfriend for him. She described Cody as nice, funny, and adventurous. She claimed that he had an edge to him that she found attractive. But she also mistook his stubbornness for independence. Ashley described her sex with Cody as "great" at first. She said she felt as if she was "lassoing a wild horse."

According to the genogram, Ashley was indeed somewhat conservative and cautious in life. She never experimented with drugs or drank very much, even in college. She reported that she had never experienced any sexual abuse and prior to her SIAD, and that she never had any sexual issues. She also claimed that she used to be orgasmic with Cody. As mentioned, her desire began to drop soon after the birth of her son.

Ashely's father was described as "a nice man" – a firefighter – who despite his erratic hours had time to spend with Ashley and her younger sister. She described her mother, however, as very controlling and demanding. "It's mom's way or the highway." When Leigh asked Ashley if her father ever challenged his wife, Ashely said that was too passive to do so. Leigh attributed this power differential to the fact that her mother was an educated woman with a master's degree who came from a somewhat wealthy family. Her father, on the other hand, was from a middle-class working family. He joined the local fire company soon after high school.

Leigh admired her mother and had a soft spot for her father. But her mother's power often overwhelmed her and made her angry at times. Leigh claimed that her parents got along well. She believed her parents had a good sex life, and that there was no substance or use or abuse issues.

According to the couple's genogram, Cody was an emergency medical technician (EMT) with a side job giving sky diving lessons. His father was a police officer, and his mother was a nurse. Cody was the middle of three children. He claimed that his father was his "best friend" and that he admired him. He said that his father did not seem to be afraid of anything and would often challenge himself. He said that his mother was more practical but also enjoyed taking risks. He said that following nursing school his mother hitchhiked across the country by herself and then enlisted in the Navy for a couple of years.

Cody graduated from college but admittedly drank and partied more than he studied. He said that his parents encouraged him to get his degree but did not put any pressure on him to get stellar grades. According to the genogram, Cody said that his father was surprised Cody made it to graduation. Not because he didn't think Cody was smart enough, but because he saw Cody as a free spirit, working outdoors with his hands rather than pinned down in an office. He even thought Cody would make a good police officer, but Cody felt the job was too dangerous for him. Apparently, his father was once shot trying to thwart a bank robbery.

Unlike Ashley, Cody dated many women over the years beginning in high school but was never serious about anybody until he met Ashley. In fact, most of his experiences were "hookups." Cody said that it was a miracle that he never contracted any sexually transmitted diseases (STDs).

Cody found Ashley to be both practical and exciting. He said that she always gave good advice. He also said she used to be a great sexual partner, open to anything although neither partner reported any paraphilias or fetishes.

Cody denied any substance abuse issues in his family of origin. While he did say that his parents enjoyed a glass of wine in the evenings, he said that he never saw either parent drunk. He also denied ever experiencing any sexual abuse or sexual dysfunction. He said that he was just as attracted to Ashley as he has ever been and he would have sex with her as often as she would allow.

Cody did, however, complain that since Ashley's desire for him has waned, her affection has gone with it. He said that she used to put her arm around him and hold his hand, but that she has stopped these behaviors as well. Cody said that he was more sad than angry about Ashley's withdrawal. He said that he does masturbate but his fantasies are usually about Ashley and the return of her desire for him.

I felt that Leigh did a good job gathering information about Ashley and Cody on the couple's genogram. I did, however, have a couple of questions for her to ask the couple as depicted in the following dialogue. Because Lori joined in, to avoid confusion I have labeled Leigh, Supervisee #1, and Lori, Supervisee #2:

Supervisor: You're seem to have a lot to work on Ashley. Do you feel the same?

Supervisee #1: Yes, I do but I could have gotten more. I was too afraid to push the couple.

Supervisor: What would you have asked if you weren't afraid?

Supervisee #1: I wanted to ask Ashley more about her feelings about her controlling mother and passive father. I suspected she was repressing some strong feelings about their dynamic.

Supervisor: Good. Follow up. I don't think that you will offend her, if you don't push too hard. She probably isn't differentiated enough to handle too much negativity about her parents. Remember, she is a "good girl." Anything else?

Supervisee #1: I wonder if there is any post-partum depression that might be responsible for her change in loss of arousal.

Supervisor: Yes, and I would also ask Ashley if she has experienced a general loss of interest in sex or is her loss specific to Cody. I'd like to know if there is anything that is bothering her about Cody.

Supervisee #1: Oaky.

Supervisee #2: This woman really bothers me.

Supervisee #1: Who, Ashley?

Supervisee #2: Yes, I can't stand her.

Supervisee #1: I like her.

Supervisor: You're being triggered by something Lori. What is it?

Supervisee #2: I'm not sure.

Supervisor: Sounds like a countertransference opportunity to me. Can you help us to better understand what you are sensing? Your input might be very important to the case.

Supervisee #2: Again, I'm not sure yet. Let me think about it some more.

Supervisee #1: Wow. That was intense.

The following week Leigh reported back on some of the questions we had for the couple. And she was right about Ashley. In answer to the question about Ashley's feelings about her parents' dynamic she had a rage for her mother. She felt that she, her sister, and her father were victimized by her. She was not, however, ready to give her father responsibility in the dynamic.

Leigh also reported that Ashely's loss of sexual interest was global and not specifically related to Cody. But she did admit that she was angry at Cody for taking such risks with his life. She felt being an EMT was exciting enough and came with certain risks. But to teach skydiving in his spare time was especially scary. She added that she did not want to control Cody, but that he made her anxious. She claimed he is not thinking about his family.

Lori said that she had thought about her strong reaction to Ashley and realized that she too had very controlling parents and that she could not wait to go to college to be free of them. She even claimed that her parents tried to choose her college major and were critical of every boyfriend she ever had. "I guess they didn't believe that I could make any good decisions on my own," she said sarcastically.

I acknowledged Lori's feelings and promised to keep her perspective in mind. Leigh, however, was less than enthused. Leigh countered that Ashley was simply expressing her anxiety, not telling Cody what to do. She added that Lori was favoring Cody and although he seemed to be a good guy, he must be playing a role in the couple's dynamic. Leigh was right that Lori had lost her therapeutic balance. But I thought rather than try to play this out at this point, more information about the couple was needed.

Step 3. Searching for Contradictions

Supervisor: In my model of treatment contradictions tend to lead to conflict. Can either of you identify any?

Supervisee# 1: I just don't see Ashley as controlling as Lori does. I would think I would recognize control given that my mother is so controlling.

Supervisee#2: Sometimes when you are standing so close to a mirror you can't see yourself.

Supervisee #1: Okay, but give me some proof.

Supervisee #2: Maybe Leigh is having a countertransference reaction. You didn't mention this.

Supervisee #1: (Laughs). No need to get snippy.

Supervisor: Lori could be right. Say more Lori.

Supervisee #2: Maybe like Ashley, Leigh is protecting her father.

Supervisee #1: I'm not siding with either partner.

Supervisor: Okay, I suspect we are not going to get anywhere on this until we get more information. For now, let's get back to locating contradictions. Something I picked up is that Ashley initially liked Cody for his adventurous spirit but now sees it as dangerous.

Supervisee #1: Yes. That's very interesting. And Cody was taken with Ashley's practicality and exciting personality, but I wonder if he's upset that she now wants him to tone down his risk-taking.

Supervisor: Check that out.

Step 4. Uncovering the Shared Internal Conflict

Supervisor: Leigh did you ask Cody if he was upset with Leigh?

Supervisee 1#: Yes. He is upset with her because he thinks she is trying to control his career.

Supervisee #2: See, I was right. But I don't want to say I told you so.
Supervisor: (Laughs). You can say it, Lori. I think we have a mutual conflict here.
Supervisee #1: They both want control, but they don't.
Supervisor: Yes. I suspect a control vs. out-of-control conflict is operating. But what does this have to do with the couple's sexual issue?

Step 5. Connecting the Conflict to the Sexual Symptom

Supervisee #1: Could this be Ashely's unconscious way of controlling Cody's risk-taking behavior?
Supervisor: It could be. But it's not working because the couple have no idea that the two are related. It will be up to you to help them to see the correlation.
Supervisee #1: I'm not sure the best way to do this.
Supervisor: So, let's talk about how to intervene.

Step 6. Suggesting Interventions

Supervisor: I would suggest that you ask Ashley about her anger and anxiety related to Cody's risk-taking behavior. Maybe she felt similar feelings for her father who was also in a dangerous field. Does the onset of Ashley's FSIAD mean anything to you now?
Supervisee #1: Maybe having a kid made her even more anxious about losing Cody.
Supervisor: And angry too.
Supervisee #1: But she hasn't put her foot down.
Supervisor: Because she is in conflict. She doesn't want to be like her mother, but she is too afraid to do nothing. She wants control over the situation, but not too much. I guess you could say that Ashley is using her foot to step on Cody's sex life.
Supervisee #1: I see it.
Supervisee #2: So how is Cody responsible for this?
Supervisor: Can you answer that question Leigh?
Supervisee #1: He isn't attuned to Ashley's concerns. He was raised in a family that supported risk-taking and he doesn't want to be controlled at any cost. But the more risk-taking, the less sex he will get.
Supervisor: I agree Leigh. And you will have to get Ashley to confront Cody about this.

Leigh exposed the couple's conflict about control and did a great job in encouraging Ashely's to express her concerns to Cody in an empathic way. She helped Ashley to explain to Cody that she did not wish to control him, but that she was scared for both her and their child. Cody initially made it about extra income, but Leigh helped him to see that it had become more about being controlled. He eventually gave up skydiving and as a compromise he took on more hours in his job as an EMT. Leigh was pleasantly surprised that the couple's sex life improved, as were the couple.

Hopefully the detailed case studies provided have made clear that there is vital need for a structured, integrative model of supervision that combines couple therapy and sex therapy. The two fields are inextricably linked, and the professional literature and clinical examples support this combination. Moreover, these linked fields present some of the most complex and challenging cases in all of psychotherapy which merit duel-trained supervisors who can adequately guide supervisees to work and thrive in the context of couple and sex therapy. As depicted in the Epilogue, times are growing even more complex, and the need for sophisticated training and supervision will no doubt grow with them.

Epilogue

Supervision has become more technologically advanced over the years, and the use of this technology has grown significantly. Soheilian et al. (2022) wrote: "The global pandemic, COVID-19, changed how clinical supervisors conducted supervision. Clinical supervisors, most with limited to no training in telesupervision, shifted from providing primarily in-person clinical supervision, to telesupervision" (p. 17). According to Sipila-Thomas and Brodhead (2023), 31.9% of the supervisors in their study provided telehealth supervision prior to the pandemic, and of those supervisors, 90.9% indicated they would continue to do so after the pandemic.

Telesupervision may be subject to interruptions from outsiders, enable distractions, increase the risk of confidential breaches, and detract from the intimacy of in-person supervision. But it can also afford supervisors and supervisees flexibility of scheduling and reduce supervisee intimidation and inhibition. I have found the latter especially important in the supervision of sexual issues which are more liable to generate feelings of shame and embarrassment (Appleton et al., 2021; Augusterfer et al., 2020; Perle & Zheng, 2023).

Telesupervision also affords greater access for training. Both individual and group supervision can now be conducted with supervisees across states and countries. Some supervisees thought it worth seeking supervision across time zones. For example, I know of a supervisee from Australia who sought supervision from a colleague of mine in the United States – a 14-hour time-zone difference exists between these countries. This is an admirable commitment requiring emotional, physical, and financial sacrifice. I also know of other supervisees from Israel, Latvia, Lebanon, Lithuania, Russia, and the United Kingdom who have sought telesupervision from supervisors in the United States.

Change usually does not come easy, however. Supervisors with little to no technological experience have been forced to become knowledgeable in areas in which they have no previous training. In this sense, they must continue to apply their traditional supervisory knowledge and maintain their clinical acumen with fewer nonverbal cues, while they strive to achieve some level of technological competence (Perle & Zheng, 2023).

Despite the negative aspects, telesupervision in its many forms, such as supervision *via* video conferencing, is here to stay. But even more controversial technologies will no doubt have a greater impact on clinical supervision. Artificial intelligence (AI), for example, may one day limit the need for human supervisors. Skepticism from the therapeutic community notwithstanding, Sheperis and Sadeh-Sharvit (2023) reported that chatbots and virtual assistants are becoming increasingly popular. The John S. McCain National Defense Authorization Act for Fiscal Year 2019 (2018) provides the following definition of AI:

- Any artificial system that performs tasks under varying and unpredictable circumstances without significant human oversight or that can learn from experience and improve performance when exposed to data sets.
- An artificial system developed in computer software, physical hardware, or other context that solves tasks requiring human-like perception, cognition, planning, learning, communication, or physical action.
- An artificial system designed to think or act like a human, including cognitive architectures and neural networks.
- A set of techniques, including machine learning, that is designed to approximate a cognitive task.
- An artificial system designed to act rationally, including an intelligent software agent or embodied robot that achieves goals using perception, planning, reasoning, learning, communicating, decision-making, and acting.

Scholars have been advocating for the integration of AI in existing telemental health protocols. Sheperis and Sadeh-Sharvit (2023) found: "AI can improve the accuracy of diagnosis, automate routine tasks, and personalize treatment plans, potentially enhancing the accessibility and quality of mental health care" (p. 1). The authors found it to be specifically helpful in conceptualizing cases, evaluating session quality, and in writing progress notes. In a study assessing the integration of AI in a telemental health training clinic, Guinn et al. (2024) found that AI can help to improve therapeutic skills in beginner clinicians. Many of these potential attributes could be easily applicable to supervision.

AI, however, also comes with its challenges. The biggest concerns include (1) issues around privacy and confidentiality, especially when used in the mental health field; (2) the complexity of successfully integrating AI into existing practices; and (3) replacing the human element. Several clinicians and scholars are especially worried about the loss of empathy and emotional support in the clinical and supervision process (Cornish, 2024; Montemayor et al., 2021; Sheperis & Sadeh-Sharvit, 2023). Montemayor et al. (2021) claimed that empathy cannot be replaced by "any of the technological and theoretical approaches that shape the current application of Al in clinical medicine in which care for patients is fundamental" (p. 1353). Supervisees also have some concern that AI might be "weaponized against them" and supervisors fear "their input would be lessened" (Cornish, 2024, p. 6).

While I have mentioned some of the pros and cons of AI use in psychotherapy, there are some issues that may apply specifically to AI and the integration of couple and sex therapy that supervisors and supervisees should be aware of. Couple therapy seems to offer unique challenges to the integration of AI because it relies primarily on the understanding of relational dynamics and especially the balancing of a couple, the emotional state of the couple, and the therapeutic alliance between the therapist and the two partners that make up the couple.

Chung (2025) found that AI, especially ChatGPT and other chatbots, present risks and limitations in couple therapy. AI may misinterpret emotional nuances such as sarcasm and body language – cues that are especially important in couple work. And they are usually unaware of underlying issues that may be behind a couple's symptoms. The author added that AI is not intuitive and thus may miss implied messages or nuances that a human couple therapist is more likely to notice. In addition, AI is not much use in a high-conflict crisis, especially when a partner's safety is at issue. Vowels et al. (2024) agreed that AI is not a great tool to use for risk assessment or reaching collaborative solutions.

Because of the potential for exposure, some couples with sexual problems are even less likely to appreciate and embrace AI in therapy. Others, however, may prefer communicating with an anonymous chatbot rather than the potential embarrassment of facing a human therapist. According to Döring et al. (2024), using AI might be easier for someone who is looking for fast, affordable, accessible, and anonymous, sexual information. The authors wrote:

> An additional advantage of online searches for sexual information is the shame and guilt-free experience of being able to ask everything and anything sexuality-related without being judged. This may be particularly important for people interested in sexual kinks and fetishes that are often omitted, misunderstood or stigmatized even by professional sex educators.
>
> (p. 4)

I believe that all supervisors and supervisees who work with couples should take the advent of AI seriously. Specifically, they should consider the potential complexities and limitations mentioned when contemplating its use of AI in the integration of couple and sex therapy supervision. Colvin and Benjamin (2025) asserted that AI cannot and should not replace human interaction but instead serve to enhance the therapeutic delivery system. But recent studies have found that AI can do more than expected. Hatch et al. (2025), for example, discovered that clinical responses to couples written by ChatGPT were generally rated higher than those written by couple therapists. Even when evaluated, the therapists could not find fault with the generated responses. And Vowels et al. (2024) found that ChatGPT rated high on attributes such as therapeutic skills and human-likeness.

While it is hard to predict the full impact AI will have, the American Psychological Association (APA) (2025) has prepared by developing ethical guidelines for AI use. It will, therefore, not be long before therapists, no matter the specialty, will be asked to integrate AI into their practices, and supervisors will be required to act as gatekeepers.

References

American Psychological Association. (APA). (2025). *Ethical guidelines for AI in the professional practice of health psychology*. www.apa.org/topics/artificial-intelligence-machine-learning/ethical-guidance-professional-practice.pdf

Appleton, R., Williams, J., Vera San Juan, N., Needle, J. J., Schlief, M., Jordan, H., Rains, L. S., Goulding, L., Badhan, M., Roxburgh, E., Barnett, P., Spyrideonidis, S., Tomaskova, M., Mo, J., Harju-Seppänen, J., Haime, Z., Casetta, C., Papamichail, A., Lloyd-Evans, B., Simpson, A., Sevdalis, N., Gaughran, F., & Johnson, S. (2021). Implementation, adoption, and perceptions of telemental health during the COVID-19 pandemic: Systematic review. *Journal of Medical Internet Research*, *23*(12), e31746. doi: 10.2196/31746

Augusterfer, E. F., O'Neal, C. R., Martin, S. W., Sheikh, T. L., & Mollica, R. F. (2020). The role of telemental health, tele-consultation, and tele-supervision in post-disaster and low-resource settings. *Current Psychiatry Reports*, 22, 85, 1–10. doi: 10.1007/s11920-020-020-01209-5

Chung, M. (2025, August 5). The ride of AI for couples therapy. *Talkspace* . www.talkspace.com/blog/ai-couples-therapy/

Colvin, A. D., & Benjamin, C. (2025). Exploring the use of AI avatars by marriage and family therapist practitioners as a therapeutic intervention. *Family Relations*, *74*, 1341–1353. https://doi.org/10.1111/fare.13145

Cornish, M. (2024, July 16). How eleos supercharges clinical supervision: A study. *Eleos*. https://eleos.health/blog-posts/enhancing-therapy-supervision-with-ai/

Döring, N., Lee, T. D., Vowles, L. M., Vowles, M. J., & Marcantonio, T. L. (2024). The impact of artificial intelligence on human sexuality: A five-year literature review 2020–2024. *Current Sexual Health Reports*, *17*, 1–39. https://doi.org/10.1007/s11930-024-00397-y

Guinn, V., Bunge, J. R., Sheparis, D. S., Assenheim-Dagan, L., & Sadeh-Sharvit, S. (2024). Integrating artificial intelligence in a telemental health clinic. *PsyArXiv*. https://doi.org/10.31234/osf.io/mk87x

Hatch, S. G., Goodman, Z. T., Vowels, L., Hatch, H. D., Brown, A. L., Guttman, S., Le, Y., Bailey, B., Bailey, R. J., Esplin, C. R., Harris, S. M., Holt, Jr., P., McLaughlin, M., O'Connell, P., Rothman, K., Ritchie, L., Top, Jr., N., & Braithwaite, S. R. (2025). When ELIZA meets therapists: A Turing test for the heart and mind. *PLOS Mental Health*, *2*(8), e0000426. https://doi.org/10.1371/journal.pmen.0000426

John S. McCain National Defense Authorization Act for Fiscal Year 2019, § 238(g), Pub. L No. 115-232, 132 Stat. 1636. (2018). www.congress.gov/115/plaws/publ232/PLAW-115publ232.pdf

Montemayor, C., Halpern, J., & Fairweather, A. (2021). In principle obstacles for empathic AI: Why we can't replace human empathy in healthcare. *AI & Society*, *37*, 1353–1359. doi: 10.1007/s00146-021-01230-z

Perle, J. G., & Zheng, W. (2023). A primer for understanding and utilizing telesupervision with healthcare trainees. *Journal of Technology in Behavioral Science*, *9*. 46–52. https://doi.org/10.1007/s41347-023-00322-5

Sheparis, D. S., & Sadeh-Sharvit, S. (2023). Using AI-supported supervision in a university telemental health training clinic. *Journal of Technology in Counselor Education and Su*pervision. *4*, 1–10. https://doi.org/10.61888/2692-4129.1093

Sipila-Thomas, E. S., & Brodhead, M. T. (2023). A survey of barriers experienced while providing supervision via telehealth: Implications for future research and practice. *Behavioral Analysis Practice*, *17*, 70–86. https://doi.org/10.1007/s40617-023-00860-7

Soheilian, S. S., O'Shaughnessy, Lehmann, J. S., & Rivero, M. (2022). Examining the impact of COVID-19 on supervisees' experiences of clinical supervision. *Training and Education in Professional Psychology*, *17*, 167–175. https://doi.org/10.1037/tep0000418

Vowles, L. M., Francois-Walcott, R. R. R., & Darwiche, J. (2024). AI in relationship counselling: Evaluating ChatGPT's therapeutic capabilities in providing relationship advice. *Computers in Human Behavior: Artificial Humans*, 2, 1–9. www.journals.elsevier.com/computers-in-human-behavior-artificial-humans

Index

Note: Page numbers in *italics* refers to figures.

For Product Safety Concerns and Information please contact our EU
representative GPSR@taylorandfrancis.com
Taylor & Francis Verlag GmbH, Kaufingerstraße 24, 80331 München, Germany

www.ingramcontent.com/pod-product-compliance
Ingram Content Group UK Ltd.
Pitfield, Milton Keynes, MK11 3LW, UK
UKHW022354190926
475702UK00015B/2279
* 9 7 8 1 0 4 1 0 7 8 8 9 0 *